The Ultimate

CROCK POT

Cookbook for Beginners 2023

800 Hot, Affordable and Delicious Recipes for Homemade Slow Cooking Meals On a Budget

Lizeth B. Barton

Copyright© 2023 By Lizeth B. Barton

All rights reserved worldwide.

No part of this book may be reproduced or transmitted in any form or by any means, electronic or mechanical, including photo- copying, recording or by any information storage and retrieval system, without written permission from the publisher, except for the inclusion of brief quotations in a review.

Warning-Disclaimer

The purpose of this book is to educate and entertain. The author or publisher does not guarantee that anyone following the techniques, suggestions, tips, ideas, or strategies will become successful. The author and publisher shall have neither liability or responsibility to anyone with respect to any loss or damage caused, or alleged to be caused, directly or indirectly by the information contained in this book.

CONTENT

Chapter 1   Breakfasts   1

Chapter 2   Snacks and Appetizers   11

Chapter 3   Vegetables and Sides   18

Chapter 4   Stews and Soups   35

Chapter 5   Beans and Grains   55

Chapter 6   Beef, Pork, and Lamb   61

Chapter 7   Pizzas, Wraps, and Sandwiches   85

Chapter 8   Poultry   88

Chapter 9   Fish and Seafood   104

Chapter 10   Desserts   109

Appendix Measurement Conversion Chart   118

Chapter 1　Breakfasts

Sweet Potato Home Fries

Prep time: 15 minutes | Cook time: 6 to 8 hours | Serves 4 to 6

3 tablespoons extra-virgin olive oil, plus more for coating the crock pot
2 pounds (907 g) sweet potatoes, diced
1 red bell pepper, seeded and diced
½ medium onion, finely diced
1 teaspoon garlic powder
1 teaspoon sea salt
1 teaspoon dried rosemary, minced
½ teaspoon freshly ground black pepper

1. Coat the crock pot with a thin layer of olive oil. 2. Put the sweet potatoes in the crock pot, along with the red bell pepper and onion. Drizzle the olive oil as evenly as possible over the vegetables. 3. Sprinkle in the garlic powder, salt, rosemary, and pepper. Toss evenly to coat the sweet potatoes in the oil and seasonings. 4. Cover the cooker and set to low. Cook for 6 to 8 hours and serve.

Chicken-Apple Breakfast Sausage

Prep time: 15 minutes | Cook time: 6 to 8 hours | Serves 4 to 6

1 pound (454 g) ground chicken
½ medium apple, peeled and minced
1 teaspoon sea salt
½ teaspoon freshly ground black pepper
½ teaspoon dried parsley flakes
½ teaspoon garlic powder
½ teaspoon dried basil leaves
¼ teaspoon ground cinnamon

1. In a large bowl, combine the chicken, apple, salt, pepper, parsley flakes, garlic powder, basil, and cinnamon. Mix well. Press the chicken mixture into the bottom of your crock pot, ensuring it's a thin layer throughout. 2. Cover the cooker and set to low. Cook for 6 to 8 hours, or until the meat is completely cooked through. 3. Using a silicone spatula, loosen the chicken from around the edges and transfer to a cutting board. Cut into desired shapes (sticks or circles are common) and serve.

Golden Beet and Spinach Frittata

Prep time: 15 minutes | Cook time: 5 to 7 hours | Serves 4 to 6

1 tablespoon extra-virgin olive oil
8 large eggs
1 cup packed fresh spinach leaves, chopped
1 cup diced peeled golden beets
½ medium onion, diced
¼ cup unsweetened almond milk
¾ teaspoon sea salt
½ teaspoon garlic powder
½ teaspoon dried basil leaves
Freshly ground black pepper, to taste

1. Coat the crock pot with the olive oil. 2. In a large bowl, combine the eggs, spinach, beets, onion, almond milk, salt, garlic powder, and basil, and season with pepper. Whisk together and pour the custard into the crock pot. 3. Cover the cooker and set to low. Cook for 5 to 7 hours, or until the eggs are completely set, and serve.

Morning Millet

Prep time: 15 minutes | Cook time: 7 to 8 hours | Serves 4

1 cup millet
2 cups water
2 cups full-fat coconut milk
½ teaspoon sea salt
½ teaspoon ground cinnamon
½ teaspoon ground ginger
¼ teaspoon vanilla extract
½ cup fresh blueberries

1. In your crock pot, combine the millet, water, coconut milk, salt, cinnamon, ginger, and vanilla. Stir well. 2. Cover the cooker and set to low. Cook for 7 to 8 hours. 3. Stir in the blueberries to warm at the end and serve.

Carrot and Fennel Quinoa Breakfast Casserole

Prep time: 15 minutes | Cook time: 5 to 7 hours | Serves 4 to 6

6 large eggs
½ cup quinoa, rinsed well
1½ cups unsweetened almond milk
½ teaspoon sea salt
½ teaspoon garlic powder
¼ teaspoon dried oregano
Freshly ground black pepper, to taste
1 fennel bulb, finely sliced
3 medium carrots, diced
1 tablespoon extra-virgin olive oil

1. In a medium bowl, whisk the eggs. 2. Add the quinoa, almond milk, salt, garlic powder, and oregano, and season with pepper. Whisk well until all ingredients are combined. 3. Stir in the fennel and carrots. 4. Coat the crock pot with the olive oil, and slowly pour in the egg mixture. 5. Cover the cooker and set to low. Cook for 5 to 7 hours and serve.

Simple Steel-Cut Oats

Prep time: 15 minutes | Cook time: 6 to 8 hours | Serves 4 to 6

1 tablespoon coconut oil
4 cups boiling water
½ teaspoon sea salt
1 cup steel-cut oats

1. Coat the crock pot with the coconut oil. 2. In your crock pot, combine the boiling water, salt, and oats. 3. Cover the cooker and set to warm (or low if there is no warm setting). Cook for 6 to 8 hours and serve.

German Chocolate Cake Protein Oats

Prep time: 15 minutes | Cook time: 6 to 8 hours | Serves 4 to 6

1 tablespoon coconut oil
2 cups rolled oats
2½ cups water
2 cups full-fat coconut milk
¼ cup unsweetened cacao powder

2 tablespoons collagen peptides
¼ teaspoon sea salt
2 tablespoons pecans
2 tablespoons unsweetened shredded coconu

1. Coat the crock pot with the coconut oil. 2. In your crock pot, combine the oats, water, coconut milk, cacao powder, collagen peptides, and salt. Stir to combine. 3. Cover the cooker and set to low. Cook for 6 to 8 hours. 4. Sprinkle the pecans and coconut on top and serve.

Nutty Granola with Power Seeds and Dried Fruit

Prep time: 15 minutes | Cook time: 6 hours | Makes 10 cups

1 overripe banana, peeled
3 tablespoons water
6 cups old-fashioned oats
½ cup chopped pecans
½ cup chopped walnuts
½ cup raw cashews
½ cup slivered or chopped raw almonds
½ cup unsweetened coconut flakes
3 tablespoons ground flaxseed
3 tablespoons raw pepitas
3 tablespoons raw sunflower seeds
3 tablespoons chia seeds
½ cup maple syrup (optional)
½ cup aquafaba
½ cup raisins
½ cup currants
½ cup unsweetened dried cherries

1. In the bottom of the crock pot, mash together the banana and water. Add the oats, pecans, walnuts, cashews, almonds, coconut, flaxseed, pepitas, sunflower seeds, chia seeds, and maple syrup (if using). 2. In a small bowl, use an electric beater to whip the aquafaba into almost-stiff peaks, about 5 minutes. Add it to the crock pot and stir to combine. 3. To keep the condensation that forms on the inside of the lid away from the granola, stretch a clean dish towel or several layers of paper towels over the top of the crock pot, but not touching the food, and place the lid on top of the towel(s). Cook on Low for 6 hours, stirring every hour to make sure the granola does not burn and replacing the damp towels as needed. 4. After 6 hours, the granola will be darker in color. Transfer it to a parchment-lined baking sheet, spread it out, and let it cool for up to 1 hour. Once it's completely cool and crispy, sprinkle on the raisins, currants, and dried cherries and stir to combine. Store in a large airtight container for up to 2 weeks.

Maple, Apple, and Walnut Great Grains

Prep time: 10 minutes | Cook time: 3 to 4 hours | Serves 4 to 6

2 large apples
½ cup quinoa, rinsed
½ cup steel-cut oats
½ cup wheat berries
½ cup pearl barley
½ cup bulgur wheat
1 tablespoon ground flaxseed
2 teaspoons ground cinnamon
½ teaspoon ground or grated nutmeg
7 cups water
⅓ cup maple syrup (optional)
½ cup chopped walnuts
½ cup raisins
Unsweetened plant-based milk, for serving (optional)

1. Peel, core, and chop the apples and place them in the crock pot. Add the quinoa, oats, wheat berries, barley, bulgur wheat, flaxseed, cinnamon, nutmeg, water, and maple syrup (if using). Stir gently. Cover and cook on High for 3 to 4 hours or on Low for 7 to 8 hours. 2. Before serving, stir in the walnuts and raisins. Spoon into a bowl and add your favorite milk (if using).

Strawberries and Cream Overnight Oatmeal

Prep time: 5 minutes | Cook time: 4 to 5 hours | Serves 4 to 6

Nonstick cooking spray (optional)
1¼ cups steel-cut oats
4 cups water
1⅔ cups unsweetened plant-based milk
2 teaspoons vanilla extract
¼ cup maple syrup (optional)
3 tablespoons ground flaxseed
1 pound (454 g) fresh strawberries, stemmed and sliced

1. Coat the inside of the crock pot with cooking spray (if using) or line it with a crock pot liner. 2. Place the oats, water, milk, vanilla, and maple syrup (if using) in the crock pot. Cover and cook on High for 4 to 5 hours or on Low for 8 to 9 hours. 3. When ready to serve, stir the flaxseed into the oatmeal and portion into bowls. Top each with 3 to 5 sliced strawberries.

Blueberry, Cinnamon, and Pecan French Toast

Prep time: 10 minutes | Cook time: 2 to 3 hours | Serves 4 to 6

2 tablespoons ground flaxseed
5 tablespoons water
1 (16-ounce / 454-g) loaf crusty whole-grain bread
1 overripe banana, peeled
1 (14½-ounce / 411-g) can full-fat coconut milk
1 cup unsweetened plant-based milk
1 tablespoon chia seeds
1 teaspoon ground cinnamon
1 tablespoon vanilla extract
Nonstick cooking spray (optional)
2 cups fresh or frozen blueberries, divided
¼ cup chopped pecans, for serving
Maple syrup, for serving (optional)

1. In a small bowl or ramekin, stir together the flaxseed and water to form flax eggs. Let rest while preparing the remaining ingredients. 2. Slice the bread into 1- to 2-inch chunks and place in a large casserole dish deep enough to have the bread submerged in the custard. 3. Place the banana, coconut milk, plant-based milk, chia seeds, cinnamon, vanilla, and flax eggs in a blender. Blend to combine and pour over the bread. Cover and refrigerate for at least 30 minutes to allow the bread to soak up the custard. 4. Coat the inside of the crock pot with cooking spray (if using) or line it with a crock pot liner. Remove the bread and custard mixture from refrigerator and place half in the bottom of the crock pot. Add 1 cup of blueberries, then layer the remaining half of the bread and custard mixture. Top with the remaining 1 cup of blueberries. Cover and cook on High for 2 to 3 hours or on Low for 4 to 5 hours. 5. To serve, top each portion with a tablespoon of pecans and a drizzle of maple syrup (if using).

Potato and Veggie Breakfast Casserole

Prep time: 10 minutes | Cook time: 4 to 5 hours | Serves 4 to 6

1 medium red bell pepper, diced
1 medium onion, diced
1 (8-ounce / 227-g) package white button or cremini mushrooms, quartered
3 cups chopped kale
Ground black pepper
Salt (optional)
1 teaspoon garlic powder, divided
1 teaspoon onion powder, divided
1 teaspoon paprika, divided
1 (14-ounce / 397-g) package extra-firm tofu, drained
1 teaspoon ground turmeric
8 small Yukon Gold or red potatoes (about 2 pounds / 907 g), unpeeled and sliced into half-inch rounds

1. Place the bell pepper, onion, mushrooms, and kale in the crock pot. Season with pepper and salt (if using). Add ½ teaspoon each of the garlic powder, onion powder, and paprika. Mix to distribute the seasonings. 2. Crumble the tofu directly into the crock pot. Sprinkle the tofu with the turmeric and stir until the tofu is coated. Then mix the tofu and veggies together. 3. Layer the potatoes on top of the veggies and tofu. Sprinkle with the remaining ½ teaspoon each of garlic powder, onion powder, and paprika. Season again with salt (if using) and pepper. Cover and cook on High for 4 to 5 hours or on Low for 7 to 8 hours.

Sweet Potato and Black Bean Hash

Prep time: 10 minutes | Cook time: 2 to 3 hours | Serves 4 to 6

1 shallot, diced
2 cups peeled, chopped sweet potatoes (about 1 large or 2 small)
1 medium bell pepper (any color), diced
2 garlic cloves, minced
1 (14½-ounce / 411-g) can black beans, drained and rinsed
1 teaspoon paprika
½ teaspoon onion powder
½ teaspoon garlic powder
¼ cup store-bought low-sodium vegetable broth
4 to 6 tablespoons unsweetened plant-based milk

1. Place the shallot, sweet potatoes, bell pepper, garlic, beans, paprika, onion powder, garlic powder, and broth in the crock pot. Stir to combine. Cover and cook on Low for 2 to 3 hours, until the potatoes are soft. 2. Remove the lid and add the milk, starting with 4 tablespoons, and stir to combine. You're looking for a creamy sauce to develop. Add more milk as needed and allow to heat through for a few minutes before serving.

Southwestern-Style Breakfast Burritos

Prep time: 10 minutes | Cook time: 2 to 3 hours | Serves 4 to 6

1 medium onion, diced
1 medium red bell pepper, diced
3 garlic cloves, minced
1 (10-ounce / 283-g) package frozen corn
1 (14-ounce / 397-g) can pinto beans, drained and rinsed
1 (14-ounce / 397-g) can no-salt-added diced tomatoes
2 handfuls chopped kale (about 2 heaping cups)
1 (14-ounce / 397-g) package extra-firm tofu
1 teaspoon ground turmeric
1 tablespoon chili powder
3 tablespoons nutritional yeast
Salt (optional)
Ground black pepper
6 to 8 (10-inch) whole-grain tortillas

1. Place the onion, bell pepper, and garlic in the crock pot. Add the corn, beans, tomatoes, and kale. Crumble the tofu over the vegetables to look like scrambled eggs. Sprinkle the turmeric over the tofu and stir to coat, until the tofu is the color of scrambled eggs. Add the chili powder, nutritional yeast, salt (if using), and black pepper. Stir to combine. Cover and cook on High for 2 to 3 hours or on Low for 5 to 6 hours. 2. Using a slotted spoon to drain off excess liquid, scoop about ⅓ cup of burrito filling onto the center of each tortilla. Roll the bottom of the tortilla to cover the filling, fold one side over the filling, and continue rolling to close.

Oatmeal

Prep time: 5 minutes | Cook time: 6 to 8 hours | Serves 4

Nonstick cooking spray
1 cup steel-cut oats
2½ cups water
2 tablespoons honey (or maple syrup if vegan)
½ teaspoon pure vanilla extract
1 teaspoon ground cinnamon

1. Spray the crock pot generously with nonstick cooking spray. 2. In the crock pot, combine the oats, water, honey, vanilla, and cinnamon. Stir to mix well. 3. Cook on low for 6 to 8 hours and serve.

Protein Oatmeal Bake

Prep time: 5 minutes | Cook time: 6 to 8 hours | Serves 8

Nonstick cooking spray
2 cups steel-cut oats
2 teaspoons protein powder
1 teaspoon baking powder
1 teaspoon ground cinnamon
½ teaspoon salt
2 cups almond milk
¼ cup honey
1 ripe banana, mashed
1 large egg
1 tablespoon pure vanilla extract

1. Spray the crock pot generously with nonstick cooking spray. 2. In a large bowl, mix together the oats, protein powder, baking powder, cinnamon, salt, milk, honey, banana, egg, and vanilla. Pour the mixture into the crock pot. 3. Cook on low for 6 to 8 hours, or until the oatmeal is set, and serve.

Egg White Vegetable Frittata

Prep time: 10 minutes | Cook time: 6 to 8 hours | Serves 8 to 12

Nonstick cooking spray
2 cups egg whites (from about 12 large eggs)
1½ cups chopped vegetables (spinach, tomatoes, bell peppers, mushrooms, etc.)

½ cup grated low-fat Cheddar cheese
½ cup low-fat or skim milk
1 garlic clove, minced
¼ cup diced onion
Salt, to taste
Freshly ground black pepper, to taste

1. Spray the crock pot generously with nonstick cooking spray. 2. In a large bowl, whisk together the egg whites, vegetables, cheese, milk, garlic, and onion. Season lightly with salt and pepper, and pour into the crock pot. 3. Cook on low for 6 to 8 hours, or until the eggs are set, and serve.

Breakfast Sausage

Prep time: 5 minutes | Cook time: 6 to 8 hours | Serves 8

1 pound (454 g) lean ground pork
1 garlic clove, minced
1 teaspoon salt
1 teaspoon dried thyme
½ teaspoon dried oregano
½ teaspoon onion powder
¼ teaspoon freshly ground black pepper
¼ teaspoon paprika
¼ teaspoon ground cinnamon

1. In a large mixing bowl, combine the pork, garlic, salt, thyme, oregano, onion powder, pepper, paprika, and cinnamon. 2. Press the meat mixture evenly into the bottom of the crock pot. 3. Cook on low for 6 to 8 hours, or until the meat is completely cooked through. 4. Blot any extra grease off the top, if needed, using a paper towel. 5. Transfer the meat to a cutting board, cut the sausage into squares or circles, and serve.

Savory Basil Oatmeal

Prep time: 10 minutes | Cook time: 8 hours | Serves 8

3 cups steel-cut oatmeal
2 shallots, peeled and minced
5 cups vegetable broth
1 cup water
1 teaspoon dried basil leaves
½ teaspoon dried thyme leaves
¼ teaspoon salt
¼ teaspoon freshly ground black pepper
½ cup grated Parmesan cheese
2 cups chopped baby spinach leaves
2 tablespoons chopped fresh basil

1. In a 6-quart crock pot, mix the oatmeal, shallots, vegetable broth, water, basil, thyme, salt, and pepper. Cover and cook on low for 7 to 8 hours, or until the oatmeal is tender. 2. Stir in the Parmesan cheese, spinach, and basil, and let stand, covered, for another 5 minutes. Stir and serve.

Root Vegetable Hash

Prep time: 20 minutes | Cook time: 8 hours | Serves 8

4 Yukon Gold potatoes, chopped
2 russet potatoes, chopped
1 large parsnip, peeled and chopped
3 large carrots, peeled and chopped
2 onions, chopped
2 garlic cloves, minced
2 tablespoons olive oil
¼ cup vegetable broth
½ teaspoon salt
1 teaspoon dried thyme leaves

1. In a 6-quart crock pot, mix all of the ingredients. Cover and cook on low for 7 to 8 hours. 2. Stir the hash well and serve.

Eggs in Purgatory

Prep time: 15 minutes | Cook time: 8 hours | Serves 8

2½ pounds (1.1 kg) Roma tomatoes, chopped
2 onions, chopped
2 garlic cloves, chopped
1 teaspoon paprika
½ teaspoon ground cumin
½ teaspoon dried marjoram leaves
1 cup vegetable broth
8 large eggs
2 red chili peppers, minced
½ cup chopped flat-leaf parsley

1. In a 6-quart crock pot, mix the tomatoes, onions, garlic, paprika, cumin, marjoram, and vegetable broth, and stir to mix. Cover and cook on low for 7 to 8 hours, or until a sauce has formed. 2. One at a time, break the eggs into the sauce; do not stir. 3. Cover and cook on high until the egg whites are completely set and the yolk is thickened, about 20 minutes. Sprinkle the eggs with the minced red chili peppers. 4. Sprinkle with the parsley and serve.

Baked Berry Oatmeal

Prep time: 15 minutes | Cook time: 6 hours | Serves 12

7 cups rolled oats
4 eggs
1½ cups almond milk
2 tablespoons melted coconut oil
⅓ cup honey
¼ teaspoon salt
1 teaspoon ground cinnamon
¼ teaspoon ground ginger
1½ cups dried blueberries
1 cup dried cherries

1. Grease a 6-quart crock pot with plain vegetable oil. 2. In a large bowl, place the rolled oats. 3. In a medium bowl, mix the eggs, almond milk, coconut oil, honey, salt, cinnamon, and ginger. Mix until well combined. Pour this mixture over the oats. 4. Gently stir in the dried blueberries and dried cherries. Pour into the prepared crock pot. 5. Cover and cook on low for 4 to 6 hours, or until the oatmeal mixture is set and the edges start to brown.

Cranberry-Quinoa Hot Cereal

Prep time: 15 minutes | Cook time: 8 hours | Serves 12

3 cups quinoa, rinsed and drained
2 cups unsweetened apple juice
4 cups canned coconut milk
2 cups water
¼ cup honey
1 teaspoon vanilla extract
1 teaspoon ground cinnamon
½ teaspoon salt
1½ cups dried cranberries

1. In a 6-quart crock pot, mix all of the ingredients. Cover and cook on low for 6 to 8 hours or until the quinoa is creamy.

Mediterranean Strata

Prep time: 20 minutes | Cook time: 7 hours | Serves 10

8 cups whole-wheat bread, cut into cubes
1 onion, finely chopped
3 garlic cloves, minced
2 red bell peppers, stemmed, seeded, and chopped
2 cups chopped baby spinach leaves
4 eggs
2 egg whites
2 tablespoons olive oil
1½ cups 2% milk
1 cup shredded Asiago cheese

1. In a 6-quart crock pot, mix the bread cubes, onion, garlic, bell peppers, and spinach. 2. In a medium bowl, mix the eggs, egg whites, olive oil, and milk, and beat well. Pour this mixture into the crock pot. Sprinkle with the cheese. 3. Cover and cook on low for 5 to 7 hours, or until a food thermometer registers 165°F (74°C) and the strata is set and puffed. 4. Scoop the strata out of the crock pot to serve.

Mixed Berry Honey Granola

Prep time: 15 minutes | Cook time: 5 hours | Makes 20 cups

10 cups rolled oats
2 cups whole almonds
2 cups whole walnuts
2 cups macadamia nuts
½ cup honey
2 teaspoons ground cinnamon
¼ teaspoon ground cardamom
1 tablespoon vanilla extract
2 cups dried blueberries
2 cups dried cherries

1. In a 6-quart crock pot, mix the oatmeal, almonds, walnuts, and macadamia nuts. 2. In a small bowl, mix the honey, cinnamon, cardamom, and vanilla. Drizzle this mixture over the oatmeal mixture in the crock pot and stir with a spatula to coat. 3. Partially cover the crock pot. Cook on low for 3½ to 5 hours, stirring twice during cooking time, until the oatmeal and nuts are toasted. 4. Remove the granola from the crock pot and spread on two large baking sheets. Add the dried blueberries and cherries to the granola and stir gently. 5. Let the granola cool, then store in an airtight container at room temperature up to one week.

Quinoa-Kale-Egg Casserole

Prep time: 20 minutes | Cook time: 8 hours | Serves 8

3 cups 2% milk
1½ cups vegetable broth
11 eggs
1½ cups quinoa, rinsed and drained
3 cups chopped kale
1 leek, chopped
1 red bell pepper, stemmed, seeded, and chopped
3 garlic cloves, minced
1½ cups shredded Havarti cheese

1. Grease a 6-quart crock pot with vegetable oil and set aside. 2. In a large bowl, mix the milk, vegetable broth, and eggs, and beat well with a wire whisk. 3. Stir in the quinoa, kale, leek, bell pepper, garlic, and cheese. Pour this mixture into the prepared crock pot. 4. Cover and cook on low for 6 to 8 hours, or until a food thermometer registers 165°F (74°C) and the mixture is set.

Egg and Potato Strata

Prep time: 20 minutes | Cook time: 8 hours | Serves 8

8 Yukon Gold potatoes, peeled and diced
1 onion, minced
2 red bell peppers, stemmed, seeded, and minced
3 Roma tomatoes, seeded and chopped
3 garlic cloves, minced
1½ cups shredded Swiss cheese
8 eggs
2 egg whites
1 teaspoon dried marjoram leaves
1 cup 2% milk

1. In a 6-quart crock pot, layer the diced potatoes, onion, bell peppers, tomatoes, garlic, and cheese. 2. In a medium bowl, mix the eggs, egg whites, marjoram, and milk well with a wire whisk. Pour this mixture into the crock pot. 3. Cover and cook on low for 6 to 8 hours, or until a food thermometer registers 165°F (74°C) and the potatoes are tender. 4. Scoop out of the crock pot to serve.

Apple French Toast Bake

Prep time: 20 minutes | Cook time: 5 hours | Serves 8

¼ cup coconut sugar
1 teaspoon ground cinnamon
¼ teaspoon ground cardamom
10 slices whole-wheat bread, cubed
2 Granny Smith apples, peeled and diced
8 eggs
1 cup canned coconut milk
1 cup unsweetened apple juice
2 teaspoons vanilla extract
1 cup granola

1. Grease a 6-quart crock pot with plain vegetable oil. 2. In a small bowl, mix the coconut sugar, cinnamon, and cardamom well. 3. In the crock pot, layer the bread, apples, and coconut sugar mixture. 4. In a large bowl, mix the eggs, coconut milk, apple juice, and vanilla, and mix well. Pour this mixture slowly over the food in the crock pot. Sprinkle the granola on top. 5. Cover and cook on low for 4 to 5 hours, or until a food thermometer registers 165°F (74°C). 6. Scoop the mixture from the crock pot to serve.

Pumpkin Pie Baked Oatmeal

Prep time: 15 minutes | Cook time: 8 hours | Serves 10

3 cups steel-cut oats
1 (16-ounce / 454-g) can solid pack pumpkin
2 cups canned coconut milk
4 cups water
¼ cup honey
2 teaspoons vanilla extract
¼ teaspoon salt
1 teaspoon ground cinnamon
½ teaspoon ground ginger
1 cup granola

1. Grease a 6-quart crock pot with plain vegetable oil. 2. Put the oats into the crock pot. 3. In a medium bowl, mix the canned pumpkin and coconut milk with a wire whisk until blended. Then stir in the water, honey, vanilla, salt, cinnamon, and ginger. Mix until well combined. Pour this mixture into the crock pot over the oats and stir. Top with the granola. 4. Cover and cook on low for 6 to 8 hours, or until the oatmeal is tender and the edges start to brown.

French Vegetable Omelet

Prep time: 20 minutes | Cook time: 4 hours | Serves 6

12 eggs, beaten
⅓ cup 2% milk
½ teaspoon dried thyme leaves
½ teaspoon dried tarragon leaves
¼ teaspoon salt
1 cup chopped fresh asparagus
1 yellow bell pepper, stemmed, seeded, and chopped
1 small zucchini, peeled and diced
2 shallots, peeled and minced
½ cup grated Parmesan cheese

1. Grease the inside of a 6-quart crock pot with plain vegetable oil. 2. In a large bowl, mix the eggs, milk, thyme, tarragon, and salt, and mix well with an eggbeater or wire whisk until well combined. 3. Add the asparagus, bell pepper, zucchini, and shallots. Pour into the crock pot. 4. Cover and cook on low for 3 to 4 hours, or until the eggs are set. 5. Sprinkle with the Parmesan cheese; cover and cook for another 5 to 10 minutes or until the cheese starts to melt.

Egg and Wild Rice Casserole

Prep time: 20 minutes | Cook time: 7 hours | Serves 6

3 cups plain cooked wild rice
2 cups sliced mushrooms
1 red bell pepper, stemmed, seeded, and chopped
1 onion, minced
2 garlic cloves, minced
11 eggs
1 teaspoon dried thyme leaves
¼ teaspoon salt
1½ cups shredded Swiss cheese

1. In a 6-quart crock pot, layer the wild rice, mushrooms, bell pepper, onion, and garlic. 2. In a large bowl, beat the eggs with the thyme and salt. Pour into the crock pot. Top with the cheese. 3. Cover and cook on low for 5 to 7 hours, or until a food thermometer registers 165ºF (74ºC) and the casserole is set.

Cornmeal Mush

Prep time: 10 minutes | Cook time: 4 to 6 hours | Serves 15 to 18

2 cups cornmeal
2 teaspoons salt
2 cups cold water
6 cups hot water

1. Combine cornmeal, salt, and cold water. 2. Stir in hot water. Pour into greased slow cooker. 3. Cover. Cook on high 1 hour, then stir again and cook on low 3 to 4 hours or cook on low 5 to 6 hours, stirring once every hour during the first 2 hours. 4. Serve hot.

Banana Bread Oatmeal

Prep time: 20 minutes | Cook time: 8 hours | Serves 8

4 cups coconut milk
4 cups water
2 cups steel cut oats
3 ripe bananas, peeled and mashed
⅓ cup coconut sugar
2 teaspoons ground cinnamon
½ teaspoon ground nutmeg
2 teaspoons vanilla extract
1 cup chopped pecans

1. Combine the coconut milk and water in a 6-quart crock pot. Add the steel cut oats, bananas, coconut sugar, cinnamon, nutmeg, vanilla, and pecans. 2. Cover and cook on low for 7 to 8 hours or until the oats are very tender. Stir well before serving.

Blueberry Apple Waffle Topping

Prep time: 10 minutes | Cook time: 3 hours | Serves 10 to 12

1 quart natural applesauce, unsweetened
2 Granny Smith apples, unpeeled, cored, and sliced
1 pint fresh or frozen blueberries
Nonfat cooking spray
½ tablespoon ground cinnamon
½ cup pure maple syrup
1 teaspoon almond flavoring
½ cup walnuts, chopped

1. Stir together applesauce, apples, and blueberries in slow cooker sprayed with nonfat cooking spray. 2. Add cinnamon and maple syrup. 3. Cover. Cook on low 3 hours. 4. Add almond flavoring and walnuts just before serving.

Hot Wheat Berry Cereal

Prep time: 5 minutes | Cook time: 10 hours | Serves 4

1 cup wheat berries
5 cups water

1. Rinse and sort berries. Cover with water and soak all day (or 8 hours) in slow cooker. 2. Cover. Cook on low overnight (or 10 hours). 3. Drain, if needed. Serve.

Streusel Cake

Prep time: 10 minutes | Cook time: 3 to 4 hours | Serves 8 to 10

1 (16-ounce / 454-g) package pound cake mix, prepared according to package directions
¼ cup packed brown sugar
1 tablespoon flour
¼ cup chopped nuts
1 teaspoon cinnamon

1. Liberally grease and flour a 2-pound (907-g) coffee can, or slow cooker baking insert, that fits into your slow cooker. Pour prepared cake mix into coffee can or baking insert. 2. In a small bowl, mix brown sugar, flour, nuts, and cinnamon together. Sprinkle over top of cake mix. 3. Place coffee tin or baking insert in slow cooker. Cover top of tin or insert with several layers of paper towels. 4. Cover cooker itself and cook on high 3 to 4 hours, or until toothpick inserted in center of cake comes out clean. 5. Remove baking tin from slow cooker and allow to cool for 30 minutes before cutting into wedges to serve.

Hot Applesauce Breakfast

Prep time: 15 minutes | Cook time: 8 to 10 hours | Serves 8

10 apples, peeled and sliced
½ to 1 cup sugar
1 tablespoon ground cinnamon
¼ teaspoon ground nutmeg

1. Combine ingredients in slow cooker. 2. Cover. Cook on low 8 to 10 hours.

Egg and Broccoli Casserole

Prep time: 15 minutes | Cook time: 2½ to 3 hours | Serves 6

1 (24-ounce / 680-g) carton small-curd cottage cheese
1 (10-ounce / 283-g) package frozen chopped broccoli, thawed and drained
2 cups shredded Cheddar cheese
6 eggs, beaten
⅓ cup flour
¼ cup butter, melted
3 tablespoons finely chopped onion
½ teaspoon salt
Shredded cheese (optional)

1. Combine first 8 ingredients. Pour into greased slow cooker. 2. Cover and cook on high 1 hour. Stir. Reduce heat to low. Cover and cook 2½ to 3 hours, or until temperature reaches 160°F (71°C) and eggs are set. 3. Sprinkle with cheese and serve.

Overnight Steel-Cut Oats

Prep time: 5 minutes | Cook time: 8 hours | Serves 4 to 5

1 cup dry steel-cut oats
4 cups water

1. Combine ingredients in slow cooker. 2. Cover and cook on low overnight, or for 8 hours. 3. Stir before serving. Serve with your other favorite toppings.

Welsh Rarebit

Prep time: 10 minutes | Cook time: 1½ to 2½ hours | Serves 6 to 8

1 (12-ounce / 340-g) can beer
1 tablespoon dry mustard
1 teaspoon Worcestershire sauce
½ teaspoon salt
⅛ teaspoon black or white pepper
1 pound (454 g) American cheese, cubed
1 pound (454 g) sharp Cheddar cheese, cubed
English muffins or toast
Tomato slices
Bacon, cooked until crisp
Fresh steamed asparagus spears

1. In slow cooker, combine beer, mustard, 2. Worcestershire sauce, salt, and pepper. Cover and cook on high 1 to 2 hours, until mixture boils. 3. Add cheese, a little at a time, stirring constantly until all the cheese melts. 4. Heat on high 20 to 30 minutes with cover off, stirring frequently. 5. Serve hot over toasted English muffins or over toasted bread cut into triangles. Garnish with tomato slices, strips of crisp bacon and steamed asparagus spears.

Smoky Breakfast Casserole

Prep time: 15 minutes | Cook time: 3 hours | Serves 8 to 10

6 eggs, beaten
1 pound (454 g) little smokies (cocktail wieners), or 1½ pounds (680 g) bulk sausage, browned and drained
1½ cups milk
1 cup shredded Cheddar cheese
8 slices bread, torn into pieces
1 teaspoon salt
½ teaspoon dry mustard
1 cup shredded Mozzarella cheese

1. Mix together all ingredients except Mozzarella cheese. Pour into greased slow cooker. 2. Sprinkle Mozzarella cheese over top. 3. Cover and cook 2 hours on high, and then 1 hour on low.

Overnight Apple Oatmeal

Prep time: 10 minutes | Cook time: 6 to 8 hours | Serves 4

2 cups skim or 2% milk
2 tablespoons honey, or ¼ cup brown sugar
1 tablespoon margarine
¼ teaspoon salt
½ teaspoon ground cinnamon
1 cup dry rolled oats
1 cup apples, chopped
½ cup raisins (optional)
¼ cup walnuts, chopped
½ cup fat-free half-and-half

1. Spray inside of slow cooker with nonfat cooking spray. 2. In a mixing bowl, combine all ingredients except half-and-half. Pour into cooker. 3. Cover and cook on low overnight, ideally 6 to 8 hours. The oatmeal is ready to eat in the morning. 4. Stir in the half-and-half just before serving.

Polenta

Prep time: 10 minutes | Cook time: 2 to 9 hours | Serves 8 to 10

4 tablespoons melted butter, divided
¼ teaspoon paprika
6 cups boiling water
2 cups dry cornmeal
2 teaspoons salt

1. Use 1 tablespoon butter to lightly grease the inside of the slow cooker. Sprinkle in paprika. Turn to high setting. 2. Add remaining ingredients to slow cooker in the order listed, including 1 tablespoon butter. Stir well. 3. Cover and cook on high 2 to 3 hours, or on low 6 to 9 hours. Stir occasionally. 4. Pour hot cooked polenta into 2 lightly greased loaf pans. Chill 8 hours or overnight. 5. To serve, cut into ¼-inch-thick slices. Melt 2 tablespoons butter in large nonstick skillet, then lay in slices and cook until browned. Turn to brown other side. 6. For breakfast, serve with your choice of sweetener.

Dulce Leche

Prep time: 5 minutes | Cook time: 2 hours | Makes 2½ cups

2 (14-ounce / 397-g) cans sweetened condensed milk

Cookies, for serving

1. Place unopened cans of milk in slow cooker. Fill cooker with warm water so that it comes above the cans by 1½ to 2 inches. 2. Cover cooker. Cook on high 2 hours. 3. Cool unopened cans. 4. When opened, the contents should be thick and spreadable. Use as a filling between 2 cookies.

Breakfast Wassail

Prep time: 5 minutes | Cook time: 3 hours | Makes 4 quarts

1 (64-ounce / 1.8-kg) bottle cranberry juice
1 (32-ounce / 907-g) bottle apple juice
1 (12-ounce / 340-g) can frozen pineapple juice concentrate
1 (12-ounce / 340-g) can frozen lemonade concentrate
3 to 4 cinnamon sticks
1 quart water (optional)

1. Combine all ingredients except water in slow cooker. Add water if mixture is too sweet. 2. Cover. Cook on low 3 hours.

Easy Egg and Sausage Puff

Prep time: 15 minutes | Cook time: 2 to 2½ hours | Serves 6

1 pound (454 g) loose sausage
6 eggs
1 cup all-purpose baking mix
1 cup shredded Cheddar cheese
2 cups milk
¼ teaspoon dry mustard (optional)
Nonstick cooking spray

1. Brown sausage in nonstick skillet. Break up chunks of meat as it cooks. Drain. 2. Meanwhile, spray interior of slow cooker with nonstick cooking spray. 3. Mix all ingredients in slow cooker. 4. Cover and cook on high 1 hour. Turn to low and cook 1 to 1½ hours, or until the dish is fully cooked in the center.

Breakfast Prunes

Prep time: 10 minutes | Cook time: 8 to 10 hours | Serves 6

2 cups orange juice
¼ cup orange marmalade
1 teaspoon ground cinnamon
¼ teaspoon ground cloves
¼ teaspoon ground nutmeg
1 cup water
1 (12-ounce / 340-g) package pitted dried prunes
2 thin lemon slices

1. Combine orange juice, marmalade, cinnamon, cloves, nutmeg, and water in slow cooker. 2. Stir in prunes and lemon slices. 3. Cover. Cook on low 8 to 10 hours, or overnight. 4. Serve warm as a breakfast food, or warm or chilled as a side dish with a meal later in the day.

Slow Cooker Oatmeal

Prep time: 15 minutes | Cook time: 8 to 9 hours | Serves 7 to 8

2 cups dry rolled oats
4 cups water
1 large apple, peeled and chopped
1 cup raisins
1 teaspoon cinnamon
1 to 2 tablespoons orange zest

1. Combine all ingredients in your slow cooker. 2. Cover and cook on low 8 to 9 hours. 3. Serve topped with brown sugar, if you wish, and milk.

"Baked" Oatmeal

Prep time: 10 minutes | Cook time: 2½ to 3 hours | Serves 4 to 6

⅓ cup oil
½ cup sugar
1 large egg, beaten
2 cups dry quick oats
1½ teaspoons baking powder
½ teaspoon salt
¾ cup milk

1. Pour the oil into the slow cooker to grease bottom and sides. 2. Add remaining ingredients. Mix well. 3. Cook on low 2½ to 3 hours.

Blueberry Fancy

Prep time: 15 minutes | Cook time: 3 to 4 hours | Serves 12

1 loaf Italian bread, cubed, divided
1 pint blueberries, divided
8 ounces (227 g) cream cheese, cubed, divided
6 eggs
1½ cups milk

1. Place half the bread cubes in the slow cooker. 2. Drop half the blueberries over top the bread. 3. Sprinkle half the cream cheese cubes over the blueberries. 4. Repeat all 3 layers. 5. In a mixing bowl, whisk together eggs and milk. Pour over all ingredients. 6. Cover and cook on low until the dish is set. 7. Serve.

Breakfast Oatmeal

Prep time: 5 minutes | Cook time: 8 hours | Serves 6

2 cups dry rolled oats
4 cups water
1 teaspoon salt
½ to 1 cup chopped dates, or raisins, or cranberries, or a mixture of any of these fruits

1. Combine all ingredients in slow cooker. 2. Cover and cook on low overnight, or for 8 hours.

Breakfast Fruit Compote

Prep time: 5 minutes | Cook time: 2 to 7 hours | Serves 8 to 9

1 (12-ounce / 340-g) package dried apricots
1 (12-ounce / 340-g) package pitted dried plums
1 (11-ounce / 312-g) can mandarin oranges in light syrup, undrained
1 (29-ounce / 822-g) can sliced peaches in light syrup, undrained
¼ cup white raisins
10 maraschino cherries

1. Combine all ingredients in slow cooker. Mix well. 2. Cover. Cook on low 6 to 7 hours, or on high 2 to 3 hours.

Chapter 2 Snacks and Appetizers

Rosemary-Onion Jam

Prep time: 5 minutes | Cook time: 6 to 7 hours | Makes 3 to 4 cups

4 to 6 large sweet onions (about 3 pounds / 1.4 kg), sliced into half-moons
2 garlic cloves, minced
½ cup maple syrup (optional)
¼ cup balsamic vinegar
1 teaspoon finely chopped fresh rosemary (about 2 sprigs), or dried

1. Put the onions in the crock pot. Add the garlic. 2. In a small bowl, stir together the maple syrup (if using), vinegar, and rosemary. Pour the mixture into the crock pot and toss gently to coat the onions. Cover and cook on High for 6 to 7 hours or on Low for 10 to 12 hours, until the onions are deep brown. 3. Transfer the mixture to a blender, or use an immersion blender, and blend into a chunky jam consistency. Store in glass jars or plastic containers in the refrigerator for up to 1 month.

Eggplant Caponata Bruschetta

Prep time: 20 minutes | Cook time: 2 to 3 hours | Serves 4 to 8

1 medium eggplant, unpeeled and chopped
1 medium onion, diced
2 small zucchini, diced
3 celery stalks, diced
4 garlic cloves, minced
1 cup sliced pitted green olives
2 (14½-ounce / 411-g) cans diced tomatoes
2 tablespoons capers, drained
¼ cup red wine vinegar
1 tablespoon maple syrup (optional)
1 teaspoon dried basil
1 teaspoon dried oregano
Ground black pepper
Salt (optional)
1 long thin loaf crusty whole-grain bread
3 tablespoons chopped fresh flat-leaf parsley

1. Put the eggplant, onion, zucchini, celery, garlic, and olives in the crock pot. Pour in the tomatoes. Add the capers, vinegar, maple syrup (if using), basil, oregano, pepper, and salt (if using). Stir well to combine. Cover and cook on High for 2 to 3 hours or on Low for 5 to 6 hours. 2. Preheat the oven to 375ºF (190ºC). Slice the bread into ½-inch slices and place them on a baking sheet. Toast in the oven, keeping an eye on the bread so it doesn't burn. Flip the bread and toast the other side to make it into crostini. 3. After the caponata finishes cooking, stir in the parsley. Spoon about 2 tablespoons of caponata onto each piece of crostini and serve immediately.

Pineapple, Peach, and Mango Salsa

Prep time: 15 minutes | Cook time: 2 to 3 hours | Makes about 6 cups

medium onion, finely diced
2 garlic cloves, minced
1 medium orange, red, or yellow bell pepper, finely diced
1 (20-ounce / 567-g) can crushed pineapple in juice
1 (15-ounce / 425-g) can no-sugar-added mango in juice, drained and finely diced
1 (15-ounce / 425-g) can no-sugar-added sliced peaches in juice, drained and finely diced
½ teaspoon ground cumin
1 teaspoon paprika
Juice of 1 lime
3 to 4 tablespoons chopped fresh mint (about 10 to 15 leaves)

1. Put the onion, garlic, and bell pepper in the crock pot. Add the pineapple and its juices, the mango, and the peaches. Sprinkle the cumin and paprika into the crock pot. Add the lime juice and stir well to combine. 2. Cover and cook on Low for 2 to 3 hours, or until the onion and peppers are cooked through and softened. Let the salsa cool slightly, then stir in the mint just before serving.

White Bean Tzatziki Dip

Prep time: 10 minutes | Cook time: 1 to 2 hours | Makes about 8 cups

4 (14½-ounce / 411-g) cans white beans, drained and rinsed
8 garlic cloves, minced
1 medium onion, coarsely chopped
¼ cup store-bought low-sodium vegetable broth, plus more as needed
Juice from one lemon, divided
2 teaspoons dried dill, divided
Salt (optional)
1 cucumber, peeled and finely diced

1. Place the beans, garlic, onion, broth, and half the lemon juice in a blender. Blend until creamy, about 1 minute, adding up to ¼ cup of additional broth as needed to make the mixture creamy. 2. Transfer the mixture to the crock pot, stir in 1 teaspoon of dill, and season with salt (if using). Cover and cook on Low for 1 to 2 hours until heated through. 3. Meanwhile, in a medium bowl, mix the cucumber with the remaining 1 teaspoon of dill and the remaining half of the lemon juice. Toss to coat. Season with salt (if using). 4. Spoon the dip from the crock pot into a serving bowl and top with the cucumber mixture before serving.

Sweet 'n' Spicy Crunchy Snack Mix

Prep time: 5 minutes | Cook time: 1½ hours | Makes 5½ cups

1 cup raw cashews
1 cup raw almonds
1 cup raw pecan halves
1 cup walnuts
½ cup raw pepitas
½ cup raw sunflower seeds
¼ cup aquafaba
¼ cup maple syrup (optional)
1 teaspoon miso paste
1 teaspoon garlic powder
1 teaspoon paprika
2 teaspoons ground ginger

1. Put the cashews, almonds, pecans, walnuts, pepitas, and sunflower seeds in the crock pot. 2. In a deep bowl, whisk or use an immersion blender to beat the aquafaba until foamy, about 1 minute. Add the maple syrup (if using), miso paste, garlic powder, paprika, and ginger and whisk or blend to combine. Pour over the nuts in the crock pot and gently toss, making sure all the nuts and seeds are coated. 3. Stretch a clean dish towel or several layers of paper towels over the top of the crock pot, but not touching the food, and place the lid on top. Cook on Low for 1½ hours, stirring every 20 to 30 minutes to keep the nuts from burning. After each stir, dry any condensation under the lid and replace the towels before re-covering. 4. Line a rimmed baking sheet with parchment paper. Transfer the snack mix to the baking sheet to cool. Store in an airtight container for up to 2 weeks.

Crispy Chickpea Snackers

Prep time: 10 minutes | Cook time: 4 to 6 hours | Makes 7 to 8 cups

4 (14½-ounce / 411-g) cans chickpeas, drained and rinsed
Juice of 2 lemons
1 tablespoon garlic powder
1 tablespoon onion powder
2 teaspoons paprika
Salt (optional)

1. Put the chickpeas into the crock pot. Add the lemon juice, garlic powder, onion powder, and paprika. Season with salt (if using). Toss gently to thoroughly coat every chickpea with the seasoning. 2. Cover the crock pot and, using a wooden spoon or a chopstick, prop open the lid to allow the steam to escape. Cook on High for 4 to 6 hours or on Low for 8 to 10 hours, stirring every 30 to 45 minutes to keep the chickpeas from burning.

Spiced Glazed Carrots

Prep time: 10 minutes | Cook time: 2 to 3 hours | Serves 4 to 6

2 pounds (907 g) fresh baby carrots or frozen cut carrots
⅓ cup no-sugar-added apricot preserves, such as Polaner All Fruit brand
2 tablespoons orange juice
1 tablespoon balsamic vinegar
1 tablespoon maple syrup (optional)
¼ teaspoon ground cinnamon
¼ teaspoon ground nutmeg
¼ teaspoon ground turmeric
½ teaspoon ground ginger
1 teaspoon dried thyme
1 tablespoon cornstarch
2 tablespoons water

1. Place the carrots into the crock pot. In a measuring cup or medium bowl, stir together the apricot preserves, orange juice, vinegar, maple syrup (if using), cinnamon, nutmeg, turmeric, ginger, and thyme. Pour the sauce into the crock pot and stir to coat the carrots. Cover and cook on High for 2 to 3 hours or on Low for 4 to 6 hours. 2. During the last 30 minutes of cooking, add the cornstarch and water to a small lidded jar. Cover and shake the jar well to form a slurry and pour it into the crock pot, stirring occasionally to thicken the sauce and form a glaze.

Classic Italian Mushrooms

Prep time: 10 minutes | Cook time: 2 hours | Serves 4 to 6

2 pounds (907 g) white button mushrooms, stemmed
4 garlic cloves, minced
1 medium onion, sliced into half-moons
3 to 5 tablespoons store-bought low-sodium vegetable broth
3 teaspoons Italian seasoning
Ground black pepper
Salt (optional)

1. Cut any extra-large mushrooms in half. Place the mushrooms in the crock pot. Add the garlic and onion. 2. Pour in the broth and sprinkle with the Italian seasoning. Season with black pepper and salt (if using). Stir to combine. Cover and cook on Low for 2 hours, or until the mushrooms are cooked through.

Spinach and Artichoke Dip

Prep time: 20 minutes | Cook time: 5 hours | Serves 10

1 (15-ounce / 425-g) BPA-free can no-salt-added cannellini beans, drained and rinsed
1 red onion, chopped
3 garlic cloves, minced
2 (14-ounce / 397-g) BPA-free cans no-salt-added artichoke hearts, drained and quartered
1 (10-ounce / 283-g) bag chopped frozen spinach, thawed and drained
½ cup sour cream
2 tablespoons freshly squeezed lemon juice
2 tablespoons olive oil
1 cup shredded Swiss cheese

1. In a 6-quart crock pot, mash the beans using a potato masher. 2. Stir in the onion, garlic, and artichoke hearts. 3. Stir in the spinach, sour cream, lemon juice, olive oil, and Swiss cheese. 4. Cover and cook on low for 4 to 5 hours, or until the dip is hot and bubbling.

Tex-Mex Nacho Dip

Prep time: 20 minutes | Cook time: 8 hours | Serves 12

4 (5-ounce / 142-g) boneless, skinless chicken breasts
3 onions, chopped
6 garlic cloves, minced
2 jalapeño peppers, minced
½ cup chicken stock
2 tablespoons chili powder
1 (15-ounce / 425-g) BPA-free can no-salt-added black beans, drained and rinsed
1 cup plain Greek yogurt
1 cup shredded Monterey Jack cheese
2 avocados, peeled and chopped

1. In a 6-quart crock pot, mix the chicken, onions, garlic, and jalapeño peppers. Add the chicken stock and chili powder. Cover and cook on low for 5 to 7 hours, or until the chicken registers 165°F (74°C) on a food thermometer. 2. Remove the chicken from the crock pot and shred it using two forks. Return the chicken to the crock pot. 3. Add the black beans, yogurt, and cheese. Cover and cook on low 1 hour longer, until hot. 4. Top with the avocados and serve.

Spiced Chocolate-Nut Clusters

Prep time: 20 minutes | Cook time: 2 hours | Makes 60 candies

4 pounds (1.8 kg) dairy-free 70% to 80% cacao dark chocolate, chopped
¼ cup coconut oil
2 teaspoons vanilla extract
1 teaspoon ground cinnamon
¼ teaspoon ground cloves
4 cups roasted cashews
3 cups coarsely chopped pecans

1. In a 6-quart crock pot, mix the chopped chocolate, coconut oil, vanilla, cinnamon, and cloves. Cover and cook on low for 2 hours, or until the chocolate melts. 2. Stir the chocolate mixture until it is smooth. 3. Stir in the cashews and pecans. 4. Drop the mixture by tablespoons onto waxed paper or parchment paper. Let stand until set.

Mole Chicken Bites

Prep time: 20 minutes | Cook time: 6 hours | Serves 8

2 onions, chopped
6 garlic cloves, minced
4 large tomatoes, seeded and chopped
2 dried red chilies, crushed
1 jalapeño pepper, minced
2 tablespoons chili powder
3 tablespoons cocoa powder
2 tablespoons coconut sugar
½ cup chicken stock
6 (5-ounce / 142-g) boneless, skinless chicken breasts

1. In a 6-quart crock pot, mix the onions, garlic, tomatoes, chili peppers, and jalapeño peppers. 2. In a medium bowl, mix the chili powder, cocoa powder, coconut sugar, and chicken stock. 3. Cut the chicken breasts into 1-inch strips crosswise and add to the crock pot. Pour the chicken stock mixture over all. 4. Cover and cook on low for 4 to 6 hours, or until the chicken registers 165ºF (74ºC) on a food thermometer. Serve with toothpicks or little plates and forks.

Spiced Nut Mix

Prep time: 20 minutes | Cook time: 3 hours | Makes 12 cups

3 cups raw cashews
3 cups walnuts
3 cups pecans
3 cups macadamia nuts
¼ cup melted unsalted butter
½ cup coconut sugar
2 tablespoons chili powder
2 teaspoons paprika
¼ teaspoon cayenne pepper

1. In a 6-quart crock pot, mix the cashews, walnuts, pecans, and macadamia nuts. Drizzle with the melted butter and toss. 2. In a small bowl, mix the coconut sugar, chili powder, paprika, and cayenne pepper until well combined. Sprinkle over the nuts and toss. 3. Partially cover the crock pot and cook on low for 2 to 3 hours, stirring twice during cooking time, until the nuts are golden and toasted.

Slow Cooker Candy

Prep time: 10 minutes | Cook time: 2 hours | Makes 80 to 100 pieces

1½ pounds (680 g) almond bark, broken
1 (4-ounce / 113-g) Baker's Brand German sweet chocolate bar, broken
8 ounces (227 g) chocolate chips
8 ounces (227 g) peanut butter chips
2 pounds (907 g) lightly salted or unsalted peanuts

1. Spray inside of cooker with nonstick cooking spray. 2. Layer ingredients into slow cooker in the order given above. 3. Cook on low 2 hours. Do not stir or lift the lid during the cooking time. 4. After 2 hours, mix well. 5. Drop by teaspoonfuls onto waxed paper. Refrigerate for approximately 45 minutes before serving or storing.

Tangy Meatballs

Prep time: 15 minutes | Cook time: 2 to 4 hours | Makes 50 to 60 meatballs

2 pounds (907 g) precooked meatballs
1 (16-ounce / 454-g) bottle barbecue sauce
8 ounces (227 g) grape jelly

1. Place meatballs in slow cooker. 2. Combine barbecue sauce and jelly in medium-sized mixing bowl. 3. Pour over meatballs and stir well. 4. Cover and cook on high 2 hours, or on low 4 hours. 5. Turn to low and serve.

Tangy Cocktail Franks

Prep time: 10 minutes | Cook time: 1 to 2 hours | Serves 12

1 (14-ounce / 397-g) jar currant jelly
¼ cup prepared mustard
3 tablespoons dry sherry
¼ teaspoon ground allspice
1 (30-ounce / 850-g) can unsweetened pineapple chunks
1 (6-ounce / 170-g) package low-sodium cocktail franks

1. Melt jelly in slow cooker turned on high. Stir in seasonings until blended. 2. Drain pineapple chunks and any liquid in cocktail franks package. Discard juice. Gently stir pineapple and franks into slow cooker. 3. Cover. Cook on low 1 to 2 hours. 4. Serve and enjoy.

Mini Hot Dogs and Meatballs

Prep time: 5 minutes | Cook time: 2 to 3 hours | Serves 15

36 frozen cooked Italian meatballs (½-ounce / 14-g each)
1 (16-ounce / 454-g) package miniature hot dogs or little smoked sausages
1 (26-ounce / 737-g) jar meatless spaghetti sauce
1 (18-ounce / 510-g) bottle barbecue sauce
1 (12-ounce / 340-g) bottle chili sauce

1. Combine all ingredients in slow cooker. 2. Cover and cook on high 2 hours, or on low 3 hours, until heated through.

Simmered Smoked Sausages

Prep time: 15 minutes | Cook time: 4 hours | Serves 16 to 20

2 (16-ounce / 454-g) packages miniature smoked sausage links
1 cup brown sugar, packed
½ cup ketchup
¼ cup prepared horseradish

1. Place sausages in slow cooker. 2. Combine remaining ingredients in a bowl and pour over sausages. 3. Cover and cook on low for 4 hours.

Butterscotch Haystacks

Prep time: 15 minutes | Cook time: 15 minutes | Makes 3 dozen pieces

2 (6-ounce / 170-g) packages butterscotch chips
¾ cup chopped almonds
1 (5-ounce / 142-g) can chow mein noodles

1. Turn cooker to high. Place chips in slow cooker. Stir every few minutes until they're melted. 2. When the chips are completely melted, gently stir in almonds and noodles. 3. When well mixed, drop by teaspoonfuls onto waxed paper. 4. Let stand until haystacks are set, or speed things up by placing them in the fridge until set. 5. Serve, or store in a covered container, placing waxed paper between layers of candy. Keep in a cool, dry place.

Apple Kielbasa

Prep time: 15 minutes | Cook time: 6 to 8 hours | Serves 12

2 pounds (907 g) fully cooked kielbasa sausage, cut into 1-inch pieces
¾ cup brown sugar
1 cup chunky applesauce
2 cloves garlic, minced

1. Combine all ingredients in slow cooker. 2. Cover and cook on low 6 to 8 hours until thoroughly heated.

Cider Cheese Fondue—for a Buffet Table

Prep time: 15 minutes | Cook time: 4 minutes | Serves 4

¾ cup apple juice or cider
2 cups shredded Cheddar cheese
1 cup shredded Swiss cheese
1 tablespoon cornstarch
⅛ teaspoon pepper
1 pound (454 g) loaf French bread, cut into chunks

1. In a large saucepan, bring cider to a boil. Reduce heat to medium low. 2. In a large mixing bowl, toss together the cheeses with cornstarch and pepper. 3. Stir mixture into cider. Cook and stir for 3 to 4 minutes, or until cheese is melted. 4. Transfer to a 1-quart slow cooker to keep warm. Stir occasionally 5. Serve with bread cubes for dipping.

Easy Barbecue Smokies

Prep time: 5 minutes | Cook time: 2 hours | Serves 12 to 16

1 (18-ounce / 510-g) bottle barbecue sauce
8 ounces (227 g) salsa
2 (16-ounce / 454-g) packages little smokies

1. Mix barbecue sauce and salsa in slow cooker. 2. Add the little smokies. 3. Heat on high for 2 hours. 4. Stir. Turn to low to serve.

Barbecued Lil' Smokies

Prep time: 5 minutes | Cook time: 4 hours | Serves 48 to 60 as an appetizer

4 (16-ounce / 454-g) packages little smokies
1 (18-ounce / 510-g) bottle barbecue sauce

1. Mix ingredients together in slow cooker. 2. Cover and cook on low for 4 hours.

Pickled Whiting

Prep time: 10 minutes | Cook time: 3 to 4 hours | Serves 24

2 onions, sliced
1 cup white vinegar
¾ cup Splenda
1 teaspoon salt
1 tablespoon allspice
2 pounds (907 g) frozen individual whiting with skin

1. Combine onions, vinegar, Splenda, salt, and allspice in bottom of slow cooker. 2. Slice frozen whiting into 2-inch slices, each with skin on. Place fish in slow cooker, pushing it down into the liquid as much as possible. 3. Cook on low 3 to 4 hours. 4. Pour cooking liquid over fish, cover, and refrigerate. Serve when well chilled.

Sweet 'n Sour Meatballs

Prep time: 10 minutes | Cook time: 2 to 4 hours | Serves 15 to 20

1 (12-ounce / 340-g) jar grape jelly
1 (12-ounce / 340-g) jar chili sauce
2 (1-pound / 454-g) bags prepared frozen meatballs, thawed

1. Combine jelly and sauce in slow cooker. Stir well. 2. Add meatballs. Stir to coat. 3. Cover and heat on low 4 hours, or on high 2 hours. Keep slow cooker on low while serving.

Chili Nuts

Prep time: 5 minutes | Cook time: 2 to 2½ hours | Makes 5 cups nuts

¼ cup butter, melted
2 (12-ounce / 340-g) cans cocktail peanuts
1 (1.6-ounce / 45-g) package chili seasoning mix

1. Pour butter over nuts in slow cooker. 2. Sprinkle in dry chili mix. Toss together. Cover. Heat on low 2 to 2½ hours. Turn to high. Remove lid and cook 10 to 15 minutes. 3. Serve warm or cool.

Party Time Artichokes

Prep time: 10 minutes | Cook time: 2½ to 4 hours | Serves 4

4 whole, fresh artichokes
1 teaspoon salt
4 tablespoons lemon juice, divided
2 tablespoons butter, melted

1. Wash and trim off the tough outer leaves and around the bottom of the artichokes. Cut off about 1 inch from the tops of each, and trim off the tips of the leaves. Spread the top leaves apart and use a long-handled spoon to pull out the fuzzy chokes in their centers. 2. Stand the prepared artichokes upright in the slow cooker. Sprinkle each with ¼ teaspoon salt. 3. Spoon 2 tablespoons lemon juice over the artichokes. Pour in enough water to cover the bottom half of the artichokes. 4. Cover and cook on high for 2½ to 4 hours. 5. Serve with melted butter and remaining lemon juice for dipping.

Cheesy Tomato Pizza Fondue

Prep time: 15 minutes | Cook time: 1 hour | Serves 4 to 6

1 (1-pound / 454-g) block of cheese, your choice of good melting cheese, cut in ½-inch cubes
2 cups shredded Mozzarella cheese
1 (19-ounce / 539-g) can Italian-style stewed tomatoes with juice
Loaf of Italian bread, slices toasted and then cut into 1-inch cubes

1. Place cheese cubes, shredded Mozzarella cheese, and tomatoes in a lightly greased slow cooker. 2. Cover and cook on high 45 to 60 minutes, or until cheese is melted. 3. Stir occasionally and scrape down sides of slow cooker with rubber spatula to prevent scorching. 4. Reduce heat to low and serve. (Fondue will keep a smooth consistency for up to 4 hours.) 5. Serve with toasted bread cubes for dipping.

Liver Paté

Prep time: 15 minutes | Cook time: 4 to 5 hours | Makes 1½ cups paté

1 pound (454 g) chicken livers
½ cup dry wine
1 teaspoon instant chicken bouillon
1 teaspoon minced parsley
1 tablespoon instant minced onion
¼ teaspoon ground ginger
½ teaspoon seasoned salt
1 tablespoon soy sauce
¼ teaspoon dry mustard
¼ cup soft butter
1 tablespoon brandy

1. In slow cooker, combine all ingredients except butter and brandy. 2. Cover. Cook on low 4 to 5 hours. Let stand in liquid until cool. 3. Drain. Place in blender or food grinder. Add butter and brandy. Process until smooth. 4. Serve.

Mini Hot Dogs

Prep time: 5 minutes | Cook time: 4 to 5 hours | Serves 20 to 30 as an appetizer

2 cups brown sugar
1 tablespoon Worcestershire sauce
1 (14-ounce / 397-g) bottle ketchup
2 or 3 pounds (907 g or 1.4 kg) mini-hot dogs

1. In slow cooker, mix together brown sugar, 2. Worcestershire sauce, and ketchup. Stir in hot dogs. 3. Cover and cook on high 1 hour. Turn to low and cook 3 to 4 hours. 4. Serve from the cooker while turned to low.

Peanut Clusters

Prep time: 20 minutes | Cook time: 3 hours | Makes 3½ to 4 dozen pieces

2 pounds (907 g) white candy coating, chopped
1 (12-ounce / 340-g) package semi-sweet chocolate chips
1 (4-ounce / 113-g) milk chocolate bar, or 1 (4-ounce / 113-g) package German sweet chocolate, chopped
1 (24-ounce / 680-g) jar dry roasted peanuts
Nonstick cooking spray

1. Spray inside of slow cooker with nonstick cooking spray. 2. In slow cooker, combine white candy coating, chocolate chips, and milk chocolate. 3. Cover and cook on low 3 hours. Stir every 15 minutes. 4. Add peanuts to melted chocolate. Mix well. 5. Drop by tablespoonfuls onto waxed paper. Cool until set. Serve immediately, or store in a tightly covered container, separating layers with waxed paper. Keep cool and dry.

All American Snack

Prep time: 10 minutes | Cook time: 3 hours | Makes 3 quarts snack mix

3 cups thin pretzel sticks
4 cups Wheat Chex
4 cups Cheerios
1 (12-ounce / 340-g) can salted peanuts
¼ cup butter, melted
1 teaspoon garlic powder
1 teaspoon celery salt
½ teaspoon seasoned salt
2 tablespoons grated Parmesan cheese

1. Combine pretzels, cereal, and peanuts in large bowl. 2. Melt butter. Stir in garlic powder, celery salt, seasoned salt, and Parmesan cheese. Pour over pretzels and cereal. Toss until well mixed. 3. Pour into large slow cooker. Cover. Cook on low 2½ hours, stirring every 30 minutes. Remove lid and cook another 30 minutes on low. 4. Serve warm or at room temperature. Store in tightly covered container.

Meaty Buffet Favorites

Prep time: 5 minutes | Cook time: 2 hours | Serves 24

1 cup tomato sauce
1 teaspoon Worcestershire sauce
½ teaspoon prepared mustard

2 tablespoons brown sugar
1 pound (454 g) prepared meatballs or mini-wieners

1. Mix first four ingredients in slow cooker. 2. Add meatballs or mini-wieners. 3. Cover and cook on high for 2 hours. Turn to low and serve as an appetizer from the slow cooker.

Chapter 3 Vegetables and Sides

Turkish Stuffed Eggplant

Prep time: 10 minutes | Cook time: 2 hours 10 minutes | Serves 6

½ cup extra-virgin olive oil
3 small eggplants
1 teaspoon sea salt
½ teaspoon black pepper
1 large yellow onion, finely chopped
4 garlic cloves, minced
1 (15-ounce / 425-g) can diced tomatoes, with the juice
¼ cup finely chopped fresh flat-leaf parsley
6 (8-inch) round pita breads, quartered and toasted
1 cup plain Greek yogurt

1. Pour ¼ cup of the olive oil into the crock pot, and generously coat the interior of the crock. 2. Cut each eggplant in half lengthwise. You can leave the stem on. Score the cut side of each half every ¼ inch, being careful not to cut through the skin. 3. Arrange the eggplant halves, skin-side down, in the crock pot. Sprinkle with 1 teaspoon salt and ½ teaspoon pepper. 4. In a large skillet, heat the remaining ¼ cup olive oil over medium-high heat. Sauté the onion and garlic for 3 minutes, or until the onion begins to soften. 5. Add the tomatoes and parsley to the skillet. Season with salt and pepper. Sauté for another 5 minutes, until the liquid has almost evaporated. 6. Using a large spoon, spoon the tomato mixture over the eggplants, covering each half with some of the mixture. 7. Cover and cook on high for 2 hours or on low for 4 hours. When the dish is finished, the eggplant should feel very tender when you insert the tip of a sharp knife into the thickest part. 8. Uncover the crock pot, and let the eggplant rest for 10 minutes. Then transfer the eggplant to a serving dish. If there is any juice in the bottom of the cooker, spoon it over the eggplant. Serve hot with toasted pita wedges and yogurt on the side.

Barley-Stuffed Cabbage Rolls with Pine Nuts and Currants

Prep time: 15 minutes | Cook time: 2 hours | Serves 4

1 large head green cabbage, cored
1 tablespoon olive oil
1 large yellow onion, chopped
3 cups cooked pearl barley
3 ounces (85 g) feta cheese, crumbled
½ cup dried currants
2 tablespoons pine nuts, toasted
2 tablespoons chopped fresh flat-leaf parsley
½ teaspoon sea salt
½ teaspoon black pepper
½ cup apple juice
1 tablespoon apple cider vinegar
1 (15-ounce / 425-g) can crushed tomatoes, with the juice

1. Steam the cabbage head in a large pot over boiling water for 8 minutes. Remove to a cutting board and let cool slightly. 2. Remove 16 leaves from the cabbage head (reserve the rest of the cabbage for another use). Cut off the raised portion of the center vein of each cabbage leaf (do not cut out the vein). 3. Heat the oil in a large nonstick lidded skillet over medium heat. Add the onion, cover, and cook 6 minutes, or until tender. Remove to a large bowl. 4. Stir the barley, feta cheese, currants, pine nuts, and parsley into the onion mixture. Season with ¼ teaspoon of the salt and ¼ teaspoon of the pepper. 5. Place cabbage leaves on a work surface. On 1 cabbage leaf, spoon about ⅓ cup of the barley mixture into the center. Fold in the edges of the leaf over the barley mixture and roll the cabbage leaf up as if you were making a burrito. Repeat for the remaining 15 cabbage leaves and filling. 6. Arrange the cabbage rolls in the crock pot. 7. Combine the remaining ¼ teaspoon salt, ¼ teaspoon pepper, the apple juice, apple cider vinegar, and tomatoes. Pour the apple juice mixture evenly over the cabbage rolls. 8. Cover and cook on high 2 hours or on low for 6 to 8 hours. Serve hot.

Lemon-Rosemary Beets

Prep time: 10 minutes | Cook time: 8 hours | Serves 7

2 pounds (907 g) beets, peeled and cut into wedges
2 tablespoons fresh lemon juice
2 tablespoons extra-virgin olive oil
2 tablespoons honey
1 tablespoon apple cider vinegar
¾ teaspoon sea salt
½ teaspoon black pepper
2 sprigs fresh rosemary
½ teaspoon lemon zest

1. Place the beets in the crock pot. 2. Whisk the lemon juice, extra-virgin olive oil, honey, apple cider vinegar, salt, and pepper together in a small bowl. Pour over the beets. 3. Add the sprigs of rosemary to the crock pot. 4. Cover and cook on low for 8 hours, or until the beets are tender. 5. Remove and discard the rosemary sprigs. Stir in the lemon zest. Serve hot.

Root Vegetable Tagine

Prep time: 30 minutes | Cook time: 9 hours | Serves 8

1 pound parsnips, peeled and chopped into bite-size pieces
1 pound turnips, peeled and chopped into bite-size pieces
2 medium yellow onions, chopped into bite-size pieces
1 pound carrots, peeled and chopped into bite-size pieces
6 dried apricots, chopped
6 figs, chopped
1 teaspoon ground turmeric
1 teaspoon ground cumin
½ teaspoon ground ginger
½ teaspoon ground cinnamon
¼ teaspoon cayenne pepper
1 tablespoon dried parsley
1 tablespoon dried cilantro (or 2 tablespoons chopped fresh cilantro)
1¾ cups vegetable stock

1. Combine the parsnips, turnips, onions, carrots, apricots, and figs in the crock pot. Sprinkle with the turmeric, cumin, ginger, cinnamon, cayenne pepper, parsley, and cilantro. 2. Pour in the vegetable stock. Cover and cook for 9 hours on low. the vegetables will be very tender. Serve hot.

Onion Potatoes

Prep time: 20 minutes | Cook time: 5 to 6 hours | Serves 6

6 medium potatoes, diced
⅓ cup olive oil
1 envelope dry onion soup mix

1. Combine potatoes and olive oil in plastic bag. Shake well. 2. Add onion soup mix. Shake well. 3. Pour into slow cooker. 4. Cover and cook on low 5 to 6 hours.

Barbecue Beans

Prep time: 15 minutes | Cook time: 8 hours | Serves 8

5 cups cooked pinto beans, rinsed
1 onion, finely chopped
6 garlic cloves, minced
3 jalapeño peppers, seeded and finely chopped
1 (14-ounce / 397-g) can tomato sauce
¼ cup blackstrap molasses
½ teaspoon liquid smoke
2 teaspoons smoked paprika
¼ teaspoon sea salt
⅛ teaspoon cayenne pepper

1. In your crock pot, combine all the ingredients. 2. Cover and cook on low for 8 hours.

Vegetable Terrine

Prep time: 30 minutes | Cook time: 5 to 7 hours | Serves 6

1 small eggplant, thinly sliced lengthwise
2 green bell peppers, halved, seeded, and sliced
2 red bell peppers, halved, seeded, and sliced
1 portobello mushroom, cut into ¼-inch-thick slices
1 zucchini, thinly sliced lengthwise
1 large red onion, cut into ¼-inch-thick rounds
2 yellow squash, thinly sliced lengthwise
4 large tomatoes, sliced
1 teaspoon sea salt
¼ teaspoon freshly ground black pepper
Nonstick cooking spray
1 cup grated Parmesan cheese
2 tablespoons extra-virgin olive oil
1 tablespoon red wine vinegar
2 teaspoons freshly squeezed lemon juice
1 teaspoon dried basil
1 garlic clove, minced

1. Season the eggplant, green and red bell peppers, mushroom, zucchini, onion, squash, and tomatoes with salt and black pepper, but keep all the vegetables separate. 2. Generously coat a slow-cooker insert with cooking spray, or line the bottom and sides with parchment paper or aluminum foil. 3. Starting with half of the eggplant, line the bottom of the prepared crock pot with overlapping slices. Sprinkle with 2 tablespoons of Parmesan cheese. 4. Add a second layer using half of the green and red bell peppers. Sprinkle with 2 more tablespoons of Parmesan cheese. 5. Add a third layer using half of the mushroom slices. Sprinkle with 2 more tablespoons of Parmesan cheese. 6. Add a fourth layer using half of the zucchini slices. Sprinkle with 2 more tablespoons of Parmesan cheese. 7. Add a fifth layer using half of the red onion slices. Sprinkle with another 2 tablespoons of Parmesan cheese. 8. Add a sixth layer using half of the yellow squash slices. Sprinkle with 2 more tablespoons of Parmesan cheese. 9. Add a final seventh layer with half of the tomato slices. Sprinkle with 2 more tablespoons of Parmesan cheese. 10. Repeat the layering with the remaining vegetables and Parmesan cheese in the same order until all of the vegetables have been used. 11. In a small bowl, whisk together the olive oil, vinegar, lemon juice, basil, and garlic until combined. Pour the mixture over the vegetables. Top with any remaining Parmesan cheese. 12. Cover the cooker and cook for 5 to 7 hours on Low heat. 13. Let cool to room temperature before slicing and serving.

Zucchini Casserole

Prep time: 20 minutes | Cook time: 3 hours | Serves 4

1 medium red onion, sliced
1 green bell pepper, cut into thin strips
4 medium zucchini, sliced
1 (15-ounce / 425-g) can diced tomatoes, with the juice
1 teaspoon sea salt
½ teaspoon black pepper
½ teaspoon basil
1 tablespoon extra-virgin olive oil
¼ cup grated Parmesan cheese

1. Combine the onion slices, bell pepper strips, zucchini slices, and tomatoes in the crock pot. Sprinkle with the salt, pepper, and basil. 2. Cover and cook on low for 3 hours. 3. Drizzle the olive oil over the casserole and sprinkle with the Parmesan. Cover and cook on low for 1½ hours more. Serve hot.

Savory Butternut Squash and Apples

Prep time: 20 minutes | Cook time: 4 hours | Serves 10

1 (3-pound / 1.4-kg) butternut squash, peeled, seeded, and cubed
4 cooking apples (granny smith or honeycrisp work well), peeled, cored, and chopped
¾ cup dried currants
½ sweet yellow onion such as vidalia, sliced thin
1 tablespoon ground cinnamon
1½ teaspoons ground nutmeg

1. Combine the squash, apples, currants, and onion in the crock pot. Sprinkle with the cinnamon and nutmeg. 2. Cook on high for 4 hours, or until the squash is tender and cooked through. Stir occasionally while cooking.

Stuffed Artichokes

Prep time: 20 minutes | Cook time: 5 to 7 hours | Serves 4 to 6

4 to 6 fresh large artichokes
½ cup bread crumbs
½ cup grated Parmesan cheese or Romano cheese
4 garlic cloves, minced
½ teaspoon sea salt
½ teaspoon freshly ground black pepper
¼ cup water
2 tablespoons extra-virgin olive oil
2 tablespoons chopped fresh parsley for garnish (optional)

1. To trim and prepare the artichokes, cut off the bottom along with 1 inch from the top of each artichoke. Pull off and discard the lowest leaves nearest the stem end. Trim off any pointy tips of artichoke leaves that are poking out. Set aside. 2. In a small bowl, stir together the bread crumbs, Parmesan cheese, garlic, salt, and pepper. 3. Spread apart the artichoke leaves and stuff the bread-crumb mixture into the spaces, down to the base. 4. Pour the water into a crock pot. 5. Place the artichokes in the crock pot in a single layer. Drizzle the olive oil over the artichokes. 6. Cover the cooker and cook for 5 to 7 hours on Low heat, or until the artichokes are tender. 7. Garnish with fresh parsley if desired.

Egg Casserole with Tomato, Spinach, and Feta

Prep time: 10 minutes | Cook time: 6 to 8 hours | Serves 6

12 large eggs	¼ teaspoon freshly ground black pepper
¼ cup milk of your choice	Nonstick cooking spray
1 cup fresh spinach, chopped	2 Roma tomatoes, sliced
¼ cup feta cheese, crumbled	
½ teaspoon sea salt	

1. In a medium bowl, whisk together the eggs, milk, spinach, feta cheese, salt, and pepper until combined. 2. Generously coat a slow-cooker insert with cooking spray. 3. Pour the egg mixture into the crock pot. Top with the tomato slices. 4. Cover the cooker and cook for 6 to 8 hours on Low heat.

Baba Ghanoush

Prep time: 15 minutes | Cook time: 2 to 4 hours | Serves 6

1 large eggplant (2 to 4 pounds / 907 g to 1.8 kg), peeled and diced	oil, plus more as needed
¼ cup freshly squeezed lemon juice	¼ teaspoon sea salt, plus more as needed
2 garlic cloves, minced	⅛ teaspoon freshly ground black pepper, plus more as needed
2 tablespoons tahini	2 tablespoons chopped fresh parsley
1 teaspoon extra-virgin olive	

1. In a crock pot, combine the eggplant, lemon juice, garlic, tahini, olive oil, salt, and pepper. Stir to mix well. 2. Cover the cooker and cook for 2 to 4 hours on Low heat. 3. Using a spoon or potato masher, mash the mixture. If you prefer a smoother texture, transfer it to a food processor and blend to your desired consistency. Taste and season with olive oil, salt, and pepper as needed. 4. Garnish with fresh parsley for serving.

Steamed Vegetables

Prep time: 10 minutes | Cook time: 5 to 7 hours | Serves 6

2 pounds (907 g) fresh vegetables of your choice, sliced	1 teaspoon sea salt
1 teaspoon dried thyme	¼ teaspoon freshly ground black pepper
1 teaspoon dried rosemary	2 tablespoons extra-virgin olive oil

1. Put the vegetables in a crock pot and season them with thyme, rosemary, salt, and pepper. 2. Drizzle the olive oil on top. 3. Cover the cooker and cook for 5 to 7 hours on Low heat, or until the vegetables are tender.

Potato Vegetable Hash

Prep time: 20 minutes | Cook time: 5 to 7 hours | Serves 4

1½ pounds (680 g) red potatoes, diced	chopped
8 ounces (227 g) green beans, trimmed and cut into ½-inch pieces	⅓ cup low-sodium vegetable broth
4 ounces (113 g) mushrooms, chopped	1 teaspoon sea salt
1 large tomato, chopped	½ teaspoon garlic powder
1 large zucchini, diced	½ teaspoon freshly ground black pepper
1 small onion, diced	¼ teaspoon red pepper flakes
1 red bell pepper, seeded and	¼ cup shredded cheese of your choice (optional)

1. In a crock pot, combine the potatoes, green beans, mushrooms, tomato, zucchini, onion, bell pepper, vegetable broth, salt, garlic powder, black pepper, and red pepper flakes. Stir to mix well. 2. Cover the cooker and cook for 5 to 7 hours on Low heat. 3. Garnish with cheese for serving (if using).

Greek Fasolakia (Green Beans)

Prep time: 10 minutes | Cook time: 6 to 8 hours | Serves 6

2 pounds (907 g) green beans, trimmed	1 teaspoon dried dill
1 (15-ounce / 425-g) can no-salt-added diced tomatoes, with juice	1 teaspoon ground cumin
	1 teaspoon dried oregano
1 large onion, chopped	1 teaspoon sea salt
4 garlic cloves, chopped	½ teaspoon freshly ground black pepper
Juice of 1 lemon	¼ cup feta cheese, crumbled

1. In a crock pot, combine the green beans, tomatoes and their juice, onion, garlic, lemon juice, dill, cumin, oregano, salt, and pepper. Stir to mix well. 2. Cover the cooker and cook for 6 to 8 hours on Low heat. 3. Top with feta cheese for serving.

Spicy Creamer Potatoes

Prep time: 10 minutes | Cook time: 8 hours | Makes 7 (1-cup) servings

2 pounds (907 g) creamer potatoes	lemon juice
1 onion, chopped	2 tablespoons water
3 garlic cloves, minced	1 tablespoon chili powder
1 chipotle chile in adobo sauce, minced	½ teaspoon ground cumin
2 tablespoons freshly squeezed	½ teaspoon salt
	⅛ teaspoon freshly ground black pepper

1. In the crock pot, combine all the ingredients and stir. 2. Cover and cook on low for 7 to 8 hours, or until the potatoes are tender, and serve.

"Baked" Sweet Potatoes

Prep time: 5 minutes | Cook time: 8 hours | Serves 4

4 medium sweet potatoes, scrubbed

1. Wrap each sweet potato in aluminum foil and put them in the crock pot. 2. Cover and cook on low for 8 hours. 3. Unwrap to serve.

Potatoes with Cumin

Prep time: 10 minutes | Cook time: 2 to 4 hours | Serves 6

2 teaspoons cumin seeds, divided
1 tablespoon coriander seeds
2 tablespoons vegetable oil
1 onion, sliced
2 fresh green chiles, sliced lengthwise
1-inch piece fresh ginger, sliced very thinly
¼ teaspoon turmeric
1 teaspoon chili powder
Sea salt
6 large potatoes, peeled and chopped into 1½-inch chunks
½ cup hot water
2 teaspoons mango powder (amchoor), or a squeeze of lemon juice
Handful fresh coriander leaves, chopped

1. Preheat the crock pot on high. 2. Meanwhile, in a dry frying pan toast 1 teaspoon of the cumin seeds along with all of the coriander seeds. Once fragrant, remove from the heat and crush in a mortar and pestle or spice grinder. 3. To the hot crock pot, add the oil, onion, sliced green chiles, ginger, and remaining 1 teaspoon of cumin seeds. Stir, and then add the roasted spice powder, turmeric, chili powder, and salt. 4. Add the cubed potatoes and mix well. Then add the water. Cover and cook on high for 2 to 3 hours, or on low for 4 hours. 5. Stir in the mango powder and garnish with coriander leaves to serve.

Balsamic Beets

Prep time: 15 minutes | Cook time: 3 to 4 hours | Serves 8

Cooking spray or 1 tablespoon extra-virgin olive oil
3 pounds (1.4 kg) beets, scrubbed, peeled, and cut into wedges
2 garlic cloves, minced
1 cup white grape or apple juice
½ cup balsamic vinegar
1 tablespoon honey
2 fresh thyme sprigs
1 teaspoon kosher salt, plus more for seasoning
½ teaspoon freshly ground black pepper, plus more for seasoning
1 tablespoon cold water
1 tablespoon cornstarch

1. Use the cooking spray or olive oil to coat the inside (bottom and sides) of the crock pot. Add the beets, garlic, juice, vinegar, honey, thyme, salt, and pepper. Stir to combine. Cover and cook on high for 3 to 4 hours. 2. About 10 minutes before serving, combine the water and cornstarch in a small bowl, stirring until no lumps remain. Add to the crock pot and continue to cook for 10 minutes, or until the sauce thickens. 3. Discard the thyme. Season with additional salt and pepper, as needed. Serve.

Spinach and Paneer Cheese

Prep time: 15 minutes | Cook time: 2 to 4 hours | Serves 6

2 pounds (907 g) fresh spinach
1½-inch piece fresh ginger, roughly chopped
5 garlic cloves, whole
2 fresh green chiles, roughly chopped
1 onion, roughly chopped
1 teaspoon salt
½ teaspoon turmeric
4 tomatoes, finely chopped
1 to 2 tablespoons cornstarch to thicken (if required)
4 tablespoons butter
1 teaspoon cumin seeds
3 garlic cloves, minced
1 tablespoon dried fenugreek leaves
2 tablespoons rapeseed oil
12 ounces (340 g) paneer, cut into cubes

1. Heat the crock pot to high and add the spinach, ginger, garlic, chiles, onion, salt, turmeric, and tomatoes. 2. Cover and cook on high for 3 hours, or on low for 6 hours. 3. Using your immersion blender or a food processor, purée the greens to a fine, glossy consistency. The aim is to have a thick and bright-green purée. If it's a little watery you may need to reduce it on the stove to thicken, or if your crock pot has a boil function, use it to boil off a little of the liquid. You can also thicken it up by sprinkling with some cornstarch. 4. Heat the butter in a pan and add the cumin seeds until they sizzle. Then add the minced garlic and stir until it just browns. Remove from the heat. Add the dried fenugreek leaves and pour everything into the saag that's in the crock pot. Whisk through. 5. Fry the cubes of paneer in a little oil in the same pan, until they are golden brown. Stir into the saag. Replace the lid and let everything sit for another 10 minutes before serving.

Lemon Chicken Soup with Orzo

Prep time: 10 minutes | Cook time: 6 to 8 hours | Serves 6

1 pound (454 g) boneless, skinless chicken thighs or 1 pound (454 g) bone-in, skinless chicken breast
4 cups low-sodium chicken broth
2 cups water
2 celery stalks, thinly sliced
1 small onion, diced
1 carrot, diced
1 garlic clove, minced
Grated zest of 1 lemon
Juice of 1 lemon
1 bay leaf
1 teaspoon sea salt
1 teaspoon dried oregano
½ teaspoon freshly ground black pepper
¾ cup dried orzo pasta
1 lemon, thinly sliced

1. In a crock pot, combine the chicken, chicken broth, water, celery, onion, carrot, garlic, lemon zest, lemon juice, bay leaf, salt, oregano, and pepper. Stir to mix well. 2. Cover the cooker and cook for 6 to 8 hours on Low heat. 3. Remove the chicken from the crock pot and shred it. (If you are using bone-in chicken, remove and discard the bones while shredding. The meat should be so tender that the bones just slide out.) 4. Return the chicken to the crock pot and add the orzo and lemon slices. 5. Replace the cover on the cooker and cook for 15 to 30 minutes on Low heat, or until the orzo is tender. 6. Remove and discard the bay leaf before serving.

Smoky Baked Beans

Prep time: 15 minutes | Cook time: 6 to 8 hours | Serves 6

Cooking spray or 1 tablespoon extra-virgin olive oil
1 pound (454 g) dried navy beans, picked over, soaked overnight, drained, and rinsed
8 thick-cut bacon slices, finely diced
1 medium onion, minced
2 garlic cloves, minced
2½ cups water
½ cup ketchup
¼ cup molasses
¼ cup maple syrup
¼ cup packed brown sugar
2 tablespoons cider vinegar
1 tablespoon prepared mustard
1¼ teaspoons kosher salt, plus more for seasoning
½ teaspoon freshly ground black pepper, plus more for seasoning

1. Use the cooking spray or olive oil to coat the inside (bottom and sides) of the crock pot. Add the beans, bacon, onion, garlic, water, ketchup, molasses, maple syrup, brown sugar, vinegar, mustard, salt, and pepper. Stir to combine. Cover and cook on low for 6 to 8 hours, or until the beans are tender when pierced with a fork. 2. Season with additional salt and pepper, as needed. Serve.

Vegetable Vindaloo

Prep time: 15 minutes | Cook time: 2 to 4 hours | Serves 6

Spice Paste:
1 teaspoon mustard seeds
1 teaspoon cumin seeds
2 teaspoons coriander seeds
4 cloves
4 dried Kashmiri chiles
1 teaspoon black peppercorns
2 onions, roughly chopped
6 garlic cloves
1-inch piece fresh ginger
4 tablespoons malt vinegar
Vindaloo:
1 tablespoon vegetable oil
1 teaspoon mustard seeds
4 medium potatoes, peeled and cut into 1-inch cubes
4 ounces (113 g) cauliflower florets
1 zucchini, diced
4 ounces (113 g) mushrooms, sliced
1 carrot, peeled and sliced
1 (14-ounce / 397-g) can kidney beans, drained and rinsed
1 teaspoon salt
1 teaspoon turmeric
½ teaspoon sugar

Make the Spice Paste: 1. Preheat the crock pot on high for 15 minutes. 2. In a blender, make the spice paste by grinding the mustard seeds, cumin seeds, coriander seeds, cloves, chiles, and peppercorns to a fine powder. 3. Then add the onions, garlic, ginger, vinegar, and a splash of water to the powder. Blend to make a paste. Make the Vindaloo: 4. Heat the oil in a frying pan (or in the crock pot if you have a sear setting). Add the mustard seeds and cook until they pop. Add all of the spice paste and cook until the paste is fragrant. 5. Put everything in the crock pot. Add the potatoes, cauliflower florets, zucchini, mushrooms, carrot, and beans. Then stir in the salt, turmeric, and sugar, plus a splash of water if needed. 6. Cover and cook on low for 3 to 4 hours, or on high for 2 hours. 7. Check the seasoning and adjust if required. Serve hot.

Apricot-Chestnut Stuffing

Prep time: 20 minutes | Cook time: 8 hours | Makes 10 (¾-cup) servings

Nonstick cooking spray
3 tablespoons butter
1 onion, chopped
1 leek, white part only, chopped
3 garlic cloves, minced
1 (16-ounce / 454-g) can whole peeled chestnuts, chopped
⅔ cup chopped dried apricots
½ cup chopped walnuts
8 slices whole-wheat bread, cut into 1-inch cubes
2 eggs, beaten
¼ cup milk
¼ cup vegetable broth
1 teaspoon salt
½ teaspoon dried thyme leaves
½ teaspoon dried basil leaves
⅛ teaspoon freshly ground black pepper

1. Spray the crock pot with the nonstick cooking spray. 2. In a medium saucepan over medium heat, melt the butter. Add the onion, leek, and garlic, and sauté, stirring, until tender, about 5 minutes. Add the mixture to the crock pot. 3. Add the chestnuts, apricots, walnuts, and bread. 4. In a small bowl, beat the eggs with the milk, broth, salt, thyme, basil, and pepper. Pour the mixture into the crock pot and stir. 5. Cover and cook on low for 7 to 8 hours, or until the stuffing registers 165°F (74°C) on a food thermometer, and serve.

Tangy-Sweet Glazed Carrots

Prep time: 10 minutes | Cook time: 3 to 4 hours | Serves 6

Cooking spray or 1 tablespoon extra-virgin olive oil
2 pounds (907 g) baby carrots
2 tablespoons butter, melted
3 sprigs fresh thyme
½ cup packed brown sugar
⅓ cup balsamic vinegar
½ teaspoon kosher salt
¼ teaspoon freshly ground black pepper
⅛ teaspoon ground cinnamon

1. Use the cooking spray or olive oil to coat the inside (bottom and sides) of the crock pot. Add the carrots, butter, and thyme to the crock pot. Stir to combine. Cover and cook on low for 3 to 4 hours, or until tender. Discard the thyme sprigs. 2. Meanwhile, mix together the brown sugar, vinegar, salt, pepper, and cinnamon. Add the mixture to the crock pot and toss with the carrots before serving.

Glazed Maple Sweet Potatoes

Prep time: 10 minutes | Cook time: 7 to 9 hours | Serves 5

5 medium sweet potatoes, cut in ½-inch-thick slices
¼ cup brown sugar, packed
¼ cup pure maple syrup
¼ cup apple cider
2 tablespoons butter

1. Place potatoes in slow cooker. 2. In a small bowl, combine brown sugar, maple syrup, and apple cider. Mix well. Pour over potatoes. Stir until all potato slices are covered. 3. Cover and cook on low 7 to 9 hours, or until potatoes are tender. 4. Stir in butter before serving.

Cheesy Creamed Corn with Bacon

Prep time: 15 minutes | Cook time: 3 hours | Serves 8

- 12 ears of corn, shucked and cut from the cob, or 2 pounds (907 g) frozen corn kernels
- 2 bacon slices, finely chopped
- 8 ounces (227 g) cream cheese, at room temperature
- 6 ounces (170 g) American cheese, finely diced
- ½ cup whole milk
- 3 ounces (85 g) sour cream
- 3 fresh thyme sprigs
- 2 bay leaves
- ¾ teaspoon kosher salt, plus more for seasoning
- ½ teaspoon freshly ground black pepper, plus more for seasoning

1. In the crock pot, combine the corn, bacon, cream cheese, cheese, milk, sour cream, thyme, and bay leaves. Season with the salt and pepper, and stir to combine. Cover and cook on low for 3 hours, until the corn is cooked and the sauce has thickened slightly. 2. Remove the cover and discard the thyme and bay leaves. Season with additional salt and pepper as needed, and serve.

Corn Pudding with Poblanos

Prep time: 15 minutes | Cook time: 3 to 4 hours | Serves 8

- Cooking spray or 1 tablespoon extra-virgin olive oil
- 1 (8-ounce / 227-g) package cream cheese, at room temperature
- 2 cups fresh corn, removed from the cob
- 2 poblano peppers, seeded, stemmed, and finely diced
- 1 (8½-ounce / 241-g) package corn muffin mix
- 1 cup whole milk
- ⅓ cup sugar
- 2 eggs, beaten
- 1 teaspoon kosher salt

1. Use the cooking spray or olive oil to coat the inside (bottom and sides) of the crock pot. To the crock pot add the cream cheese, corn, peppers, muffin mix, milk, sugar, eggs, and salt. Stir to combine. Cover and cook on low for 3 to 4 hours or until a knife inserted into the center of the pudding comes out clean. 2. Let stand for 5 minutes before serving.

Brown Rice and Vegetable Pilaf

Prep time: 20 minutes | Cook time: 5 hours | Makes 9 (¾-cup) servings

- 1 onion, minced
- 1 cup sliced cremini mushrooms
- 2 carrots, sliced
- 2 garlic cloves, minced
- 1½ cups long-grain brown rice
- 2½ cups vegetable broth
- ½ teaspoon salt
- ½ teaspoon dried marjoram leaves
- ⅛ teaspoon freshly ground black pepper
- ⅓ cup grated Parmesan cheese

1. In the crock pot, combine the onion, mushrooms, carrots, garlic, and rice. 2. Add the broth, salt, marjoram, and pepper, and stir. 3. Cover and cook on low for 5 hours, or until the rice is tender and the liquid is absorbed. 4. Stir in the cheese and serve.

Artichoke-Parmesan Dip with Crostini

Prep time: 15 minutes | Cook time: 2 hours | Serves 10

- Cooking spray or 1 tablespoon extra-virgin olive oil
- 2 (14-ounce / 397-g) cans artichokes, drained
- 1 small onion, minced
- ½ cup mayonnaise
- 6 ounces (170 g) cream cheese, at room temperature
- ¼ cup sour cream
- ½ teaspoon garlic salt, plus more for seasoning
- ¼ teaspoon freshly ground black pepper, plus more for seasoning
- ¼ teaspoon red pepper flakes
- ½ cup Mozzarella cheese
- ⅓ cup grated Parmesan cheese
- ¼ cup heavy (whipping) cream
- 1 baguette, sliced and toasted, for crostini

1. Use the cooking spray or olive oil to coat the inside (bottom and sides) of the crock pot. Pull any tough leaves from the artichokes and discard them. Add the artichokes, onion, mayonnaise, cream cheese, sour cream, garlic salt, pepper, red pepper flakes, Mozzarella, Parmesan, and heavy cream to the crock pot. Stir to combine. Cover and cook on low for 2 hours. 2. Season with additional garlic salt and pepper, as needed. Serve with the crostini.

Green Beans and Potatoes

Prep time: 20 minutes | Cook time: 6 hours | Makes 9 (¾-cup) servings

- Nonstick cooking spray
- 1 onion, chopped
- 2 garlic cloves, minced
- 1 leek, white part only, sliced thin
- 2 cups whole fresh green string beans
- 3 cups small creamer potatoes
- ½ cup vegetable broth
- 2 tablespoons freshly squeezed lemon juice
- ½ teaspoon salt
- ½ teaspoon dried thyme leaves
- ⅛ teaspoon freshly ground black pepper

1. Spray the crock pot with the nonstick cooking spray. 2. In the crock pot, combine all the ingredients. 3. Cover and cook on low for 5 to 6 hours, or until the potatoes and beans are tender, and serve.

Quick Broccoli Fix

Prep time: 15 minutes | Cook time: 5 to 6 hours | Serves 6

- 1 pound (454 g) fresh or frozen broccoli, cut up
- 1 (10¾-ounce / 305-g) can cream of mushroom soup
- ½ cup mayonnaise
- ½ cup plain yogurt
- ½ pound (227 g) sliced fresh mushrooms
- 1 cup shredded Cheddar cheese, divided
- 1 cup crushed saltine crackers
- Sliced almonds (optional)

1. Microwave broccoli for 3 minutes. Place in greased slow cooker. 2. Combine soup, mayonnaise, yogurt, mushrooms, and ½ cup cheese. Pour over broccoli. 3. Cover. Cook on low 5 to 6 hours. 4. Top with remaining cheese and crackers for last half hour of cooking time. 5. Top with sliced almonds, for a special touch, before serving.

Creamed Kale

Prep time: 20 minutes | Cook time: 3 hours | Serves 8

Cooking spray or 1 tablespoon extra-virgin olive oil
½ stick unsalted butter
2 garlic cloves, minced
½ cup heavy (whipping) cream
2 ounces (57 g) cream cheese
1½ cups whole milk
1 cup low-sodium chicken stock
4 tablespoons all-purpose flour
½ cup finely grated Parmesan cheese
½ teaspoon kosher salt, plus more for seasoning
½ teaspoon freshly ground black pepper, plus more for seasoning
¼ teaspoon ground nutmeg
¼ teaspoon red pepper flakes
2 bunches kale, washed, stemmed, and leaves torn

1. If using a crock pot with a stove-top function to make the sauce, first use the cooking spray or olive oil to coat the inside (bottom and sides) of the crock pot. In the crock pot or in a Dutch oven or heavy-bottomed pan over medium-high heat, prepare the sauce by whisking together the butter, garlic, whipping cream, cream cheese, milk, chicken stock, flour, and Parmesan until the butter and cheese are melted and the flour is incorporated, and the sauce is free of lumps. 2. If you prepared the sauce outside the crock pot, use the cooking spray or olive oil to coat the inside (bottom and sides) of the crock pot. Add the sauce to the crock pot, along with the salt, pepper, nutmeg, red pepper flakes, and kale. Stir to combine. Cover and cook on low for 3 hours. 3. Season with additional salt and pepper, as needed. Serve.

Cheesy Hash Browns

Prep time: 10 minutes | Cook time: 7 hours | Makes 9 (¾-cup) servings

Nonstick cooking spray
1 (20-ounce / 567-g) package frozen hash brown potatoes
1 onion, finely chopped
3 garlic cloves, minced
1 cup grated Colby or Gruyère cheese
1 cup milk
⅓ cup heavy cream
3 tablespoons butter
½ teaspoon dried marjoram leaves
¼ teaspoon salt
⅛ teaspoon freshly ground black pepper
½ cup sour cream

1. Spray the crock pot with the nonstick cooking spray. 2. In the crock pot, combine the hash brown potatoes, onion, and garlic, and stir. Mix in the cheese. 3. In a small saucepan over high heat, combine the milk, cream, butter, marjoram, salt, and pepper, and heat until the butter melts, about a minute. Remove from the heat and stir in the sour cream. 4. Pour the milk mixture into the crock pot. 5. Cover and cook on low for 7 hours, or until the potatoes are tender, and serve.

Root Vegetable Hash

Prep time: 20 minutes | Cook time: 8 hours | Makes 9 (¾-cup) servings

4 carrots, peeled and cut into 1-inch cubes
3 large russet potatoes, peeled and cut into 1-inch cubes
1 onion, diced
3 garlic cloves, minced
½ teaspoon salt
⅛ teaspoon freshly ground black pepper
½ teaspoon dried thyme leaves
1 sprig rosemary
½ cup vegetable broth
3 plums, cut into 1-inch pieces

1. In the crock pot, combine the carrots, potatoes, onion, and garlic. Sprinkle with the salt, pepper, and thyme, and stir. 2. Imbed the rosemary sprig in the vegetables. 3. Pour the broth over everything. 4. Cover and cook on low for 7½ hours, or until the vegetables are tender. 5. Stir in the plums, cover, and cook on low for 30 minutes, until tender. 6. Remove and discard the rosemary sprig, and serve.

Harvard Beets

Prep time: 20 minutes | Cook time: 8 hours | Makes 9 (¾-cup) servings

1½ pounds (680 g) small beets, peeled and thickly sliced
1 onion, chopped
3 garlic cloves, sliced
½ cup brown sugar
2 tablespoons cornstarch
⅓ cup orange juice
3 tablespoons freshly squeezed lemon juice
2 tablespoons honey
2 tablespoons butter
½ teaspoon salt
¼ teaspoon ground cinnamon

1. In the crock pot, combine the beets, onion, and garlic. 2. In a medium bowl, mix the brown sugar, cornstarch, orange juice, lemon juice, and honey until well combined. Pour the mixture into the crock pot. 3. Dot the top of the ingredients in the crock pot with the butter, and sprinkle with the salt and cinnamon. 4. Cover and cook on low for 8 hours, or until the beets are tender, and serve.

Mushrooms in Red Wine

Prep time: 5 minutes | Cook time: 6 hours | Serves 4

1 pound (454 g) fresh mushrooms, stemmed, trimmed, and cleaned
4 cloves garlic, minced
¼ cup onion
1 tablespoon olive oil
1 cup red wine

1. Combine all ingredients in slow cooker. 2. Cook on low 6 hours.

Fruited Wild Rice with Pecans

Prep time: 15 minutes | Cook time: 2 to 2½ hours | Serves 4

½ cup chopped onions
2 tablespoons butter
1 (6-ounce / 170-g) package long-grain and wild rice
Seasoning packet from wild rice pkg.
1½ cups hot water
⅔ cup apple juice
1 large tart apple, chopped
¼ cup raisins
¼ cup coarsely chopped pecans

1. Combine all ingredients except pecans in greased slow cooker. 2. Cover. Cook on high 2 to 2½ hours. 3. Stir in pecans. Serve.

Mashed Sweet Potatoes with Garlic

Prep time: 20 minutes | Cook time: 8 hours | Makes 7 (1-cup) servings

Nonstick cooking spray
4 large sweet potatoes, peeled and cubed
1 onion, chopped
6 garlic cloves, peeled
½ cup orange juice
2 tablespoons honey
1 teaspoon salt
⅛ teaspoon freshly ground black pepper
⅓ cup butter, at room temperature
½ cup heavy cream

1. Spray the crock pot with the nonstick cooking spray. 2. In the crock pot, combine the sweet potatoes, onion, and garlic. 3. Pour the orange juice and honey over everything, and stir. Sprinkle with the salt and pepper. 4. Cover and cook on low for 8 hours, or until the potatoes are tender. 5. Add the butter and cream, mash using a potato masher or immersion blender, and serve.

Caramelized Onions and Garlic

Prep time: 20 minutes | Cook time: 9 hours | Makes 6 (½-cup) servings

5 large onions, sliced
12 garlic cloves, peeled
2 tablespoons extra-virgin olive oil
1 tablespoon butter
½ teaspoon salt

1. Spray the crock pot with the nonstick cooking spray. 2. In the crock pot, combine all the ingredients and stir. 3. Cover and cook on low for 9 hours, until the onions and garlic are golden brown. If you're at home during the day, stir occasionally. 4. Serve.

Pumpernickel-Cranberry Stuffing

Prep time: 20 minutes | Cook time: 8 hours | Makes 10 (¾-cup) servings

2 tablespoons butter
1 tablespoon extra-virgin olive oil
1 onion, chopped
1 cup sliced celery stalk
3 garlic cloves, sliced
Nonstick cooking spray
1 cup dried cranberries
6 cups (1-inch cubes) pumpernickel bread
1 egg, beaten
½ cup vegetable broth
1 teaspoon fennel seeds
1 teaspoon salt
¼ teaspoon freshly ground black pepper

1. In a medium saucepan over medium heat, melt the butter and olive oil. Add the onion, celery, and garlic, and sauté, stirring, until tender, about 6 minutes. 2. Spray the crock pot with the nonstick cooking spray. 3. In the crock pot, stir together the onion mixture, cranberries, and bread cubes. 4. In a small bowl, beat the egg, broth, fennel seeds, salt, and pepper. Pour the mixture into the crock pot and stir. 5. Cover and cook on low for 7 to 8 hours, or until the stuffing registers 165°F (74°C) on a food thermometer, and serve.

Cornflake Cooker Potatoes

Prep time: 15 minutes | Cook time: 4 hours | Serves 4 to 6

6 to 8 potatoes, peeled
2 teaspoons salt
2 to 3 tablespoons butter
1 cup cornflakes, slightly crushed

1. Place potatoes in slow cooker. 2. Fill cooker with hot water. Sprinkle with salt. 3. Cover and cook on high 4 hours, or until potatoes are tender. 4. While potatoes are cooking, melt butter. Continue melting until butter browns, but does not burn. (Watch carefully!) Stir in cornflakes. Set aside. 5. Drain potatoes. Spoon buttered cornflakes over potatoes. or mash potatoes and then top with buttered cornflakes.

Squash Medley

Prep time: 20 minutes | Cook time: 4 to 6 hours | Serves 8

8 summer squash, each about 4-inches long, thinly sliced
½ teaspoon salt
2 tomatoes, peeled and chopped
¼ cup sliced green onions
Half a small sweet green pepper, chopped
1 chicken bouillon cube
¼ cup hot water
4 slices bacon, fried and crumbled
¼ cup fine dry bread crumbs

1. Sprinkle squash with salt. 2. In slow cooker, layer half the squash, tomatoes, onions, and pepper. Repeat layers. 3. Dissolve bouillon in hot water. Pour into slow cooker. 4. Top with bacon. Sprinkle bread crumbs over top. 5. Cover. Cook on low 4 to 6 hours.

Rustic Potatoes au Gratin

Prep time: 10 minutes | Cook time: 6 to 8 hours | Serves 6

½ cup skim milk
1 (10¾-ounce / 305-g) can light condensed Cheddar cheese soup
1 (8-ounce / 227-g) package fat-free cream cheese, softened
1 clove garlic, minced
¼ teaspoon ground nutmeg
¼ teaspoon black pepper
2 pounds (907 g) baking potatoes, cut into ¼-inch-thick slices
1 small onion, thinly sliced
Paprika
Nonfat cooking spray

1. Heat milk in small saucepan over medium heat until small bubbles form around edge of pan. Remove from heat. 2. Add soup, cream cheese, garlic, nutmeg, and pepper to pan. Stir until smooth. 3. Spray inside of slow cooker with nonfat cooking spray. Layer one-quarter of potatoes and onions on bottom of slow cooker. 4. Top with one-quarter of soup mixture. Repeat layers 3 times. 5. Cover. Cook on low 6 to 8 hours, or until potatoes are tender and most of liquid is absorbed. 6. Sprinkle with paprika before serving.

Zucchini Casserole

Prep time: 20 minutes | Cook time: 4 to 6 hours | Serves 6

2 to 3 cups thinly sliced zucchini
1 medium onion, diced
2 large carrots, shredded (enough to make 1 cup)
1 (10¾-ounce / 305-g) can 98% fat free cream of celery soup
1 (10¾-ounce / 305-g) can condensed cream of chicken soup
¼ teaspoon salt
Fat-free cooking spray

1. Spray slow cooker with fat-free cooking spray. Mix vegetables, soups, and salt together gently in slow cooker. Cover. 2. Cook on high 4 to 6 hours, or until vegetables are as crunchy or as soft as you like.

Sweet Potato Casserole

Prep time: 10 minutes | Cook time: 3 to 4 hours | Serves 8

2 (29-ounce / 822-g) cans sweet potatoes, drained and mashed
½ cup fat-free milk
⅓ cup chopped pecans
⅓ cup brown sugar
2 tablespoons brown sugar
1 tablespoon orange juice
2 eggs, beaten
2 tablespoons flour
2 teaspoons butter, melted

1. Combine sweet potatoes and 2 tablespoons brown sugar. 2. Stir in orange juice, eggs, and milk. Transfer to greased slow cooker. 3. Combine pecans, ⅓ cup brown sugar, flour, and butter. Spread over sweet potatoes. 4. Cover. Cook on high 3 to 4 hours.

Squash Casserole

Prep time: 15 minutes | Cook time: 7 to 9 hours | Serves 4 to 6

2 pounds (907 g) yellow summer squash or zucchini thinly sliced (about 6 cups)
Half a medium onion, chopped
1 cup peeled, shredded carrot
1 (10¾-ounce / 305-g) can condensed cream of chicken soup
1 cup sour cream
¼ cup flour
1 (8-ounce / 227-g) package seasoned stuffing crumbs
½ cup butter, melted

1. Combine squash, onion, carrots, and soup. 2. Mix together sour cream and flour. Stir into vegetables. 3. Toss stuffing crumbs with butter. Spread half in bottom of slow cooker. Add vegetable mixture. Top with remaining crumbs. 4. Cover. Cook on low 7 to 9 hours.

Swiss-Irish Hot Sauce

Prep time: 15 minutes | Cook time: 4 hours | Serves 6 to 8

2 medium onions, diced
5 garlic cloves, minced
¼ cup oil
1 (1-pound / 454-g) can tomatoes, puréed
1 (15-ounce / 425-g) can tomato sauce
1 (12-ounce / 340-g) can tomato paste
2 tablespoons parsley, fresh or dried
½ teaspoon red pepper
½ teaspoon black pepper
1 teaspoon chili powder
1 teaspoon dried basil
2 teaspoons Worcestershire sauce
2 teaspoons Tabasco sauce
¼ cup red wine

1. Sauté onions and garlic in oil in skillet. 2. Combine all ingredients in slow cooker. 3. Cover. Cook on low 4 hours. 4. Serve.

Cheese Potatoes and Croutons

Prep time: 15 minutes | Cook time: 8¼ hours | Serves 10

6 potatoes, peeled and cut into ¼-inch strips
2 cups sharp Cheddar cheese, shredded
1 (10¾-ounce / 305-g) can cream of chicken soup
1 small onion, chopped
7 tablespoons butter, melted, divided
1 teaspoon salt
1 teaspoon pepper
1 cup sour cream
2 cups seasoned stuffing cubes

1. Toss together potatoes and cheese. Place in slow cooker. 2. Combine soup, onion, 4 tablespoons butter, salt, and pepper. Pour over potatoes. 3. Cover. Cook on low 8 hours. 4. Stir in sour cream. Cover and heat for 10 more minutes. 5. Meanwhile, toss together stuffing cubes and 3 tablespoons butter. Sprinkle over potatoes just before serving.

Simply Sweet Potatoes

Prep time: 5 minutes | Cook time: 6 to 9 hours | Serves 4

3 large sweet potatoes
¼ cup water

1. Place unpeeled sweet potatoes into slow cooker. 2. Add ¼ cup water. 3. Cover and cook on high 1 hour. Then turn to low and cook for 5 to 8 hours, or until potatoes are tender.

Mustard Potatoes

Prep time: 5 minutes | Cook time: 2 to 4 hours | Serves 6

½ cup onions, chopped
1 tablespoon butter
1½ teaspoons prepared mustard
1 teaspoon salt
¼ teaspoon black pepper
½ cup fat-free or 2% milk
¼ pound (113 g) low-fat cheese, shredded
6 medium potatoes, cooked and grated

1. Sauté onion in butter in skillet. Add mustard, salt, pepper, milk, and cheese. 2. Place potatoes in slow cooker. Do not press down. 3. Pour mixture over potatoes. 4. Cover. Cook on low 3 to 4 hours. 5. Toss potatoes with a large spoon when ready to serve.

Stuffed Mushrooms

Prep time: 20 minutes | Cook time: 2 to 4 hours | Serves 4 to 6

8 to 10 large mushrooms
¼ teaspoon minced garlic
1 tablespoon oil
Dash of salt
Dash of pepper
Dash of cayenne pepper (optional)
¼ cup shredded Monterey Jack cheese

1. Remove stems from mushrooms and dice. 2. Heat oil in skillet. Sauté diced stems with garlic until softened. Remove skillet from heat. 3. Stir in seasonings and cheese. Stuff into mushroom shells. Place in slow cooker. 4. Cover. Heat on low 2 to 4 hours.

Pineapple Sweet Potatoes

Prep time: 5 minutes | Cook time: 2 to 4 hours | Serves 10

1 (10-ounce / 283-g) can unsweetened crushed pineapple, drained
2 tablespoons dark brown sugar
1 (40-ounce / 1.1-kg) can unsweetened yams, drained
Cooking spray

1. Mix crushed pineapples with brown sugar. 2. Combine with yams in slow cooker sprayed with cooking spray. 3. Cover. Cook on low 2 to 4 hours, or until heated through.

Golden Carrots

Prep time: 5 minutes | Cook time: 3 to 4 hours | Serves 6

1 (2-pound / 907-g) package baby carrots
½ cup golden raisins
1 stick butter, melted or softened
⅓ cup honey
2 tablespoons lemon juice
½ teaspoon ground ginger (optional)

1. Combine all ingredients in slow cooker. 2. Cover and cook on low 3 to 4 hours, or until carrots are tender-crisp.

Refrigerator Mashed Potatoes

Prep time: 30 minutes | Cook time: 2 hours | Serves 8 to 10

5 pounds (2.3 kg) potatoes
1 (8-ounce / 227-g) package cream cheese, softened
1 cup sour cream
1 teaspoon salt
¼ teaspoon pepper
¼ cup crisp bacon, crumbled
2 tablespoons butter

1. Cook and mash potatoes. 2. Add remaining ingredients except butter. Put in slow cooker. Dot with butter. 3. Cover. Cook on low 2 hours.

Special Green Beans

Prep time: 30 minutes | Cook time: 1 to 2 hours | Serves 12 to 14

4 (14½-ounce / 411-g) cans green beans, drained
1 (10¾-ounce / 305-g) can cream of mushroom soup
1 (14½-ounce / 411-g) can chicken broth
1 cup tater tots
1 (3-ounce / 85-g) can French-fried onion rings

1. Put green beans in slow cooker. 2. In a bowl, mix soup and broth together. Spread over beans. 3. Spoon tater tots over all. Top with onion rings. 4. Cover and cook on high 1 to 2 hours, or until heated through and potatoes are cooked.

Purely Artichokes

Prep time: 15 minutes | Cook time: 6 to 8 hours | Serves 4 to 6

4 to 6 artichokes
1 to 1½ teaspoons salt
1 cup lemon juice, divided
2 cups hot water
1 stick (½ cup) butter, melted

1. Wash and trim artichokes. Cut off about 1 inch from top. If you wish, trim tips of leaves. Stand chokes upright in slow cooker. 2. Sprinkle each choke with ¼ teaspoon salt and 2 tablespoons lemon juice. 3. Pour 2 cups hot water around the base of the artichokes. 4. Cover and cook on low 6 to 8 hours. 5. Serve with melted butter and lemon juice for dipping.

"Baked" Tomatoes

Prep time: 5 minutes | Cook time: ¾ to 1 hour | Serves 4

2 tomatoes, each cut in half
½ tablespoon olive oil
½ teaspoon parsley, chopped, or ¼ teaspoon dry parsley flakes
¼ teaspoon dried oregano
¼ teaspoon dried basil
Nonfat cooking spray

1. Place tomato halves in slow cooker sprayed with nonfat cooking spray. 2. Drizzle oil over tomatoes. Sprinkle with remaining ingredients. 3. Cover. Cook on high 45 minutes to 1 hour.

Green Beans with Dill

Prep time: 5 minutes | Cook time: 3 to 4 hours | Serves 8

2 quarts cut green beans, or 4 (14½-ounce / 411-g) cans cut green beans
2 teaspoons beef bouillon granules
½ teaspoon dill seed
¼ cup water
Fat-free cooking spray

1. Spray slow cooker with fat-free cooking spray. 2. Add all ingredients and mix well. 3. Cook on high 3 to 4 hours.

"Stir-Fry" Veggies

Prep time: 20 minutes | Cook time: 8 to 10 hours | Serves 8

1 (16-ounce / 454-g) bag baby carrots
4 ribs celery, chunked
1 medium onion, diced
1 (14½-ounce / 411-g) can low-sodium Italian-style stewed tomatoes
½ teaspoon dried basil
½ teaspoon dried oregano
½ teaspoon salt
1 large red or yellow bell pepper, diced
1 small head cabbage, cut up
1 pound (454 g) raw broccoli, cut up

1. Combine carrots, celery, onion, tomatoes, basil, oregano, and salt in slow cooker. 2. Cover. Cook on high 3 to 4 hours, or on low 6 to 8 hours, stirring occasionally. 3. Stir in pepper, cabbage, and broccoli. 4. Cook 1 hour more on high, or 2 hours more on low, stirring occasionally. You may need to add a little water if there is not liquid left on the veggies.

Cheesy Scalloped Potatoes

Prep time: 15 minutes | Cook time: 3 to 4 hours | Serves 8 to 10

2 tablespoons dried minced onion
1 medium clove garlic, minced
1 teaspoon salt
8 to 10 medium fresh potatoes, sliced, divided
1 (8-ounce / 227-g) package cream cheese, cubed, divided
½ cup shredded Cheddar cheese (optional)
Nonstick cooking spray

1. Spray interior of slow cooker with nonstick cooking spray. 2. In a small bowl, combine onion, garlic, and salt. 3. Layer about one-fourth of the potatoes into the slow cooker. 4. Sprinkle one-fourth of onion-garlic mixture over potatoes. 5. Spoon about one-third of cream cheese cubes over top. 6. Repeat layers, ending with the seasoning. 7. Cook on high 3 to 4 hours, or until potatoes are tender. 8. Stir potatoes to spread out the cream cheese. If you wish, you can mash the potatoes at this point. 9. If you like, sprinkle shredded cheese over top of the sliced or mashed potatoes. 10. Cover and cook an additional 10 minutes, or until the cheese is melted.

Vegetable Curry

Prep time: 15 minutes | Cook time: 3 to 10 hours | Serves 8 to 10

1 (16-ounce / 454-g) package baby carrots
3 medium potatoes, cubed
1 pound (454 g) fresh or frozen green beans, cut in 2-inch pieces
1 green pepper, chopped
1 onion, chopped
1 to 2 cloves garlic, minced
1 (15-ounce / 425-g) can garbanzo beans, drained
1 (28-ounce / 794-g) can crushed tomatoes
3 tablespoons minute tapioca
3 teaspoons curry powder
2 teaspoons salt
1¾ cups boiling water
2 teaspoons chicken bouillon granules, or 2 chicken bouillon cubes

1. Combine carrots, potatoes, green beans, pepper, onion, garlic, garbanzo beans, and crushed tomatoes in large bowl. 2. Stir in tapioca, curry powder, and salt. 3. Dissolve bouillon in boiling water. Pour over vegetables. Mix well. Spoon into large cooker, or two medium-sized ones. 4. Cover. Cook on low 8 to 10 hours, or on high 3 to 4 hours. Serve.

Orange-Glazed Carrots

Prep time: 10 minutes | Cook time: 4 to 6 hours | Serves 6 to 8

1 (32-ounce / 907-g) package baby carrots
¼ cup packed brown sugar
½ cup orange juice
1 tablespoon butter
½ to ¾ teaspoon ground cinnamon, according to your taste preference
¼ teaspoon ground nutmeg
2 tablespoons cornstarch
¼ cup water

1. Combine all ingredients except cornstarch and water in slow cooker. 2. Cover. Cook on low 4 to 6 hours, or until carrots are done to your liking. 3. Put carrots in serving dish and keep warm, reserving cooking juices. Put reserved juices in small saucepan. Bring to boil. 4. Mix cornstarch and water in small bowl until blended. Add to juices. Boil one minute or until thickened, stirring constantly. 5. Pour over carrots and serve.

Stress-Free "Baked" Potatoes

Prep time: 10 minutes | Cook time: 4 to 10 hours | Serves 12

12 potatoes
Butter, softened
Nonstick cooking spray

1. Spray slow cooker with nonstick cooking spray. 2. Rub butter over unpeeled whole potatoes. Place in slow cooker. 3. Cover and cook on high 4 to 5 hours, or on low 8 to 10 hours, or until potatoes are tender when jagged.

Zucchini in Sour Cream

Prep time: 10 minutes | Cook time: 1 to 1½ hours | Serves 6

4 cups unpeeled, sliced zucchini
1 cup fat-free sour cream
¼ cup skim milk
1 cup chopped onions
1 teaspoon salt
1 cup shredded low-fat sharp Cheddar cheese
Nonfat cooking spray

1. Parboil zucchini in microwave for 2 to 3 minutes. Turn into slow cooker sprayed with nonfat cooking spray. 2. Combine sour cream, milk, onions, and salt. Pour over zucchini and stir gently. 3. Cover. Cook on low 1 to 1½ hours. 4. Sprinkle cheese over vegetables 30 minutes before serving.

Mediterranean Eggplant

Prep time: 20 minutes | Cook time: 5 to 6 hours | Serves 8

1 medium red onion, chopped
2 cloves garlic, crushed
1 cup fresh mushrooms, sliced
2 tablespoons olive oil
1 eggplant, unpeeled, cubed
2 green bell peppers, coarsely chopped
1 (28-ounce / 794-g) can crushed tomatoes
1 (28-ounce / 794-g) can garbanzo beans, drained and rinsed
2 tablespoons fresh rosemary
1 cup chopped fresh parsley
½ cup Kalamata olives, pitted and sliced
Nonfat cooking spray

1. Sauté onion, garlic, and mushrooms in olive oil in a skillet over medium heat. Transfer to slow cooker coated with nonfat cooking spray. 2. Add eggplant, peppers, tomatoes, garbanzo beans, rosemary, and parsley. 3. Cover. Cook on low 5 to 6 hours. 4. Stir in olives just before serving. 5. Serve.

Stuffed Peppers with Beans

Prep time: 15 minutes | Cook time: 6 hours | Serves 4

4 medium green, yellow, or red sweet peppers, or a mixture of colors
1 cup rice, cooked
1 (15-ounce / 425-g) can chili beans with chili gravy
1 cup shredded cheese, divided
1 (14½-ounce / 411-g) can petite diced tomatoes, with onion, celery, and green pepper

1. Wash and dry sweet peppers. Remove tops, membranes, and seeds, but keep the peppers whole. 2. In a bowl, mix together rice, beans, and half the cheese. Spoon mixture into peppers. 3. Pour tomatoes into slow cooker. Place filled peppers on top, keeping them upright. Do not stack the peppers. 4. Cover and cook on high 3 hours. 5. Carefully lift peppers out of cooker and place on a serving platter. Spoon hot tomatoes over top. Sprinkle remaining cheese over peppers.

Sweet Potatoes and Apples

Prep time: 15 minutes | Cook time: 6 to 8 hours | Serves 8 to 10

3 large sweet potatoes, peeled and cubed
3 large tart and firm apples, peeled and sliced
½ to ¾ teaspoon salt
⅛ to ¼ teaspoon pepper
1 teaspoon sage
1 teaspoon ground cinnamon
4 tablespoons (½ stick) butter, melted
¼ cup maple syrup
Toasted sliced almonds or chopped pecans (optional)

1. Place half the sweet potatoes in slow cooker. Layer in half the apple slices. 2. Mix together seasonings. Sprinkle half over apples. 3. Mix together butter and maple syrup. Spoon half over seasonings. 4. Repeat layers. 5. Cover. Cook on low 6 to 8 hours or until potatoes are soft, stirring occasionally. 6. To add a bit of crunch, sprinkle with toasted almonds or pecans when serving. 7. Serve.

Lemon Red Potatoes

Prep time: 10 minutes | Cook time: 2½ to 3 hours | Serves 6

1½ pounds (680 g) medium red potatoes
¼ cup water
2 tablespoons butter, melted
1 tablespoon lemon juice
3 tablespoons fresh chives, snipped
Chopped fresh parsley
1 teaspoon salt
½ teaspoon black pepper

1. Cut a strip of peel from around the middle of each potato. Place potatoes and water in slow cooker. 2. Cover. Cook on high 2½ to 3 hours. 3. Drain. 4. Combine butter, lemon juice, chives, and parsley. Pour over potatoes. Toss to coat. 5. Season with salt and pepper.

Uptown Scalloped Potatoes

Prep time: 15 minutes | Cook time: 6 to 7 hours | Serves 8 to 10

5 pounds (2.3 kg) red potatoes, peeled and sliced
2 cups water
1 teaspoon cream of tartar
¼ pound (113 g) bacon, cut in 1-inch squares, browned until crisp, and drained
Dash of salt
½ pint whipping cream
1 pint half-and-half

1. Toss potatoes in water and cream of tartar. Drain. 2. Layer potatoes and bacon in large slow cooker. Sprinkle with salt. 3. Mix whipping cream and half-and-half. 4. Cover. Cook on low 6 to 7 hours.

Sweet Potato Stuffing

Prep time: 15 minutes | Cook time: 4 hours | Serves 8

½ cup chopped celery
½ cup chopped onions
¼ cup butter
6 cups dry bread cubes
1 large sweet potato, cooked, peeled, and cubed
½ cup chicken broth
¼ cup chopped pecans
½ teaspoon poultry seasoning
½ teaspoon rubbed sage
½ teaspoon salt
¼ teaspoon pepper

1. Sauté celery and onion in skillet in butter until tender. Pour into greased slow cooker. 2. Add remaining ingredients. Toss gently. 3. Cover. Cook on low 4 hours.

Mexican Hominy

Prep time: 10 minutes | Cook time: 1 hour | Serves 6 to 8

2 (29-ounce / 822-g) cans hominy, drained
1 (4-ounce / 113-g) can chopped green chilies, mild or hot
1 cup sour cream
1 (8-ounce / 227-g) jar Cheez Whiz

1. Combine ingredients in slow cooker. 2. Cover and heat on low for 1 hour, or until cheese is melted and dish is thoroughly hot.

Corn on the Cob

Prep time: 10 minutes | Cook time: 2 to 3 hours | Serves 3 to 4

6 to 8 ears of corn (in husk)
½ cup water

1. Remove silk from corn, as much as possible, but leave husks on. 2. Cut off ends of corn so ears can stand in the cooker. 3. Add water. 4. Cover. Cook on low 2 to 3 hours.

Broccoli Casserole

Prep time: 10 minutes | Cook time: 3 to 5 hours | Serves 6

1 (10-ounce / 283-g) package frozen chopped broccoli
6 eggs, beaten
(24-ounce / 680-g) carton fat-free small-curd cottage cheese
6 tablespoons flour
8 ounces (227 g) fat-free mild cheese of your choice, diced
2 green onions, chopped
½ teaspoon salt

1. Place frozen broccoli in colander. Run cold water over it until it thaws. Separate into pieces. Drain well. 2. Combine remaining ingredients in large bowl and mix until well blended. Stir in broccoli. Pour into slow cooker sprayed with fat-free cooking spray. 3. Cover. Cook on high 1 hour. Stir well, then resume cooking on low 2 to 4 hours.

Creamy Mashed Potatoes

Prep time: 15 minutes | Cook time: 3 to 5 hours | Serves 10 to 12

2 teaspoons salt
6 tablespoons (¾ stick) butter, melted
2¼ cups milk
6⅞ cups potato flakes
6 cups water
1 cup sour cream
4 to 5 ounces (113 to 142 g) cream cheese, softened

1. Combine first five ingredients as directed on potato box. 2. Whip cream cheese with electric mixer until creamy. Blend in sour cream. 3. Fold potatoes into cheese and sour cream. Beat well. Place in slow cooker. 4. Cover. Cook on low 3 to 5 hours.

Potato Filling

Prep time: 40 minutes | Cook time: 3 hours | Serves 20

1 cup celery, chopped fine
medium onion, minced
½ cup butter
2 (15-ounce / 425-g) packages low-fat bread cubes
6 eggs, beaten
1 quart fat-free milk
1 quart mashed potatoes
3 teaspoons salt
2 pinches saffron
1 cup boiling water
1 teaspoon black pepper

1. Sauté celery and onion in butter in skillet until transparent. 2. Combine sautéed mixture with bread cubes. Stir in remaining ingredients. Add more milk if mixture isn't very moist. 3. Pour into large, or several medium-sized, slow cookers. Cook on high 3 hours, stirring up from bottom every hour or so to make sure the filling isn't sticking.

Hot German Potato Salad

Prep time: 20 minutes | Cook time: 3 to 8 hours | Serves 8

6 to 7 cups potatoes, sliced
1 cup onions, chopped
1 cup celery, chopped
1 cup water
⅓ cup vinegar
¼ cup sugar
2 tablespoons quick-cooking tapioca
1 teaspoon salt
1 teaspoon celery seed
¼ teaspoon black pepper
6 slices lean turkey bacon, cooked and crumbled
¼ cup fresh parsley

1. Combine potatoes, onions, and celery in slow cooker. 2. In a bowl, combine water, vinegar, sugar, tapioca, salt, celery seed, and black pepper. 3. Pour over potatoes. Mix together gently. 4. Cover. Cook on low 6 to 8 hours, or on high 3 to 4 hours. 5. Stir in bacon and parsley just before serving.

Stuffed Acorn Squash

Prep time: 15 minutes | Cook time: 2½ hours | Serves 6

3 small carnival or acorn squash
5 tablespoons instant brown rice
3 tablespoons dried cranberries
3 tablespoons diced celery
3 tablespoons minced onion
Pinch of ground or dried sage
1 teaspoon butter, divided
3 tablespoons orange juice
½ cup water

1. Slice off points on the bottoms of squash so they will stand in slow cooker. Slice off tops and discard. Scoop out seeds. Place squash in slow cooker. 2. Combine rice, cranberries, celery, onion, and sage. Stuff into squash. 3. Dot with butter. 4. Pour 1 tablespoon orange juice into each squash. 5. Pour water into bottom of slow cooker. 6. Cover. Cook on low 2½ hours. 7. Serve.

Apricot-Glazed Carrots

Prep time: 5 minutes | Cook time: 9¼ hours | Serves 8

2 pounds (907 g) baby carrots
1 onion, chopped
½ cup water
⅓ cup honey
⅓ cup apricot preserves
2 tablespoons chopped fresh parsley

1. Place carrots and onions in slow cooker. Add water. 2. Cover and cook on low 9 hours. 3. Drain liquid from slow cooker. 4. In a small bowl, mix honey and preserves together. Pour over carrots. 5. Cover and cook on high 10 to 15 minutes. 6. Sprinkle with parsley before serving.

Orange Yams

Prep time: 15 minutes | Cook time: 3 hours | Serves 6 to 8

1 (40-ounce / 1.1-kg) can yams, drained
2 apples, cored, peeled, thinly sliced
3 tablespoons butter, melted
2 teaspoons orange zest
1 cup orange juice
2 tablespoons cornstarch
½ cup brown sugar
1 teaspoon salt
Dash of ground cinnamon and/or nutmeg

1. Place yams and apples in slow cooker. 2. Add butter and orange zest. 3. Combine remaining ingredients and pour over yams. 4. Cover. Cook on high 1 hour and on low 2 hours, or until apples are tender.

Creamy Red Potatoes

Prep time: 10 minutes | Cook time: 8 hours | Serves 4 to 6

2 pounds (907 g) small red potatoes, quartered
1 (8-ounce / 227-g) package cream cheese, softened
1 (10¾-ounce / 305-g) can cream of potato soup
1 envelope dry Ranch salad dressing mix

1. Place potatoes in slow cooker. 2. Beat together cream cheese, soup, and salad dressing mix. Stir into potatoes. 3. Cover. Cook on low 8 hours, or until potatoes are tender.

Brussels Sprouts with Pimentos

Prep time: 5 minutes | Cook time: 6 hours | Serves 8

2 pounds (907 g) Brussels sprouts
¼ teaspoon dried oregano
½ teaspoon dried basil
1 (2-ounce / 57-g) jar pimentos, drained
¼ cup, or 1 small can, sliced black olives, drained
1 tablespoon olive oil
½ cup water

1. Combine all ingredients in slow cooker. 2. Cook on low 6 hours.

Potatoes Perfect

Prep time: 15 minutes | Cook time: 3 to 10 hours | Serves 4 to 6

¼ pound (113 g) bacon, diced and browned until crisp
2 medium onions, thinly sliced
6 to 8 medium potatoes, thinly sliced
½ pound (227 g) Cheddar cheese, thinly sliced
Salt to taste
Pepper to taste
2 to 4 tablespoons butter

1. Layer half of bacon, onions, potatoes, and cheese in greased slow cooker. Season with salt and pepper to taste. 2. Dot with butter. Repeat layers. 3. Cover. Cook on low 8 to 10 hours, or on high 3 to 4 hours, or until potatoes are soft.

Very Special Spinach

Prep time: 10 minutes | Cook time: 5 hours | Serves 8

3 (10-ounce / 283-g) boxes frozen spinach, thawed and drained
2 cups cottage cheese
1½ cups shredded Cheddar cheese
3 eggs
¼ cup flour
1 teaspoon salt
½ cup butter, or margarine, melted

1. Mix together all ingredients. 2. Pour into slow cooker. 3. Cook on high 1 hour. Reduce heat to low and cook 4 more hours.

Vegetables with Pasta

Prep time: 20 minutes | Cook time: 6 hours | Serves 6

2 cups chopped zucchini
½ cup cherry tomatoes, cut in half
Half green or red bell pepper, sliced
Half medium onion, sliced
½ cup sliced fresh mushrooms
4 cloves garlic, minced
1 tablespoon olive oil
1 tablespoon Italian seasoning
1 (8-ounce / 227-g) can tomato sauce

1. Combine all ingredients in slow cooker. 2. Cook on low 6 hours, or until vegetables are tender.

"Baked" Acorn Squash

Prep time: 15 minutes | Cook time: 5 to 6 hours | Serves 4

2 acorn squash
⅔ cup cracker crumbs
½ cup coarsely chopped pecans
⅓ cup butter, melted
4 tablespoons brown sugar
½ teaspoon salt
¼ teaspoon ground nutmeg
2 tablespoons orange juice

1. Cut squash in half. Remove seeds. 2. Combine remaining ingredients. Spoon into squash halves. Place squash in slow cooker. 3. Cover. Cook on low 5 to 6 hours, or until squash is tender.

"Baked" Sweet Potatoes

Prep time: 10 minutes | Cook time: 4 to 8 hours | Serves 6 to 8

6 to 8 medium sweet potatoes
Salt to taste
Butter, for serving

1. Scrub and prick sweet potatoes with fork. Wrap each in tin foil and arrange in slow cooker. 2. Cover. Cook on low 6 to 8 hours, or on high 4 to 5 hours, or until each potato is soft. 3. Remove from foil and serve with butter and salt.

Do-Ahead Mashed Potatoes

Prep time: 45 minutes | Cook time: 3 to 4 hours | Serves 8

12 medium potatoes, washed, peeled, and quartered
1 small or medium onion, chopped
4 ounces (113 g) fat-free cream cheese
1 teaspoon salt
¼ teaspoon black pepper
1 cup skim milk

1. In a saucepan, cover potatoes and onion with water. Bring to a boil, and then simmer over medium-low heat for 30 minutes or so, until fully softened. Drain. 2. Mash potatoes and onion with a potato masher to remove chunks. 3. In a large mixing bowl, combine partially mashed potatoes, cream cheese, salt, pepper, and milk. Whip together on high for 3 minutes. 4. Transfer potatoes into slow cooker. 5. Cook on low 3 to 4 hours.

Cranberry-Orange Beets

Prep time: 15 minutes | Cook time: 3½ to 7½ hours | Serves 6

2 pounds (907 g) medium beets, peeled and quartered
½ teaspoon ground nutmeg
1 cup cranberry juice
1 teaspoon orange peel, finely shredded (optional)
2 tablespoons butter
2 tablespoons sugar
4 teaspoons cornstarch

1. Place beets in slow cooker. Sprinkle with nutmeg. 2. Add cranberry juice and orange peel. Dot with butter. 3. Cover. Cook on low 6 to 7 hours, or on high 3 to 3½ hours. 4. In small bowl, combine sugar and cornstarch. 5. Remove ½ cup of cooking liquid and stir into cornstarch. 6. Stir mixture into slow cooker. 7. Cover. Cook on high 15 to 30 minutes.

Apple Stuffing

Prep time: 20 minutes | Cook time: 4 to 5 hours | Serves 4 to 5

1 stick (½ cup) butter, divided
1 cup chopped walnuts
2 onions, chopped
1 (14-ounce / 397-g) package dry herb-seasoned stuffing mix
1½ cups applesauce
Water (optional)
Nonstick cooking spray

1. In nonstick skillet, melt 2 tablespoons of butter. Sauté walnuts over medium heat until toasted, about 5 minutes, stirring frequently. Remove from skillet and set aside. 2. Melt remaining butter in skillet. Add onions and cook 3 to 4 minutes, or until almost tender. Set aside. 3. Spray slow cooker with nonstick cooking spray. Place dry stuffing mix in slow cooker. 4. Add onion-butter mixture and stir. Add applesauce and stir. 5. Cover and cook on low 4 to 5 hours, or until heated through. Check after Stuffing has cooked for 3½ hours. If it's sticking to the cooker, drying out, or becoming too brown on the edges, stir in ½ to 1 cup water. Continue cooking. 6. Sprinkle with walnuts before serving.

"Baked" Corn

Prep time: 5 minutes | Cook time: 3 hours | Serves 8

1 quart corn (be sure to thaw and drain if using frozen corn)
2 eggs, beaten
1 teaspoon salt
1 cup fat-free milk
⅛ teaspoon black pepper
2 teaspoons oil
2 tablespoons sugar
3 tablespoons flour

1. Combine all ingredients well. Pour into slow cooker sprayed with fat-free cooking spray. 2. Cover. Cook on high 3 hours.

Bavarian Cabbage

Prep time: 10 minutes | Cook time: 3 to 8 hours | Serves 4 to 8

1 small head red cabbage, sliced
1 medium onion, chopped
3 tart apples, cored and quartered
2 teaspoons salt
1 cup hot water
2 tablespoons sugar
⅓ cup vinegar
3 tablespoons bacon drippings

1. Place all ingredients in slow cooker in order listed. 2. Cover. Cook on low 8 hours, or on high 3 hours. Stir well before serving.

Apple-Glazed Carrots

Prep time: 10 minutes | Cook time: 2½ to 3½ hours | Serves 4

1 (16-ounce / 454-g) package frozen baby carrots
¼ cup apple cider or apple juice
¼ cup apple jelly
1½ teaspoons Dijon mustard

1. Put carrots and apple juice in slow cooker. 2. Cover and cook on high 2 to 3 hours, until carrots are tender. 3. Blend jelly and mustard together in a small bowl. 4. During the last 45 minutes of cooking time, after carrots are tender, stir in blended apple jelly and mustard. Continue to heat until steaming hot.

Broccoli Delight

Prep time: 15 minutes | Cook time: 2 to 6 hours | Serves 4 to 6

1 to 2 pounds (454 to 907 g) broccoli, chopped
2 cups cauliflower, chopped
1 (10¾-ounce / 305-g) can 98% fat-free cream of celery soup
½ teaspoon salt
¼ teaspoon black pepper
1 medium onion, diced
2 to 4 garlic cloves, crushed, according to your taste preference
½ cup vegetable broth

1. Combine all ingredients in slow cooker. 2. Cook on low 4 to 6 hours, or on high 2 to 3 hours.

Chapter 3 Vegetables and Sides | 33

Super Green Beans

Prep time: 15 minutes | Cook time: 1 to 2 hours | Serves 5

2 (14½-ounce / 411-g) cans green beans, undrained
1 cup cooked cubed ham
⅓ cup finely chopped onion
1 tablespoon butter, melted, or bacon drippings

1. Place undrained beans in cooker. Add remaining ingredients and mix well. 2. Cook on high 1 to 2 hours, or until steaming hot.

Hominy and Ham

Prep time: 10 minutes | Cook time: 1½ to 3 hours | Serves 12 to 14

3 (29-ounce / 822-g) cans hominy, drained
1 (10¾-ounce / 305-g) can cream of chicken soup
½ pound (227 g) Cheddar cheese, shredded or cubed
1 pound (454 g) cubed cooked ham
2 (2¼-ounce / 64-g) cans green chilies, undrained

1. Mix all ingredients together in slow cooker. 2. Cover and cook on high for 1½ hours, or on low for 2 to 3 hours, or until bubbly and cheese is melted.

Chapter 4 — Stews and Soups

Baked Potato Soup

Prep time: 10 minutes | Cook time: 8 hours | Serves 2

2 russet potatoes, peeled and diced
½ cup minced onion
¼ cup minced celery
2 cups low-sodium chicken broth
⅛ teaspoon sea salt
1 tablespoon heavy cream
¼ cup thinly sliced scallions, white and green parts, for garnish
¼ cup grated sharp Cheddar cheese, for garnish
2 tablespoons crumbled cooked bacon, for garnish

1. Put the potatoes, onion, celery, broth, and salt in the crock pot, and stir together. 2. Cover and cook on low for 8 hours. 3. Stir in the cream and purée the soup with an immersion blender for a smooth soup. Or leave the soup chunky. 4. Serve garnished with the scallions, Cheddar cheese, and bacon.

Greek Salad Soup

Prep time: 15 minutes | Cook time: 6 to 8 hours | Serves 6

4 tomatoes, cut into wedges
2 cucumbers, cut into 1-inch-thick rounds
2 green bell peppers, seeded and diced
1 small red onion, diced
1 cup whole Kalamata olives, pitted
4 cups low-sodium chicken broth
2 cups water
1 tablespoon extra-virgin olive oil
2 teaspoons red wine vinegar
1½ teaspoons dried oregano
1 teaspoon sea salt
½ teaspoon freshly ground black pepper
4 ounces (113 g) feta cheese, crumbled

1. In a crock pot, combine the tomatoes, cucumbers, bell peppers, onion, olives, chicken broth, water, olive oil, vinegar, oregano, salt, and black pepper. Stir to mix well. 2. Cover the cooker and cook for 6 to 8 hours on Low heat. 3. Top each bowl with feta cheese before serving.

Mediterranean Beef Stew with Rosemary and Balsamic Vinegar

Prep time: 15 minutes | Cook time: 8⅓ hours | Serves 6

ounces (227 g) mushrooms, sliced
1 large yellow onion, diced
2 tablespoons olive oil
2 pounds (907 g) chuck steak, trimmed and cut into bite-size pieces
1 cup beef stock
1 (15-ounce / 425-g) can diced tomatoes, with the juice
½ cup tomato sauce
¼ cup balsamic vinegar
1 (5-ounce / 142-g) can chopped black olives
½ cup thinly sliced garlic cloves
2 tablespoons finely chopped fresh rosemary (or 1 tablespoon dried rosemary)
2 tablespoons finely chopped fresh flat-leaf parsley (or 1 tablespoon dried parsley)
2 tablespoons capers, drained
Sea salt
Black pepper

1. Place the mushrooms and onion in the crock pot. 2. Heat the olive oil in a large skillet over medium-high heat. Add the beef and cook until well browned, stirring often, for 10 to 15 minutes. Don't rush the browning step, and decrease the heat to medium if the beef browns too quickly. Add the beef to the crock pot. 3. Add the beef stock to the skillet and simmer for 5 minutes or until slightly reduced, scraping up the flavorful brown bits from the bottom of the pan with a wooden spoon. Add the stock to the crock pot. 4. Add the diced tomatoes, tomato sauce, vinegar, olives, garlic, rosemary, parsley, and capers to the crock pot. Season with salt and pepper. Stir gently to combine. Cover and cook on low for 6 to 8 hours. (It is possible to cook on high for 3 to 4 hours, but the lower setting yields the best results.) Season with additional salt and pepper, if desired, and serve hot.

Chicken and Shrimp Bouillabaisse

Prep time: 20 minutes | Cook time: 7⅓ hours | Serves 2

4 boneless, skinless chicken thighs, cut into strips
1 onion, chopped
3 garlic cloves, minced
1 cup sliced fennel
2 large tomatoes, seeded and chopped
2 Yukon Gold potatoes, cubed
2 cups clam juice
½ cup dry white wine
1 teaspoon dried thyme leaves
½ teaspoon salt
⅛ teaspoon freshly ground black pepper
1 pinch saffron
½ pound (227 g) medium shrimp, peeled and deveined
1 teaspoon minced fresh rosemary leaves

1. In the crock pot, combine all the ingredients except the shrimp and rosemary, and mix well. 2. Cover and cook on low for 7 hours. 3. Add the shrimp and rosemary. Cover and cook on high for 20 minutes, or until the shrimp curl and turn pink. 4. Ladle the stew into 2 bowls and serve.

Tuscan Bean Soup with Herbs

Prep time: 15 minutes | Cook time: 8 hours | Serves 2

1 cup dried navy beans
1 onion, chopped
2 garlic cloves, minced
2 carrots, sliced
2 Yukon Gold potatoes, cubed
3 cups vegetable broth
½ teaspoon salt
⅛ teaspoon freshly ground black pepper
½ teaspoon dried thyme leaves
2 cups baby spinach leaves
2 teaspoons chopped fresh rosemary leaves
2 tablespoons chopped fresh flat-leaf parsley
2 tablespoons extra-virgin olive oil, divided

1. Sort the beans and rinse; drain well. 2. In the crock pot, combine the beans, onion, garlic, carrots, potatoes, broth, salt, pepper, and thyme. 3. Cover and cook on low for 7½ hours. 4. Add the spinach, rosemary, and parsley to the crock pot and stir. Cover and cook on low for 25 to 30 minutes more, or until the spinach wilts. 5. Ladle the soup into 2 bowls, drizzle each with 1 tablespoon of olive oil, and serve.

Rutabaga and Sweet Potato Soup with Garlicky

Prep time: 10 minutes | Cook time: 8 hours | Serves 2

2 cups peeled, diced rutabaga
1 cup peeled, diced sweet potato
1 leek, white and pale green parts only, sliced thin
⅛ teaspoon sea salt
2 cups low-sodium vegetable broth
1 sprig fresh sage, plus 1 teaspoon minced fresh sage
1 teaspoon minced garlic
2 tablespoons toasted walnuts

1. Put the rutabaga, sweet potato, leek, salt, broth, and sprig of sage into the crock pot. 2. Cover and cook on low for 8 hours. Remove the sage sprig. 3. Use an immersion blender to purée the soup until smooth. 4. Place the 1 teaspoon minced fresh sage, garlic, and walnuts into a mortar and pestle and grind them into a paste. Serve each bowl of soup garnished with the walnut mixture.

Chicken Stew with Gnocchi

Prep time: 15 minutes | Cook time: 8 hours | Serves 2

4 boneless, skinless chicken thighs, cubed
1 leek, white part only, chopped
2 garlic cloves, minced
1 sweet potato, peeled and chopped
½ cup chopped tomato
½ teaspoon salt
½ teaspoon dried basil leaves
⅛ teaspoon freshly ground black pepper
3 cups chicken stock
1 cup potato gnocchi

1. In the crock pot, combine all the ingredients except the gnocchi. 2. Cover and cook on low for 7½ hours. 3. Add the gnocchi. Cover and cook on high for 25 to 30 minutes more, or until the gnocchi are tender. 4. Ladle the stew into 2 bowls and serve.

Chicken and Pasta Soup

Prep time: 10 minutes | Cook time: 5 hours 18 minutes | Serves 6

6 boneless skinless chicken thighs
4 carrots, cut into 1-inch pieces
4 stalks celery, cut into ½-inch pieces
1 medium yellow onion, halved
2 garlic cloves, minced
2 bay leaves
Sea salt
Black pepper
6 cups chicken stock
½ cup small pasta like stelline or alphabet
¼ cup chopped fresh flat-leaf parsley

1. In the crock pot, place the chicken, carrots, celery, onion, and garlic. Add the bay leaves and season with salt and pepper. 2. Add the chicken stock. Cover and cook on high for 4 to 5 hours, or on low for 7 to 8 hours, until the chicken is cooked through and tender. 3. About 20 minutes before serving, transfer the chicken to a bowl. Let the chicken cool until it can comfortably be handled. 4. Remove and discard the onion and bay leaves. If the crock pot is on the low setting, turn it to high. 5. Add the pasta to the crock pot, cover, and cook until tender, 15 to 18 minutes. 6. Meanwhile, shred the chicken. 7. Stir the chicken into the soup along with the parsley. When the chicken is heated through, about 5 minutes, serve the soup hot.

Red Curry Butternut Squash Soup

Prep time: 15 minutes | Cook time: 8 hours | Serves 2

2 cups cubed butternut squash
½ cup diced onion
1 teaspoon minced garlic
1 teaspoon minced ginger
2 cups low-sodium chicken broth
1 teaspoon Thai red curry paste
1 teaspoon fish sauce
½ cup coconut milk
1 teaspoon freshly squeezed lime juice
¼ cup fresh cilantro, for garnish

1. Put the butternut squash, onion, garlic, ginger, broth, curry paste, fish sauce, and coconut milk in the crock pot. Stir gently to combine. 2. Cover and cook on low for 8 hours. 3. Just before serving, stir in the lime juice and garnish the soup with the cilantro.

Chickpea Stew

Prep time: 10 minutes | Cook time: 6 to 8 hours | Serves 6

2 cups dried chickpeas, rinsed
4 cups low-sodium vegetable broth or low-sodium chicken broth
1 tablespoon extra-virgin olive oil
1 small onion, diced
1 green bell pepper, seeded and chopped
2 garlic cloves, minced
1 tablespoon drained capers
1 teaspoon ground cumin
1 teaspoon ground turmeric
½ teaspoon ground coriander
½ teaspoon sea salt
¼ teaspoon freshly ground black pepper

1. In a crock pot, combine the chickpeas, vegetable broth, olive oil, onion, bell pepper, garlic, capers, cumin, turmeric, coriander, salt, and black pepper. Stir to mix well. 2. Cover the cooker and cook for 6 to 8 hours on Low heat.

Wild Rice–Meatball Soup

Prep time: 15 minutes | Cook time: 8 hours | Serves 2

½ pound (227 g) frozen fully cooked meatballs
1 onion, chopped
2 large tomatoes, seeded and chopped
2 garlic cloves, minced
½ cup wild rice, rinsed
1 carrot, sliced
3 cups beef stock
1 bay leaf
½ teaspoon dried marjoram leaves
½ teaspoon salt
⅛ teaspoon freshly ground black pepper

1. In the crock pot, combine all the ingredients. 2. Cover and cook on low for 8 hours, or until the vegetables are tender. 3. Remove the bay leaf, ladle the soup into 2 bowls, and serve.

Minestrone with Parmigiano-Reggiano

Prep time: 25 minutes | Cook time: 3 to 8 hours | Serves 8

2 tablespoons extra-virgin olive oil
3 cloves garlic, minced
1 cup coarsely chopped sweet onion
1 cup coarsely chopped carrots
1 cup coarsely chopped celery
1 tablespoon finely chopped fresh rosemary
1 (14- to 15-ounce / 397- to 425-g) can plum tomatoes, with their juice
¼ cup dry white wine
2 medium zucchini, cut into ½-inch rounds
1 (14- to 15-ounce / 397- to 425-g) can small white beans, drained and rinsed
1 head escarole or Savoy cabbage, cut into small pieces
8 ounces (227 g) green beans, ends snipped, cut into 1-inch pieces
1 medium head cauliflower, cut into florets
Rind from Parmigiano-Reggiano cheese, cut into ½-inch pieces, plus ½ to 1 cup finely grated Parmigiano-Reggiano cheese, for garnish
2 cups vegetable broth
1 teaspoon salt
½ teaspoon freshly ground black pepper
8 ounces (227 g) cooked small pasta (shells, ditalini, or other short tubular pasta)

1. Heat the oil in a large skillet over medium-high heat. Add the garlic, onion, carrots, celery, and rosemary and sauté until the vegetables begin to soften, 4 to 5 minutes. 2. Add the tomatoes and wine and allow some of the liquid to evaporate in the pan. 3. Transfer the contents of the skillet to the insert of a 5- to 7-quart crock pot. Add the zucchini, white beans, cabbage, green beans, cauliflower, Parmigiano-Reggiano rind, broth, salt, and pepper. 4. Cover the crock pot and cook on high for 3 to 4 hours or on low for 6 to 8 hours. 5. Stir in the cooked pasta at the end of the cooking time, cover, and set on warm until ready to serve. Serve the soup garnished with the grated Parmigiano-Reggiano.

Mediterranean Vegetable Soup

Prep time: 20 minutes | Cook time: 6 to 8 hours | Serves 6

1 (28-ounce / 794-g) can no-salt-added diced tomatoes
2 cups low-sodium vegetable broth
1 green bell pepper, seeded and chopped
1 red or yellow bell pepper, seeded and chopped
4 ounces (113 g) mushrooms, sliced
2 zucchini, chopped
1 small red onion, chopped
3 garlic cloves, minced
1 tablespoon extra-virgin olive oil
2 teaspoons dried oregano
1 teaspoon paprika
1 teaspoon sea salt
½ teaspoon freshly ground black pepper
Juice of 1 lemon

1. In a crock pot, combine the tomatoes, vegetable broth, green and red bell peppers, mushrooms, zucchini, onion, garlic, olive oil, oregano, paprika, salt, and black pepper. Stir to mix well. 2. Cover the cooker and cook for 6 to 8 hours on Low heat. 3. Stir in the lemon juice before serving.

Chickpea Tagine

Prep time: 20 minutes | Cook time: 7 hours | Serves 2

1 onion, chopped
2 garlic cloves, minced
1 (15-ounce / 425-g) can chickpeas, rinsed and drained
1 large sweet potato, peeled and cubed
1 zucchini, peeled, seeded, and chopped
1 large tomato, seeded and chopped
2 cups chicken stock
1 tablespoon freshly squeezed lemon juice
½ teaspoon salt
½ teaspoon lemon zest
¼ teaspoon ground cinnamon
⅛ teaspoon freshly ground black pepper
Pinch saffron threads

1. In the crock pot, combine all the ingredients and stir. 2. Cover and cook on low for 7 hours, or until the squash and potatoes are tender. 3. Ladle the stew into 2 bowls and serve.

Potato Soup with Spinach

Prep time: 20 minutes | Cook time: 8 hours | Serves 2

4 cups vegetable broth
2 russet potatoes, peeled and cubed
1 onion, chopped
½ cup chopped leeks
2 garlic cloves, minced
½ teaspoon salt
½ teaspoon dried marjoram
⅛ teaspoon freshly ground black pepper
2 cups baby spinach leaves

1. In the crock pot, combine the broth, potatoes, onion, leeks, garlic, salt, marjoram, and pepper, and stir. 2. Cover and cook on low for 7½ hours. 3. Using an immersion blender or potato masher, blend or mash the ingredients so the soup is fairly smooth but still has texture. 4. Add the spinach, cover, and cook on low for another 20 to 30 minutes, or until the spinach is wilted. 5. Ladle the soup into 2 bowls and serve.

Pumpkin Black Bean Chili

Prep time: 15 minutes | Cook time: 8 hours | Serves 2

1 cup canned black beans, drained and rinsed
1 cup canned fire-roasted diced tomatoes, drained
1 cup unsweetened pumpkin purée
½ cup diced onion
½ cup diced green bell pepper
1 teaspoon minced garlic
1 teaspoon ground Ancho chile
1 teaspoon smoked paprika
⅛ teaspoon cinnamon
⅛ teaspoon sea salt
¼ cup shredded Cheddar cheese, for garnish
2 tablespoons sour cream, for garnish
¼ cup roughly chopped fresh cilantro, for garnish

1. Put the beans, tomatoes, pumpkin, onion, bell pepper, garlic, chili powder, paprika, cinnamon, and salt in the crock pot, and stir to combine. 2. Cover and cook on low for 8 hours. 3. Garnish each serving with the Cheddar cheese, sour cream, and fresh cilantro.

Southern Italian Chicken Stew

Prep time: 15 minutes | Cook time: 4 hours 18 minutes | Serves 4

2 teaspoons olive oil
4 skinless chicken breasts, cut into 1-inch pieces
1 teaspoon garlic powder
¼ teaspoon black pepper
½ teaspoon sea salt
2 teaspoons dried oregano
1 (28-ounce / 794-g) can diced tomatoes with the juice
1 yellow onion, diced
2 cloves garlic, minced
1 (8-ounce / 227-g) package pasta
1 (14-ounce / 397-g) can artichoke hearts, drained and quartered
1 (6-ounce / 170-g) can black olives, drained

1. Heat the olive oil in a large skillet over medium-high heat. 2. Sprinkle the chicken pieces with the garlic powder, black pepper, sea salt, and oregano. 3. Sauté the chicken for 6 to 8 minutes, turning frequently, until browned on all sides. Remove to a paper towel–lined plate to drain. 4. Place the chicken in the crock pot. Top with the tomatoes, onion, and garlic. Cover and cook on low for 4 hours. 5. After 3 hours, add the pasta to the crock pot. Cover and continue cooking. 6. After 4 hours, stir in the artichoke hearts and olives. Turn up the heat to high. Cover and cook for 10 minutes more, or until the artichokes and olives are heated through. Serve hot.

Sweet Spiced Lentil Soup

Prep time: 10 minutes | Cook time: 8 hours | Serves 2

1 cup dried lentils, rinsed and sorted
1 apple, cored, peeled, and diced
1 cup diced onion
¼ cup diced celery
1 teaspoon fresh thyme
¼ teaspoon ground cinnamon
¼ teaspoon ground allspice
⅛ teaspoon sea salt
¼ cup dry red wine
3 cups low-sodium chicken or vegetable broth

1. Put all the ingredients into the crock pot and stir to combine. 2. Cover and cook on low for 6 to 8 hours, until the lentils are very soft.

Kale and Cannellini Stew with Farro

Prep time: 20 minutes | Cook time: 2 hours | Serves 6

4 cups vegetable or chicken stock
1 (14-ounce / 397-g) can diced fire-roasted tomatoes
1 cup farro, rinsed
1 large yellow onion, chopped
2 medium carrots, halved lengthwise and thinly sliced crosswise
2 stalks celery, coarsely chopped
4 cloves garlic, minced
½ teaspoon red pepper flakes
¼ teaspoon sea salt
4 cups fresh kale, stemmed and coarsely chopped
1 (15-ounce / 425-g) can cannellini beans, rinsed and drained
3 tablespoons fresh lemon juice
½ cup crumbled feta cheese
Fresh flat-leaf parsley or basil, chopped, for garnish

1. Combine the stock, tomatoes, farro, onion, carrots, celery, and garlic in the crock pot. 2. Add the red pepper flakes and ¼ teaspoon salt. 3. Cover and cook on high for 2 hours, or until the farro is tender yet chewy. 4. Add the kale, cannellini, and lemon juice and stir. Cover and cook 1 additional hour. 5. Serve hot, sprinkled with the feta cheese and parsley.

Corn and Red Pepper Chowder

Prep time: 15 minutes | Cook time: 8 hours | Serves 2

½ cup diced onion
1 cup diced roasted red bell pepper
2 Yukon Gold potatoes, peeled and diced
2 cups frozen corn kernels, thawed, divided
2 cups low-sodium chicken broth
1 teaspoon smoked paprika
½ teaspoon ground cumin
½ teaspoon ground coriander
⅛ teaspoon sea salt
Freshly ground black pepper
1 teaspoon red wine vinegar
2 tablespoons heavy cream (optional)
¼ cup thinly sliced scallions, white and green parts

1. Combine the onion, bell pepper, potatoes, 1 cup of corn kernels, broth, paprika, cumin, coriander, salt, and a few grinds of black pepper in the crock pot and stir to combine. 2. Cover and cook on low for 8 hours. 3. Add the vinegar and heavy cream (if using) and purée the soup with an immersion blender. Stir in the remaining 1 cup of corn kernels and the scallions just before

Garlicky Chicken Kale Soup

Prep time: 15 minutes | Cook time: 6 hours | Serves 2

2 boneless, skinless chicken thighs, diced
1 small onion, halved and sliced thin
2 carrots, peeled and diced
6 garlic cloves, roughly chopped
2 cups low-sodium chicken broth
⅛ teaspoon sea salt
⅛ teaspoon red pepper flakes
Zest of 1 lemon
Juice of 1 lemon
2 cups shredded fresh kale

1. Put the chicken, onion, carrots, garlic, broth, salt, red pepper flakes, and lemon zest in the crock pot and stir to combine. 2. Cover and cook on low for 6 hours. 3. Stir in the lemon juice and kale just before serving.

Crab Meat Soup

Prep time: 10 minutes | Cook time: 5 to 6 hours | Serves 8

2 (10¾-ounce / 305-g) cans cream of tomato soup
2 (10½-ounce / 298-g) cans split pea soup
3 cans milk
1 cup heavy cream
1 or 2 (6-ounce / 170-g) cans crab meat, drained
¼ cup sherry (optional)

1. Pour soups into slow cooker. Add milk and stir to mix. 2. Cover and cook on low for 4 hours, or until hot. 3. Stir in cream and crab meat. Continue to cook on low for 1 hour, or until heated through.

Chapter 4 Stews and Soups | 39

Mushroom Soup

Prep time: 10 minutes | Cook time: 8 hours | Serves 2

1 ounce (28 g) dried wild mushrooms
8 ounces (227 g) cremini mushrooms, washed and quartered
2 cups low-sodium chicken broth
2 tablespoons dry sherry (optional)
1 onion, halved, cut into thin half circles
2 garlic cloves, minced
1 teaspoon fresh thyme
½ teaspoon minced fresh rosemary
⅛ teaspoon sea salt
¼ cup heavy cream

1. Put the wild mushrooms, cremini mushrooms, broth, sherry (if using), onion, garlic, thyme, rosemary, and salt in the crock pot and stir to combine. 2. Cover and cook on low for 8 hours. 3. Stir in the heavy cream just before serving.

Steak and Black Bean Chili

Prep time: 15 minutes | Cook time: 7½ hours | Serves 2

1 pound (454 g) sirloin tip steak, cubed
1 onion, chopped
2 garlic cloves, minced
1 jalapeño pepper, minced
1 chipotle chili in adobo sauce, minced
2 tablespoons adobo sauce
1 (15-ounce / 425-g) can black beans, rinsed and drained
1 (15-ounce / 425-g) can diced tomatoes with green chiles
1 (8-ounce / 227-g) can tomato sauce
1 teaspoons chili powder
½ teaspoon dried oregano
½ teaspoon salt
⅛ teaspoon freshly ground black pepper
⅛ teaspoon ground cayenne pepper
1 tablespoon cornstarch
¼ cup water

1. In the crock pot, combine all the ingredients except the cornstarch and water, and stir. 2. Cover and cook on low for 7 hours. 3. In a small bowl, stir together the cornstarch and water. Stir the mixture into the crock pot. 4. Cover and cook on high for 20 to 30 minutes, or until thickened, and serve.

Indian Cauliflower-Potato Soup

Prep time: 20 minutes | Cook time: 8 hours | Serves 2

1 onion, chopped
2 garlic cloves, sliced
2 teaspoons grated fresh ginger
1 tablespoon green curry paste
2 Yukon Gold potatoes, peeled and cubed
2 cups cauliflower florets
3 cups vegetable broth
1 bay leaf
½ teaspoon salt
⅛ teaspoon freshly ground black pepper
½ cup light cream

1. In the crock pot, combine all the ingredients except the light cream. 2. Cover and cook on low for 8 hours. 3. Remove and discard the bay leaf. 4. Using an immersion blender or potato masher, blend or mash the soup until just a bit of texture remains. 5. Stir in the cream, ladle the soup into 2 bowls, and serve.

Lentil-Vegetable Soup

Prep time: 15 minutes | Cook time: 8 hours | Serves 2

½ cup dried lentils
1 cup chopped grape tomatoes
2 carrots, chopped
2 celery stalks, chopped
1 onion, chopped
3 garlic cloves, sliced
1 bay leaf
½ teaspoon dried thyme leaves
½ teaspoon dried marjoram
½ teaspoon salt
2 cups vegetable broth
1 cup water
2 tablespoons minced fresh thyme leaves

1. Sort the lentils and rinse; drain well. 2. In the crock pot, combine the lentils with all the remaining ingredients except the fresh thyme leaves. 3. Cover and cook on low for 8 hours, or until the lentils and vegetables are tender. 4. Remove and discard the bay leaf, stir in the fresh thyme leaves, ladle the soup into 2 bowls and serve.

Minced Beef or Lamb Soup

Prep time: 20 minutes | Cook time: 6 to 8 hours | Serves 6

1 pound (454 g) raw ground beef or lamb
12 ounces (340 g) new red potatoes, halved, or 1 (15-ounce / 425-g) can reduced-sodium chickpeas, drained and rinsed
4 cups low-sodium beef broth
2 cups water
2 carrots, diced
2 celery stalks, diced
2 zucchini, cut into 1-inch pieces
1 large tomato, chopped
1 small onion, diced
2 garlic cloves, minced
¼ cup no-salt-added tomato paste
1 teaspoon sea salt
1 teaspoon dried oregano
1 teaspoon dried basil
½ teaspoon freshly ground black pepper
½ teaspoon dried thyme
2 bay leaves

1. In a large skillet over medium-high heat, cook the ground meat for 3 to 5 minutes, stirring and breaking it up with a spoon until it has browned and is no longer pink. Drain any grease and put the meat in a crock pot. 2. Add the potatoes, beef broth, water, carrots, celery, zucchini, tomato, onion, garlic, tomato paste, salt, oregano, basil, pepper, thyme, and bay leaves to the ground meat. Stir to mix well. 3. Cover the cooker and cook for 6 to 8 hours on Low heat. 4. Remove and discard the bay leaves before serving.

Moroccan Fish Stew

Prep time: 10 minutes | Cook time: 3 to 5 hours | Serves 6

1 pound (454 g) fresh fish fillets of your choice, cut into 2-inch pieces
3 cups low-sodium vegetable broth or low-sodium chicken broth
1 (15-ounce / 425-g) can no-salt-added diced tomatoes
1 bell pepper, any color, seeded and diced
1 small onion, diced
1 garlic clove, minced
1 teaspoon ground coriander
1 teaspoon sea salt
1 teaspoon paprika
½ teaspoon ground turmeric

½ teaspoon freshly ground black pepper

¼ cup fresh cilantro

1. In a crock pot, combine the fish, vegetable broth, tomatoes, bell pepper, onion, garlic, coriander, salt, paprika, turmeric, and black pepper. Stir to mix well. 2. Cover the cooker and cook for 3 to 5 hours on Low heat. 3. Garnish with the fresh cilantro for serving.

Vietnamese Beef and Noodle Soup

Prep time: 15 minutes | Cook time: 8 hours | Serves 2

½ pound (227 g) chuck eye roast, cut into 1-inch pieces
1 onion, chopped
3 radishes, sliced
3 garlic cloves, minced
1 serrano chile, minced
1 tablespoon grated fresh ginger
1 tablespoon freshly squeezed lime juice
2 teaspoons fish sauce
1 star anise pod
3 cups beef stock
½ teaspoon dried basil leaves
½ teaspoon dried marjoram leaves
½ teaspoon salt
¼ teaspoon freshly ground black pepper
½ (12-ounce / 340-g) package udon noodles or spaghetti
1 tablespoon minced fresh basil leaves
1 tablespoon minced fresh mint

1. In the crock pot, combine the beef, onion, radishes, garlic, chile, ginger, lime juice, fish sauce, star anise, stock, basil, marjoram, salt, and pepper. 2. Cover and cook on low for 7½ hours. 3. Add the udon noodles and stir. Cover and cook on high for 20 minutes, or until the noodles are tender. 4. Stir in the fresh basil and mint, ladle the soup into 2 bowls, and serve.

Chipotle Black Bean Soup

Prep time: 10 minutes | Cook time: 8 hours | Serves 2

2 cups canned black beans, drained but not rinsed
1 teaspoon smoked paprika
1 teaspoon ground cumin
1 teaspoon ground coriander
1 teaspoon ground chipotle pepper
1 tablespoon tomato paste
½ cup diced onion
1 tablespoon minced garlic
⅛ teaspoon sea salt
2 cups low-sodium chicken or vegetable broth
Juice of ½ lime
1 small avocado, diced, for garnish

1. Put the black beans, paprika, cumin, coriander, chipotle chili, tomato paste, onion, garlic, salt, and broth into the crock pot and stir to combine. 2. Cover and cook on low for 6 to 8 hours, until some of the beans are broken down but others still retain their shape. 3. Just before serving, stir in the lime juice. Garnish each serving with the avocado slices.

Chicken Fajita Soup

Prep time: 25 minutes | Cook time: 8 hours | Serves 2

2 bone-in, skinless chicken thighs
½ cup frozen corn, thawed
½ cup canned fire-roasted diced tomatoes
½ cup canned black beans, drained and rinsed
½ cup diced onions
¼ teaspoon red chili flakes
2 garlic cloves, minced
2 cups low-sodium chicken broth
1 tablespoon ground cumin
1 teaspoon smoked paprika
⅛ teaspoon sea salt
2 tablespoons shredded sharp Cheddar cheese
¼ cup minced fresh cilantro
1 tablespoon freshly squeezed lime juice
1 cup corn tortilla chips, for garnish
Sour cream, for garnish (optional)

1. Put the chicken, corn, tomatoes, beans, onions, red chili flakes, garlic, broth, cumin, and paprika in the crock pot and stir to combine. 2. Cover and cook on low for 8 hours. 3. Remove the chicken to a cutting board. Stir the cheese into the soup. While the cheese melts, shred the chicken with a fork. Stir the meat back into the soup along with the cilantro and lime juice. 4. Serve the soup garnished with the tortilla chips and a dollop of sour cream.

French Vegetable Stew

Prep time: 20 minutes | Cook time: 7 hours | Serves 2

1 small eggplant, peeled and cubed
1 onion, chopped
2 large tomatoes, seeded and chopped
1 red bell pepper, chopped
1 yellow bell pepper, chopped
1 small yellow summer squash, chopped
2 garlic cloves, minced
½ teaspoon dried basil leaves
½ teaspoon dried thyme leaves
½ teaspoon salt
⅛ teaspoon freshly ground black pepper
¼ cup dry white wine
2 cups vegetable broth
2 tablespoons extra-virgin olive oil, divided

1. In the crock pot, combine all the ingredients except the olive oil, and stir well. 2. Cover and cook on low for 7 hours. 3. Ladle the stew into 2 bowls, drizzle each with 1 tablespoon of olive oil, and serve.

Rosemary Parsnip Bisque with Toasted Bread Crumbs

Prep time: 10 minutes | Cook time: 8 hours | Serves 2

4 parsnips, peeled and cut into large chunks
½ cup diced onion
¼ cup diced celery
1 garlic clove, smashed
2 teaspoons fresh rosemary, divided
2 cups low-sodium chicken broth
⅛ teaspoon sea salt
2 tablespoons heavy cream
Freshly ground black pepper
¼ cup panko bread crumbs

1. Put the parsnips, onion, celery, garlic, and 1 teaspoon of rosemary in the crock pot. Add the broth and salt and stir to combine. 2. Cover and cook on low for 8 hours. 3. Stir in the heavy cream and purée the soup with an immersion blender. 4. In a small bowl, mix together the remaining 1 teaspoon of rosemary, a few grinds of the black pepper, and the bread crumbs. Sprinkle some of this mixture over each serving of the soup.

Mediterranean Vegetable Stew

Prep time: 20 minutes | Cook time: 8 to 10 hours | Serves 10

- 1 butternut squash, peeled, seeded, and cubed
- 2 cups unpeeled cubed eggplant
- 2 cups cubed zucchini
- 10 ounces (283 g) fresh okra, cut into slices
- 1 (8-ounce / 227-g) can tomato sauce
- 1 large yellow onion, chopped
- 1 ripe tomato, chopped
- 1 carrot, thinly sliced
- ½ cup vegetable stock
- ⅓ cup raisins
- 2 cloves garlic, minced
- ½ teaspoon ground cumin
- ½ teaspoon ground turmeric
- ¼ teaspoon red pepper flakes
- ¼ teaspoon ground cinnamon
- 1 teaspoon paprika

1. In the crock pot, combine the butternut squash, eggplant, zucchini, okra, tomato sauce, onion, tomato, carrot, vegetable stock, raisins, and garlic. Sprinkle in the cumin, turmeric, red pepper flakes, cinnamon, and paprika. 2. Cover and cook on low for 8 to 10 hours, or until the vegetables are fork-tender. Serve hot.

Chicken Clam Chowder

Prep time: 20 minutes | Cook time: 4 to 9 hours | Serves 10

- 6 slices lean turkey bacon, diced
- ¼ pound (113 g) lean ham, cubed
- 2 cups chopped onions
- 2 cups diced celery
- ½ teaspoon salt
- ¼ teaspoon black pepper
- 2 cups diced potatoes
- 2 cups cooked, lean chicken, diced
- 4 cups fat-free, low-sodium clam juice, or 2 cans clams with juice
- 1 (1-pound / 454-g) can whole-kernel corn with liquid
- ¾ cup flour
- 4 cups fat-free milk
- 4 cups shredded fat-free Cheddar or Monterey Jack cheese
- ½ cup fat-free evaporated milk
- 2 tablespoons fresh parsley

1. Sauté bacon, ham, onions, and celery in nonstick skillet until bacon is crisp and onions and celery are limp. Add salt and pepper. 2. Combine all ingredients in slow cooker except flour, milk, cheese, evaporated milk, and parsley. 3. Cover. Cook on low 6 to 8 hours, or on high 3 to 4 hours. 4. Whisk flour into milk. Stir into soup, along with cheese, evaporated milk, and parsley. Cook 1 more hour on high.

Taco Chicken Soup

Prep time: 10 minutes | Cook time: 5 to 7 hours | Serves 4 to 6

- 1 envelope dry reduced-sodium taco seasoning
- 1 (32-ounce / 907-g) can low-sodium V-8 juice
- 1 (16-ounce / 454-g) jar salsa
- 1 (15-ounce / 425-g) can black beans
- 1 cup frozen corn
- 1 cup frozen peas
- 2 whole chicken breasts, cooked and shredded

1. Combine all ingredients except corn, peas, and chicken in slow cooker. 2. Cover. Cook on low 4 to 6 hours. Add remaining vegetables and chicken 1 hour before serving.

Nancy's Vegetable Beef Soup

Prep time: 10 minutes | Cook time: 8 hours | Serves 6 to 8

- 1 (2-pound / 907-g) roast cut into bite-sized pieces, or 2 pounds (907 g) stewing meat
- 1 (15-ounce / 425-g) can corn
- 1 (15-ounce / 425-g) can green beans
- 1 (1-pound / 454-g) bag frozen peas
- 1 (40-ounce / 1.1-kg) can stewed tomatoes
- 5 beef bouillon cubes
- Tabasco to taste
- 2 teaspoons salt

1. Combine all ingredients in slow cooker. Do not drain vegetables. 2. Add water to fill slow cooker to within 3 inches of top 3. Cover. Cook on low 8 hours, or until meat is tender and vegetables are soft.

Southwest Corn Soup

Prep time: 10 minutes | Cook time: 4 hours | Serves 6

- 2 (4-ounce / 113-g) cans chopped green chilies, undrained
- 2 small zucchini, cut into bite-sized pieces
- 1 medium onion, thinly sliced
- 3 cloves garlic, minced
- 1 teaspoon ground cumin
- 3 (14½-ounce / 411-g) cans fat-free, sodium-reduced chicken broth
- 1½ to 2 cups cooked turkey, shredded
- 1 (15-ounce / 425-g) can chickpeas or black beans, rinsed and drained
- 1 (10-ounce / 283-g) package frozen corn
- 1 teaspoon dried oregano
- ½ cup chopped cilantro

1. Combine all ingredients in slow cooker. 2. Cook on low 4 hours.

All-Together Chicken Rice Soup

Prep time: 30 minutes | Cook time: 4 to 5 hours | Serves 14

- 3 quarts hot water
- 1 medium onion, finely chopped
- 2 to 3 celery ribs, finely chopped
- 2 sprigs finely chopped fresh parsley
- 1 clove garlic, crushed
- 2 teaspoons salt
- ½ cup thinly sliced carrots
- 4 large skinless chicken legs and thighs
- ½ cup chopped fresh parsley
- 3 cups hot cooked rice

1. Combine water, onion, celery, 2 sprigs parsley, garlic, salt, carrots, and chicken in slow cooker. 2. Cover. Cook on high 4 to 5 hours. 3. Remove chicken when tender and debone. 4. Stir cut-up chicken back into soup. Add ½ cup fresh chopped parsley 5. To serve, ladle soup into bowls. Add a rounded tablespoonful of hot cooked rice to each bowl.

Minestrone

Prep time: 20 minutes | Cook time: 4 to 9 hours | Serves 8 to 10

1 large onion, chopped	frozen green beans
4 carrots, sliced	2 to 3 cups chopped cabbage
3 ribs celery, sliced	1 medium zucchini, sliced
2 garlic cloves, minced	8 cups water
1 tablespoon olive oil	2 tablespoons parsley
1 (6-ounce / 170-g) can tomato paste	2 tablespoons Italian spice
	1 teaspoon salt, or more
1 (14½-ounce / 411-g) can chicken, beef, or vegetable broth	½ teaspoon pepper
	¾ cup dry acini di pepe (small round pasta)
1 (24-ounce / 680-g) can pinto beans, undrained	Grated Parmesan or Asiago cheese
1 (10-ounce / 283-g) package	

1. Sauté onion, carrots, celery, and garlic in oil until tender. 2. Combine all ingredients except pasta and cheese in slow cooker. 3. Cover. Cook 4 to 5 hours on high or 8 to 9 hours on low, adding pasta 1 hour before cooking is complete. 4. Top individual servings with cheese.

Chicken Corn Soup

Prep time: 15 minutes | Cook time: 8 to 9 hours | Serves 4 to 6

2 whole boneless, skinless chicken breasts, cubed	1 (12-ounce / 340-g) can cream-style corn
1 onion, chopped	1 (14-ounce / 397-g) whole-kernel corn
1 garlic clove, minced	
2 carrots, sliced	3 cups chicken stock
2 ribs celery, chopped	¼ cup chopped Italian parsley
2 medium potatoes, cubed	1 teaspoon salt
1 teaspoon mixed dried herbs	¼ teaspoon pepper
⅓ cup tomato sauce	

1. Combine all ingredients except parsley, salt, and pepper in slow cooker. 2. Cover. Cook on low 8 to 9 hours, or until chicken is tender. 3. Add parsley and seasonings 30 minutes before serving.

Steak Soup

Prep time: 20 minutes | Cook time: 4 to 12 hours | Serves 10 to 12

2 pounds (907 g) coarsely ground chuck, browned and drained	1 (10-ounce / 283-g) package frozen mixed vegetables
	5 tablespoons beef-based granules, or 5 beef bouillon cubes
5 cups water	
1 large onion, chopped	
4 ribs celery, chopped	½ teaspoon pepper
3 carrots, sliced	½ cup butter, melted
2 (14½-ounce / 411-g) cans diced tomatoes	½ cup flour
	2 teaspoons salt

1. Combine chuck, water, onion, celery, carrots, tomatoes, mixed vegetables, beef granules, and pepper in slow cooker. 2. Cover. Cook on low 8 to 12 hours, or on high 4 to 6 hours. 3. One hour before serving, turn to high. Make a paste of melted butter and flour. Stir until smooth. Pour into slow cooker and stir until well blended. Add salt. 4. Cover. Continue cooking on high until thickened.

Vegetarian Minestrone Soup

Prep time: 15 minutes | Cook time: 6 to 8 hours | Serves 6

6 cups vegetable broth	kidney beans, drained
2 carrots, chopped	1 tablespoon parsley
2 large onions, chopped	½ teaspoon dried thyme
3 ribs celery, chopped	1 teaspoon dried oregano
2 garlic cloves, minced	1 (28-ounce / 794-g) can crushed Italian tomatoes
1 small zucchini, cubed	
1 handful fresh kale, chopped	1 teaspoon salt
½ cup dry barley	¼ teaspoon pepper
1 can chickpeas or white	Shredded cheese

1. Combine all ingredients except cheese in slow cooker. 2. Cover. Cook on low 6 to 8 hours, or until vegetables are tender. 3. Sprinkle individual servings with shredded cheese.

Taco Soup with Hominy

Prep time: 15 minutes | Cook time: 4 hours | Serves 8

1 pound (454 g) ground beef	beans, undrained
1 envelope dry ranch dressing mix	1 (24-ounce / 680-g) can hominy, undrained
1 envelope dry taco seasoning mix	1 (14½-ounce / 411-g) can stewed tomatoes, undrained
3 (12-ounce / 340-g) cans Rotel tomatoes, undrained	1 onion, chopped
	2 cups water
2 (24-ounce / 680-g) cans pinto	

1. Brown meat in skillet. Pour into slow cooker. 2. Add remaining ingredients. Mix well. 3. Cover. Cook on low 4 hours.

Sausage-Vegetable Stew

Prep time: 30 minutes | Cook time: 3 to 10 hours | Serves 10

1 pound (454 g) sausage (regular, turkey, or smoked)	4 cups green beans, cooked
	1 (28-ounce / 794-g) can tomato sauce
4 cups potatoes, cooked and cubed	
	1 teaspoon onion powder
4 cups carrots, cooked and sliced	¼ or ½ teaspoon black pepper, according to your taste

1. Slice sausage into 1½-inch pieces. Place in slow cooker. 2. Add cooked vegetables. Pour tomato sauce over top. 3. Sprinkle with onion powder and pepper. Stir. 4. Cook on high 3 to 4 hours, or on low 8 to 10 hours.

Split Pea Soup with Ham

Prep time: 15 minutes | Cook time: 7 hours | Serves 2

1½ cups dried split peas
1 onion, chopped
2 garlic cloves, minced
1 bay leaf
1 cup chopped cooked ham
4 cups chicken stock
½ teaspoon dried thyme leaves
1 tablespoon freshly squeezed lemon juice
⅛ teaspoon freshly ground black pepper
1 cup garlic croutons

1. Sort the peas to remove any twigs, dirt, or stones. Rinse well and drain. 2. In the crock pot, combine the peas, onion, garlic, bay leaf, ham, stock, thyme, lemon juice, and pepper, and stir. 3. Cover and cook on low for 7 hours, or until the split peas dissolve and the soup is thick. 4. Remove the bay leaf, ladle the soup into 2 bowls, top with the croutons, and serve.

Crab Soup

Prep time: 20 minutes | Cook time: 8 to 10 hours | Serves 10

1 pound (454 g) carrots, sliced
½ bunch celery, sliced
1 large onion, diced
2 (10-ounce / 283-g) bags frozen mixed vegetables, or your choice of frozen vegetables
1 (12-ounce / 340-g) can tomato juice
1 pound (454 g) ham, cubed
1 pound (454 g) beef, cubed
6 slices bacon, chopped
1 teaspoon salt
¼ teaspoon pepper
1 tablespoon Old Bay seasoning
1 pound (454 g) claw crab meat

1. Combine all ingredients except seasonings and crab meat in large slow cooker. Pour in water until cooker is half-full. 2. Add spices. Stir in thoroughly. Put crab on top. 3. Cover. Cook on low 8 to 10 hours. 4. Stir well and serve.

Veggie Surprise Beef Stew

Prep time: 20 minutes | Cook time: 5½ to 6½ hours | Serves 5

¾ pound (340 g) lean stewing meat, trimmed of fat and cut into ½-inch cubes
2 teaspoons canola oil
1 (14½-ounce / 411-g) can low-sodium, low-fat beef broth
1 (14½-ounce / 411-g) can low-sodium stewed tomatoes
1½ cups butternut squash, peeled and cubed
1 cup frozen corn
½ cup chopped carrots
Dash of salt
Dash of black pepper
Dash of dried oregano
2 tablespoons cornstarch
¼ cup water

1. In a skillet, brown stewing meat in canola oil over medium heat. Transfer to slow cooker. 2. Add beef broth, vegetables, salt, pepper, and oregano. 3. Cover. Cook on high 5 to 6 hours. 4. Combine cornstarch and water until smooth. Stir into stew. 5. Cover. Cook on high 30 minutes.

Spicy Potato Soup

Prep time: 15 minutes | Cook time: 5 to 10 hours | Serves 6 to 8

1 pound (454 g) ground beef or bulk sausage, browned
4 cups cubed peeled potatoes
1 small onion, chopped
3 (8-ounce / 227-g) cans tomato sauce
2 teaspoons salt
1½ teaspoons pepper
½ teaspoon hot pepper sauce
Water

1. Combine all ingredients except water in slow cooker. Add enough water to cover ingredients. 2. Cover. Cook on low 8 to 10 hours, or on high 5 hours, until potatoes are tender.

Aunt Thelma's Homemade Soup

Prep time: 15 minutes | Cook time: 4½ hours | Serves 10 to 12

7 cups water
4 chicken or vegetable bouillon cubes
1 cup thinly sliced carrots
1 (1-pound / 454-g) package frozen peas
1 (1-pound / 454-g) package frozen corn
1 (1-pound / 454-g) package frozen lima beans
1 bay leaf
¼ teaspoon dill seed
1 (28-ounce / 794-g) can whole tomatoes
1 cup diced raw potatoes
1 cup chopped onions
2 to 3 teaspoons salt
½ teaspoon dried basil
¼ teaspoon pepper
2 tablespoons cornstarch
¼ cup cold water

1. Combine all ingredients except cornstarch and ¼ cup water in slow cooker. 2. Cover. Simmer on high 4 hours, or until vegetables are tender. 3. Thirty minutes before end of cooking time, mix cornstarch and cold water together until smooth. Remove 1 cup broth from cooker and mix with cornstarch-water. When smooth, stir into soup. Cover and continue cooking another half hour. 4. Serve.

Karen's Split Pea Soup

Prep time: 15 minutes | Cook time: 7 hours | Serves 6

2 carrots
2 ribs celery
1 onion
1 parsnip
1 leek (keep 3 inches of green)
1 ripe tomato
1 ham hock
1¾ cups dried split peas, washed with stones removed
2 tablespoons olive oil
1 bay leaf
1 teaspoon dried thyme
4 cups chicken broth
4 cups water
1 teaspoon salt
¼ teaspoon pepper
2 teaspoons chopped fresh parsley

1. Cut all vegetables into ¼-inch pieces and place in slow cooker. Add remaining ingredients except salt, pepper, and parsley. 2. Cover. Cook on high 7 hours. 3. Remove ham hock. Shred meat from bone and return meat to pot. 4. Season soup with salt and pepper. Stir in parsley. Serve immediately.

Pumpkin Soup

Prep time: 5 minutes | Cook time: 5 to 6 hours | Serves 6

¼ cup chopped green bell pepper
1 small onion, finely chopped
2 cups low-sodium chicken stock or broth, fat removed
2 cups pumpkin purée
2 cups skim milk
⅛ teaspoon dried thyme
¼ teaspoon ground nutmeg
½ teaspoon salt
2 tablespoons cornstarch
¼ cup cold water
1 teaspoon chopped fresh parsley

1. Combine all ingredients except cornstarch, cold water, and fresh parsley in slow cooker. Mix well. 2. Cover. Cook on low 5 to 6 hours. 3. During the last hour add cornstarch mixed with water and stir until soup thickens. 4. Just before serving, stir in fresh parsley.

Bratwurst Stew

Prep time: 15 minutes | Cook time: 3 to 4 hours | Serves 8

2 (10¾-ounce / 305-g) cans fat-free chicken broth
4 medium carrots, sliced
2 ribs of celery, cut in chunks
1 medium onion, chopped
1 teaspoon dried basil
½ teaspoon garlic powder
3 cups chopped cabbage
2 (1-pound / 454-g) cans Great Northern beans, drained
5 fully cooked bratwurst links, cut into ½-inch slices

1. Combine all ingredients in slow cooker. 2. Cook on high 3 to 4 hours, or until veggies are tender.

Curried Lima and Potato Soup

Prep time: 15 minutes | Cook time: 4 to 10 hours | Serves 6

1½ cups dried large lima beans
4 cups water, divided
5 to 6 medium potatoes, finely chopped
½ head cauliflower (optional)
2 cups sour cream
2 tablespoons curry
1 to 2 teaspoons salt and pepper, to taste

1. In a medium saucepan, bring dried beans to a boil in 2 cups water. Boil, uncovered, for 2 minutes. Cover, turn off heat, and wait 2 hours. 2. Drain water. Place beans in slow cooker. 3. Add 2 cups fresh water. Cover and cook 2 hours on high. 4. During the last hour of cooking, add diced potatoes and cauliflower florets. Cook longer if vegetables are not as tender as you like after 1 hour. 5. Ten minutes before serving, add sour cream, curry, and salt and pepper to taste.

Joyce's Minestrone

Prep time: 15 minutes | Cook time: 4 to 16 hours | Serves 6

3½ cups beef broth
1 (28-ounce / 794-g) can crushed tomatoes
2 medium carrots, thinly sliced
½ cup chopped onion
½ cup chopped celery
2 medium potatoes, thinly sliced
1 to 2 garlic cloves, minced
1 (16-ounce / 454-g) can red kidney beans, drained
2 ounces (57 g) thin spaghetti, broken into 2-inch pieces
2 tablespoons parsley flakes
2 to 3 teaspoons dried basil
1 to 2 teaspoons dried oregano
1 bay leaf

1. Combine all ingredients in slow cooker. 2. Cover. Cook on low 10 to 16 hours, or on high 4 to 6 hours. 3. Remove bay leaf. Serve.

Chet's Trucker Stew

Prep time: 15 minutes | Cook time: 2 to 3 hours | Serves 8

1 pound (454 g) bulk pork sausage, cooked and drained
1 pound (454 g) ground beef, cooked and drained
1 (31-ounce / 879-g) can pork and beans
1 (16-ounce / 454-g) can light kidney beans
1 (16-ounce / 454-g) can dark kidney beans
1 (14½-ounce / 411-g) can waxed beans, drained
1 (14½-ounce / 411-g) can lima beans, drained
1 cup ketchup
1 cup brown sugar
1 tablespoon spicy prepared mustard

1. Combine all ingredients in slow cooker. 2. Cover. Simmer on high 2 to 3 hours.

Fresh Tomato Soup

Prep time: 10 minutes | Cook time: 6 to 8 hours | Serves 6

5 cups ripe, diced tomatoes (your choice about whether or not to peel them)
1 tablespoon tomato paste
4 cups salt-free chicken broth
1 carrot, grated
1 onion, minced
1 tablespoon minced garlic
1 teaspoon dried basil
Pepper to taste
1 bay leaf

1. Combine all ingredients in a slow cooker. 2. Cook on low for 6 to 8 hours. Stir once while cooking. 3. Remove bay leaf before serving.

Butternut Squash Soup

Prep time: 5 minutes | Cook time: 4 to 8 hours | Serves 4 to 6

1 (45-ounce / 1.3-kg) can chicken broth
1 medium butternut squash, peeled and cubed
1 small onion, chopped
1 teaspoon ground ginger
1 teaspoon garlic, minced (optional)
¼ teaspoon nutmeg (optional)

1. Place chicken broth and squash in slow cooker. Add remaining ingredients. 2. Cover and cook on high 4 hours, or on low 6 to 8 hours, or until squash is tender.

Ham and Potato Chowder

Prep time: 10 minutes | Cook time: 8 hours | Serves 5

1 (5-ounce / 142-g) package scalloped potatoes
Sauce mix from potato package
1 cup cooked ham, cut into narrow strips
4 cups chicken broth
1 cup chopped celery
⅓ cup chopped onions
Salt to taste
Pepper to taste
2 cups half-and-half
⅓ cup flour

1. Combine potatoes, sauce mix, ham, broth, celery, onions, salt, and pepper in slow cooker. 2. Cover. Cook on low 7 hours. 3. Combine half-and-half and flour. Gradually add to slow cooker, blending well. 4. Cover. Cook on low up to 1 hour, stirring occasionally until thickened.

Onion Soup

Prep time: 30 minutes | Cook time: 6 to 8 hours | Serves 8

3 medium onions, thinly sliced
2 tablespoons butter
2 tablespoons vegetable oil
1 teaspoon salt
1 tablespoon sugar
2 tablespoons flour
1 quart fat-free, low-sodium vegetable broth
½ cup dry white wine
Slices of French bread
½ cup grated fat-free Swiss or Parmesan cheese

1. Sauté onions in butter and oil in covered skillet until soft. Uncover. Add salt and sugar. Cook 15 minutes. Stir in flour. Cook 3 more minutes. 2. Combine onions, broth, and wine in slow cooker. 3. Cover. Cook on low 6 to 8 hours. 4. Toast bread. Sprinkle with grated cheese and then broil. 5. Dish soup into individual bowls; then float a slice of broiled bread on top of each serving of soup.

Hearty Bean Soup

Prep time: 30 minutes | Cook time: 4 to 5 hours | Serves 6

3 (15-ounce / 425-g) cans pinto beans, undrained
3 (15-ounce / 425-g) cans Great Northern beans, undrained
4 cups chicken or vegetable broth
3 potatoes, peeled and chopped
4 carrots, sliced
2 celery ribs, sliced
1 large onion, chopped
1 green pepper, chopped
1 sweet red pepper, chopped (optional)
2 garlic cloves, minced
1 teaspoon salt, or to taste
¼ teaspoon pepper, or to taste
1 bay leaf (optional)
½ teaspoon liquid barbecue smoke (optional)

1. Empty beans into 6-quart slow cooker, or divide ingredients between 2 (4- to 5-quart) cookers. 2. Cover. Cook on low while preparing vegetables. 3. Cook broth and vegetables in stockpot until vegetables are tender-crisp. Transfer to slow cooker. 4. Add remaining ingredients and mix well. 5. Cover. Cook on low 4 to 5 hours. 6. Serve.

Tomato Green Bean Soup

Prep time: 10 minutes | Cook time: 6 to 8 hours | Serves 8

1 cup chopped onions
1 cup chopped carrots
6 cups low-fat, reduced-sodium chicken broth
1 pound (454 g) fresh green beans, cut in 1-inch pieces
1 clove garlic, minced
3 cups fresh, diced tomatoes
1 teaspoon dried basil
½ teaspoon salt
¼ teaspoon black pepper

1. Combine all ingredients in slow cooker. 2. Cover. Cook on low 6 to 8 hours.

Corn Chowder

Prep time: 15 minutes | Cook time: 6 to 7 hours | Serves 4

6 slices bacon, diced
½ cup chopped onions
2 cups diced peeled potatoes
2 (10-ounce / 283-g) packages frozen corn
1 (16-ounce / 454-g) can cream-style corn
1 tablespoon sugar
1 teaspoon Worcestershire sauce
1 teaspoon seasoned salt
¼ teaspoon pepper
1 cup water

1. In skillet, brown bacon until crisp. Remove bacon, reserving drippings. 2. Add onions and potatoes to skillet and sauté for 5 minutes. Drain. 3. Combine all ingredients in slow cooker. Mix well. 4. Cover. Cook on low 6 to 7 hours.

Best Everyday Stew

Prep time: 20 minutes | Cook time: 10 hours | Serves 8

2¼ pounds (1 kg) flank steak, 1½-inch thick
8 red potatoes, small to medium in size
10 baby carrots
1 large clove garlic, diced
1 medium to large onion, chopped
1 cup baby peas
3 ribs celery, cut in 1-inch pieces
3 cups cabbage, in chunks
2 (8-ounce / 227-g) cans low-sodium tomato sauce
1 tablespoon Worcestershire sauce
2 bay leaves
¼ to ½ teaspoon dried thyme, according to your taste preference
¼ to ½ teaspoon dried basil, according to your taste preference
¼ to ½ teaspoon dried marjoram, according to your taste preference
1 tablespoon parsley
2 cups water or more, if desired
4 cubes beef or vegetable bouillon

1. Trim flank steak of fat. Cut in 1½-inch cubes. 2. Brown slowly in nonstick skillet. Quarter potatoes. 3. Combine all ingredients in large slow cooker. 4. Cover. Cook on high 1 hour. Turn to low and cook 9 additional hours.

Black Bean and Corn Soup

Prep time: 10 minutes | Cook time: 5 to 6 hours | Serves 6 to 8

- 2 (15-ounce / 425-g) cans black beans, drained and rinsed
- 1 (14½-ounce / 411-g) can Mexican stewed tomatoes, undrained
- 1 (14½-ounce / 411-g) can diced tomatoes, undrained
- 1 (11-ounce / 312-g) can whole-kernel corn, drained
- 4 green onions, sliced
- 2 to 3 tablespoons chili powder
- 1 teaspoon ground cumin
- ½ teaspoon dried minced garlic

1. Combine all ingredients in slow cooker. 2. Cover. Cook on high 5 to 6 hours.

Sauerkraut Potato Soup

Prep time: 15 minutes | Cook time: 2 to 8 hours | Serves 8

- 1 pound (454 g) smoked Polish sausage, cut into ½-inch pieces
- 5 medium potatoes, cubed
- 2 large onions, chopped
- 2 large carrots, cut into ¼-inch slices
- 1 (42-ounce / 1.2-kg) can chicken broth
- 1 (32-ounce / 907-g) can or bag sauerkraut, rinsed and drained
- 1 (6-ounce / 170-g) can tomato paste

1. Combine all ingredients in large slow cooker. Stir to combine. 2. Cover. Cook on high 2 hours, and then on low 6 to 8 hours. 3. Serve.

Green Bean and Ham Soup

Prep time: 15 minutes | Cook time: 4¼ to 6¼ hours | Serves 6

- 1 meaty ham bone, or 2 cups cubed ham
- 1½ quarts water
- 1 large onion, chopped
- 2 to 3 cups cut-up green beans
- 3 large carrots, sliced
- 2 large potatoes, peeled and cubed
- 1 tablespoon parsley
- 1 tablespoon summer savory
- ½ teaspoon salt
- ¼ teaspoon pepper
- 1 cup cream or milk

1. Combine all ingredients except cream in slow cooker. 2. Cover. Cook on high 4 to 6 hours. 3. Remove ham bone. Cut off meat and return to slow cooker. 4. Turn to low. Stir in cream or milk. Heat through and serve.

Beef Barley Stew

Prep time: 15 minutes | Cook time: 9 to 10 hours | Serves 6

- ½ pound (227 g) lean round steak, cut in ½-inch cubes
- 4 carrots, peeled and cut in ¼-inch slices
- 1 cup chopped yellow onions
- ½ cup coarsely chopped green bell peppers
- 1 clove garlic, pressed
- ½ pound (227 g) fresh button mushrooms, quartered
- ¾ cup dry pearl barley
- ½ teaspoon salt
- ¼ teaspoon ground black pepper
- ½ teaspoon dried thyme
- ½ teaspoon dried sweet basil
- 1 bay leaf
- 5 cups fat-free, low-sodium beef broth

1. Combine all ingredients in slow cooker. 2. Cover. Cook on low 9 to 10 hours.

Jeanne's Vegetable-Beef Borscht

Prep time: 20 minutes | Cook time: 8 to 10 hours | Serves 8

- 1 pound (454 g) beef roast, cooked and cubed
- Half a head of cabbage, sliced thinly
- 3 medium potatoes, diced
- 4 carrots, sliced
- 1 large onion, diced
- 1 cup tomatoes, diced
- 1 cup corn
- 1 cup green beans
- 2 cups beef broth
- 2 cups tomato juice
- ¼ teaspoon garlic powder
- ¼ teaspoon dill seed
- 2 teaspoons salt
- ½ teaspoon pepper
- Water
- Sour cream

1. Mix together all ingredients except water and sour cream. Add water to fill slow cooker three-quarters full. 2. Cover. Cook on low 8 to 10 hours. 3. Top individual servings with sour cream.

Sauerkraut Tomato Soup

Prep time: 10 minutes | Cook time: 4 to 6 hours | Serves 4

- 2 (14½-ounce / 411-g) cans stewed tomatoes
- 2 cups sauerkraut
- 1 cup diced potatoes
- 1 pound (454 g) fresh or smoked sausage, sliced

1. Combine all ingredients in slow cooker. 2. Cover and cook on low 4 to 6 hours, or until the flavors have blended and the soup is thoroughly heated.

French Market Soup

Prep time: 10 minutes | Cook time: 10 hours | Serves 8

- 2 cups dry bean mix, washed with stones removed
- 2 quarts water
- 1 ham hock
- 1 teaspoon salt
- ¼ teaspoon pepper
- 1 (16-ounce / 454-g) can tomatoes
- 1 large onion, chopped
- 1 garlic clove, minced
- 1 chili pepper, chopped, or 1 teaspoon chili powder
- ¼ cup lemon juice

1. Combine all ingredients in slow cooker. 2. Cover. Cook on low 8 hours. Turn to high and cook an additional 2 hours, or until beans are tender. 3. Debone ham, cut meat into bite-sized pieces, and stir back into soup.

Tasty Chicken Soup

Prep time: 15 minutes | Cook time: 6 to 7 hours | Serves 12

12 cups chicken broth
2 cups cooked chicken, cubed
1 cup shredded carrots
3 whole cloves
Small onion
1 (16-ounce / 454-g) bag of dry noodles, cooked (optional)

1. Place broth, chicken, and carrots in slow cooker. 2. Peel onion. Using a toothpick, poke 3 holes on the cut ends. Carefully press cloves into 3 of the holes until only their round part shows. Add to slow cooker. 3. Cover and cook on high 6 to 7 hours. 4. If you'd like a thicker soup, add a bag of cooked fine egg noodles before serving.

Black Bean and Tomato Soup

Prep time: 15 minutes | Cook time: 8 hours | Serves 6

1 (1-pound / 454-g) bag black beans
2 (10-ounce / 283-g) cans Rotel tomatoes
1 medium onion, chopped
1 medium green bell pepper, chopped
1 tablespoon minced garlic
1 (14½-ounce / 411-g) can chicken or vegetable broth
Water
Cajun seasoning to taste

1. Cover beans with water and soak for 8 hours or overnight. Drain well. Place beans in slow cooker. 2. Add tomatoes, onions, pepper, garlic, and chicken or vegetable broth. Add water just to cover beans. Add Cajun seasoning. 3. Cover. Cook on high 8 hours. Mash some of the beans before serving for a thicker consistency. 4. Serve.

Hearty Lentil and Sausage Stew

Prep time: 10 minutes | Cook time: 4 to 6 hours | Serves 6

2 cups dry lentils, picked over and rinsed
1 (14½-ounce / 411-g) can diced tomatoes
8 cups canned chicken broth or water
1 tablespoon salt
½ to 1 pound (227 to 454 g) pork or beef sausage, cut into 2-inch pieces

1. Place lentils, tomatoes, chicken broth, and salt in slow cooker. Stir to combine. Place sausage pieces on top. 2. Cover and cook on low 4 to 6 hours, or until lentils are tender but not dry or mushy.

Southwestern Bean Soup with Cornmeal Dumplings

Prep time: 20 minutes | Cook time: 4½ to 12½ hours | Serves 4

Soup:
1 (15½-ounce / 439-g) can red kidney beans, rinsed and drained
1 (15½-ounce / 439-g) can black beans, pinto beans, or Great Northern beans, rinsed and drained
3 cups water
1 (14½-ounce / 411-g) can Mexican-style stewed tomatoes
1 (10-ounce / 283-g) package frozen whole-kernel corn, thawed
1 cup sliced carrots
1 cup chopped onions
1 (4-ounce / 113-g) can chopped green chilies
2 tablespoons instant beef, chicken, or vegetable bouillon granules
1 to 2 teaspoons chili powder
2 cloves garlic, minced
Dumplings:
⅓ cup flour
¼ cup yellow cornmeal
1 teaspoon baking powder
Dash of salt
Dash of pepper
1 egg white, beaten
2 tablespoons milk
1 tablespoon oil

1. Combine 11 soup ingredients in slow cooker. 2. Cover. Cook on low 10 to 12 hours, or on high 4 to 5 hours. 3. Make dumplings by mixing together flour, cornmeal, baking powder, salt, and pepper. 4. Combine egg white, milk, and oil. Add to flour mixture. Stir with fork until just combined. 5. At the end of the soup's cooking time, turn slow cooker to high. Drop dumpling mixture by rounded teaspoonfuls to make 8 mounds atop the soup. 6. Cover. Cook for 30 minutes (do not lift cover).

Chicken Noodle Soup

Prep time: 10 minutes | Cook time: 4 to 8 hours | Serves 6 to 8

2 cups chicken, cubed
1 (15¼-ounce / 432-g) can corn, or 2 cups frozen corn
1 cup frozen peas or green beans
10 cups water
10 to 12 chicken bouillon cubes
3 tablespoons bacon drippings
½ package dry kluski (or other very sturdy) noodles

1. Combine all ingredients except noodles in slow cooker. 2. Cover. Cook on high 4 to 6 hours, or on low 6 to 8 hours. Add noodles during last 2 hours. 3. Serve.

Overnight Bean Soup

Prep time: 10 minutes | Cook time: 5¼ to 11¼ hours | Serves 6 to 8

1 pound (454 g) dry small white beans
6 cups water
2 cups boiling water
2 large carrots, diced
3 ribs celery, diced
2 teaspoons chicken bouillon granules, or 2 chicken bouillon cubes
1 bay leaf
½ teaspoon dried thyme
½ teaspoon salt
¼ teaspoon pepper
¼ cup chopped fresh parsley
1 envelope dry onion soup mix
Crispy, crumbled bacon (optional)

1. Rinse beans. Combine beans and 6 cups water in saucepan. Bring to boil. Reduce heat to low and simmer 2 minutes. Remove from heat. Cover and let stand 1 hour or overnight. 2. Place beans and soaking water in slow cooker. 3. Add 2 cups boiling water, carrots, celery, bouillon, bay leaf, thyme, salt, and pepper. Cover. Cook on high 5 to 5½ hours, or on low 10 to 11 hours, until beans are tender. 4.

Stir in parsley and soup mix. Cover. Cook on high 10 to 15 minutes. 5. Remove bay leaf. Garnish individual servings with bacon.

Low-Calorie Soup

Prep time: 15 minutes | Cook time: 5 hours | Serves 14

2 cups thinly sliced celery
2 cups chopped cabbage
1 (8-ounce / 227-g) package frozen green beans
1 onion, chopped
1 (28-ounce / 794-g) can diced tomatoes
3 envelopes dry low-sodium beef-flavored soup mix
3 tablespoons Worcestershire sauce
½ teaspoon salt
¼ teaspoon black pepper
Water to cover

1. Combine all ingredients in slow cooker. 2. Cover. Cook on high 5 hours.

Sausage-Pasta Stew

Prep time: 35 minutes | Cook time: 7¼ to 9¼ hours | Serves 8

1 pound (454 g) Italian sausage, casings removed
4 cups water
1 (26-ounce / 737-g) jar meatless spaghetti sauce
1 (16-ounce / 454-g) can kidney beans, rinsed and drained
1 medium yellow summer squash, cut in 1-inch pieces
2 medium carrots, cut in ¼-inch slices
1 medium red or green sweet pepper, diced
⅓ cup chopped onions
1½ cups spiral pasta, uncooked
1 cup frozen peas
1 teaspoon sugar
½ teaspoon salt
¼ teaspoon pepper

1. Sauté sausage in skillet until no longer pink. Drain and place in slow cooker. 2. Add water, spaghetti sauce, kidney beans, squash, carrots, pepper, and onions. Mix well. 3. Cover. Cook on low 7 to 9 hours, or until vegetables are tender. 4. Add remaining ingredients. Mix well. 5. Cover. Cook on high 15 to 20 minutes until pasta is tender.

Swiss Cheese and Veggie Soup

Prep time: 5 minutes | Cook time: 6 to 8 hours | Serves 4

2¼ cups frozen California-blend vegetables (broccoli, carrots, and cauliflower)
½ cup chopped onions
½ cup water
½ teaspoon chicken bouillon granules
1 cup skim milk
3 ounces (85 g) shredded fat-free Swiss cheese

1. Combine vegetables, onions, water, and bouillon in slow cooker. 2. Cook on low 6 to 8 hours, or until vegetables are tender. 3. Pour into blender or food processor. Add milk. Process until smooth, or chunky smooth, whichever you prefer. 4. Serve, topped with shredded cheese.

Bean and Ham Soup

Prep time: 30 minutes | Cook time: 9 to 11 hours | Serves 10

1 pound (454 g) mixed dry beans
Ham bone from half a ham butt
1½ cups ham, cubed
1 large chopped onion
¾ cup chopped celery
¾ cup sliced or chopped carrots
1 (15-ounce / 425-g) can low-sodium diced tomatoes
2 tablespoons chopped parsley
1 cup low-sodium tomato juice
5 cups water
2 tablespoons Worcestershire sauce
1 bay leaf
1 teaspoon prepared mustard
½ teaspoon chili powder
Juice of 1 lemon
1 teaspoon salt
½ teaspoon black pepper

1. Place beans in saucepan. Cover with water and soak overnight. Drain. 2. Cover beans with fresh water and cook in saucepan 30 minutes uncovered. Drain again. Discard water. 3. Combine beans with remaining ingredients in slow cooker. 4. Cover. Cook on low 9 to 11 hours. 5. Remove bay leaf and ham bone before serving.

Chicken Noodle Soup with Vegetables

Prep time: 15 minutes | Cook time: 5 to 7 hours | Serves 6

2 onions, chopped
2 cups sliced carrots
2 cups sliced celery
1 (10-ounce / 283-g) package frozen peas (optional)
2 teaspoons salt (optional)
¼ teaspoon black pepper
½ teaspoon dried basil
¼ teaspoon dried thyme
3 tablespoons dry parsley flakes
4 cups water
2½ to 3 pounds (1.1 to 1.4 kg) chicken, cut-up
1 cup thin noodles, uncooked

1. Place all ingredients in slow cooker, except chicken and noodles. 2. Remove skin and any fat from chicken pieces. Then place chicken in cooker, on top of the rest of the ingredients. 3. Cover. Cook on high 4 to 6 hours. 4. One hour before serving, remove chicken. 5. Cool slightly. Cut meat from bones. Return meat to cooker. Add noodles. 6. Cover. Cook on high 1 hour.

Wonderful Clam Chowder

Prep time: 15 minutes | Cook time: 6 to 7 hours | Serves 4 to 6

2 (12-ounce / 340-g) cans evaporated milk
1 evaporated milk can of water
2 (6-ounce / 170-g) cans whole clams, undrained
1 (6-ounce / 170-g) can minced clams, undrained
1 small onion, chopped
2 small potatoes, diced
2 tablespoons cornstarch
¼ cup water

1. Combine all ingredients except cornstarch and ¼ cup water in slow cooker. 2. Cover. Cook on low 6 to 7 hours. 3. One hour before end of cooking time, mix cornstarch and ¼ cup water together. When smooth, stir into soup. Stir until soup thickens.

Cheeseburger Soup

Prep time: 15 minutes | Cook time: 8 to 9 hours | Serves 6

1 pound (454 g) ground turkey
1 cup chopped onions
½ cup chopped green bell peppers
2 ribs celery, chopped
1 (20-ounce / 567-g) beef broth
1 cup non-fat milk
2 cups water
2 tablespoons flour
8 ounces (227 g) low-fat Cheddar cheese, shredded

1. Brown turkey in nonstick skillet. Spoon into slow cooker. 2. Add vegetables to slow cooker. 3. Heat broth, milk, and water in skillet. Sprinkle flour over liquid. Stir until smooth and let boil for 3 minutes. 4. Pour into slow cooker. 5. Cover. Cook on low 6 hours. Then add cheese and cook another 2 to 3 hours.

Kielbasa Stew

Prep time: 45 minutes | Cook time: 8 to 10 hours | Serves 6 to 8

6 strips of bacon
1 onion, chopped
1 to 1½ pounds (680 g) smoked, fully cooked kielbasa, thinly sliced
2 (15½-ounce / 439-g) cans Great Northern beans
2 (8-ounce / 227-g) cans tomato sauce
1 (4-ounce / 113-g) can chopped green chilies
2 medium carrots, thinly sliced
1 medium green pepper, chopped
½ teaspoon Italian seasoning
½ teaspoon dried thyme
½ teaspoon black pepper

1. Fry bacon in skillet until crisp. Crumble bacon and place in large slow cooker. Add onions and kielbasa to drippings in skillet. Cook until onions are soft. 2. Transfer onions and kielbasa to slow cooker. 3. Add all remaining ingredients to cooker and stir together well. 4. Cover. Cook on low 8 to 10 hours, or until vegetables are tender.

Vegetable Salmon Chowder

Prep time: 15 minutes | Cook time: 3 hours | Serves 8

1½ cups cubed potatoes
1 cup diced celery
½ cup diced onions
2 tablespoons fresh parsley, or 1 tablespoon dried parsley
½ teaspoon salt
¼ teaspoon black pepper
Water to cover
1 (16-ounce / 454-g) can pink salmon
4 cups skim milk
2 teaspoons lemon juice
2 tablespoons finely cut red bell peppers
2 tablespoons finely shredded carrots
½ cup instant potatoes

1. Combine cubed potatoes, celery, onions, parsley, salt, pepper, and water to cover in slow cooker. 2. Cook on high for 3 hours, or until soft. Add a bit more water if needed. 3. Add salmon, milk, lemon juice, red peppers, carrots, and instant potatoes. 4. Heat 1 hour more until very hot.

Shrimp Soup/Chowder

Prep time: 25 minutes | Cook time: 7 to 8 hours | Serves 12

1 medium onion, chopped
5 medium russet potatoes, peeled and cubed
1½ cups diced precooked ham
4 to 6 cups water
Salt and pepper to taste
2 pounds (907 g) shrimp, peeled, deveined, and cooked
Chowder Option:
4 tablespoons flour
1 cup heavy (whipping) cream

1. Place chopped onion in microwave-safe bowl and cook in microwave for 2 minutes on high. 2. Place onion, cubed potatoes, diced ham, and 4 cups water in slow cooker. (If you're making the Chowder option, whisk 4 tablespoons flour into 4 cups water in bowl before adding to slow cooker.) 3. Cover and cook on low for 7 hours, or until potatoes are softened. If soup base is thicker than you like, add up to 2 cups more water. 4. About 15 to 20 minutes before serving, turn heat to high and add shrimp. If making chowder, also add heavy cream. Cook until shrimp are hot, about 15 minutes.

Mexican Tomato-Corn Soup

Prep time: 10 minutes | Cook time: 6 to 8 hours | Serves 8

1 medium onion, diced
1 medium green bell pepper, diced
1 clove garlic, minced
1 cup diced carrots
1 (14½-ounce / 411-g) can low-sodium diced Italian tomatoes
2½ cups low-sodium tomato juice
1 quart low-fat, low-sodium chicken broth
3 cups corn, frozen or canned
1 (4-ounce / 113-g) can chopped chilies, undrained
1 teaspoon chili powder
1½ teaspoons ground cumin
Dash cayenne powder

1. Combine all ingredients in slow cooker. 2. Cover. Cook on low 6 to 8 hours.

Lilli's Vegetable-Beef Soup

Prep time: 25 minutes | Cook time: 8 to 10 hours | Serves 10 to 12

3 pounds (1.4 kg) stewing meat, cut in 1-inch pieces
2 tablespoons oil
4 potatoes, cubed
4 carrots, sliced
3 ribs celery, sliced
1 (14-ounce / 397-g) diced tomatoes
1 (14-ounce / 397-g) Italian tomatoes, crushed
2 medium onions, chopped
2 wedges cabbage, sliced thinly
2 beef bouillon cubes
2 tablespoons fresh parsley
1 teaspoon seasoned salt
1 teaspoon garlic salt
½ teaspoon pepper
Water

1. Brown meat in oil in skillet. Drain. 2. Combine all ingredients except water in large slow cooker. Cover with water. 3. Cover. Cook on low 8 to 10 hours.

Old-Fashioned Chicken and Dumplings

Prep time: 30 minutes | Cook time: 4¼ to 6¼ hours | Serves 8

Soup:
4 cups cooked chicken, cubed
6 cups fat-free, low-sodium chicken broth
1 tablespoon fresh parsley, or 1½ teaspoons dry parsley flakes
1 cup onions, chopped
1 cup celery, chopped
6 cups diced potatoes
1 cup green beans
1 cup carrots
1 cup peas (optional)
Dumplings: (optional)
2 cups flour (half white and half whole wheat)
1 teaspoon salt
4 teaspoons baking powder
1 egg, beaten
2 tablespoons olive oil
⅔ cup skim milk

1. Combine all soup ingredients, except peas. 2. Cover. Cook on low 4 to 6 hours. 3. Transfer to large soup kettle with lid. Add peas, if desired. Bring to a boil. Reduce to simmer. 4. To make Dumplings, combine flour, salt, and baking powder in a large bowl. 5. In a separate bowl, combine egg, olive oil, and milk until smooth. Add to flour mixture.

Double Corn and Cheddar Chowder

Prep time: 10 minutes | Cook time: 4½ hours | Serves 6

1 tablespoon butter or margarine
1 cup onions, chopped
2 tablespoons all-purpose flour
2½ cups fat-free, reduced-sodium chicken broth
1 (16-ounce / 454-g) can creamed corn
1 cup frozen corn
½ cup finely chopped red bell peppers
½ teaspoon hot pepper sauce
¾ cup shredded, reduced-fat, sharp Cheddar cheese

1. In saucepan on top of stove, melt butter or margarine. Stir in onions and sauté until wilted. Stir in flour. When well mixed, whisk in chicken broth. Stir frequently over medium heat until broth is thickened. 2. Pour into slow cooker. Mix in remaining ingredients except cheese. 3. Cook on low 4½ hours. About an hour before the end of the cooking time, stir in cheese until melted and well blended.

Busy Cook's Stew

Prep time: 30 minutes | Cook time: 6 to 8 hours | Serves 4 to 6

1 pound (454 g) boneless stew meat, cut up
1 (10¾-ounce / 305-g) can cream of mushroom soup
2 cups water
3 potatoes, cubed
3 carrots, diced
1 onion, chopped

1. Brown meat in large nonstick skillet. Don't crowd the skillet so the meat browns on all sides. (If your skillet is 10 inches or smaller, brown the beef in 2 batches.) 2. Place meat in slow cooker. Add remaining ingredients in the order listed. Stir well after each addition. 3. Cover and cook on low 6 to 8 hours, or until meat and vegetables are tender but not mushy. Stir occasionally.

Cream of Broccoli and Mushroom Soup

Prep time: 10 minutes | Cook time: 3½ to 8 hours | Serves 12

8 ounces (227 g) fresh mushrooms, sliced
2 pounds (907 g) fresh broccoli
3 (10¾-ounce / 305-g) cans 98% fat-free cream of broccoli soup
½ teaspoon dried thyme leaves, crushed (optional)
3 bay leaves (optional)
1 pint fat-free half-and-half
4 ounces (113 g) extra-lean smoked ham, chopped
¼ teaspoon black pepper

1. Combine all ingredients in slow cooker. 2. Cook on low 6 to 8 hours, or on high 3½ to 4 hours. 3. Remove bay leaves before serving.

Pork Potato Stew

Prep time: 20 minutes | Cook time: 4 hours | Serves 4

1 pound (454 g) ground pork
½ cup chopped onion
1 sweet potato, cubed and peeled
2 beef bouillon cubes
½ teaspoon dried rosemary
3 cups water

1. Place meat and onion in nonstick skillet. Brown on stovetop. 2. Place drained meat, along with onion, into slow cooker. Add remaining ingredients. 3. Cover and cook on low for 4 hours.

Easy Cheese Soup

Prep time: 10 minutes | Cook time: 4 to 6 hours | Serves 4

2 (10¾-ounce / 305-g) cans cream of mushroom or cream of chicken soup
1 cup beer or milk
1 pound (454 g) Cheddar cheese, shredded
1 teaspoon Worcestershire sauce
¼ teaspoon paprika
Croutons

1. Combine all ingredients except croutons in slow cooker. 2. Cover. Cook on low 4 to 6 hours. 3. Stir thoroughly 1 hour before serving, to make sure cheese is well distributed and melted. 4. Serve topped with croutons.

Chinese Chicken Soup

Prep time: 5 minutes | Cook time: 1 to 2 hours | Serves 6

3 (14½-ounce / 411-g) cans chicken broth
1 (16-ounce / 454-g) package frozen stir-fry vegetable blend
2 cups cooked chicken, cubed
1 teaspoon minced fresh ginger root
1 teaspoon soy sauce

1. Mix all ingredients in slow cooker. 2. Cover and cook on high for 1 to 2 hours, depending upon how crunchy or soft you like your vegetables to be.

Santa Fe Stew

Prep time: 20 minutes | Cook time: 4½ to 6½ hours | Serves 4 to 6

2 pounds (907 g) sirloin or stewing meat, cubed
2 tablespoons oil
1 large onion, diced
2 garlic cloves, minced
1½ cups water
1 tablespoon dried parsley flakes
2 beef bouillon cubes
1 teaspoon ground cumin
½ teaspoon salt
3 carrots, sliced
1 (14½-ounce / 411-g) can diced tomatoes
1 (14½-ounce / 411-g) can green beans, drained, or 1 pound (454 g) frozen green beans
1 (14½-ounce / 411-g) can corn, drained, or 1 pound (454 g) frozen corn
1 (4-ounce / 113-g) can diced green chilies
3 zucchini squash, diced (optional)

1. Brown meat, onion, and garlic in oil in saucepan until meat is no longer pink. Place in slow cooker. 2. Stir in remaining ingredients. 3. Cover. Cook on high 30 minutes. Reduce heat to low and cook 4 to 6 hours.

Barley-Cabbage Soup

Prep time: 15 minutes | Cook time: 5 to 12 hours | Serves 8

¼ cup dry pearl barley
6 cups fat-free, low-sodium meat or vegetable broth
1 cup chopped onions
3 to 4 cups finely chopped green cabbage
¼ cup chopped fresh parsley
½ teaspoon celery salt
½ teaspoon salt
⅛ teaspoon black pepper
1 tablespoon minute tapioca

1. Combine all ingredients in slow cooker. 2. Cover. Cook on low 10 to 12 hours, or on high 5 to 6 hours.

Taco Twist Soup

Prep time: 10 minutes | Cook time: 4 to 6 hours | Serves 6 to 8

1 medium onion, chopped
2 garlic cloves, minced
2 tablespoons canola or olive oil
3 cups reduced-sodium beef broth or vegetable broth
1 (15-ounce / 425-g) can black beans, rinsed and drained
1 (14½-ounce / 411-g) can diced tomatoes, undrained
1½ cups picante sauce
1 cup spiral pasta, uncooked
1 small green bell pepper, chopped
2 teaspoons chili powder
1 teaspoon ground cumin
½ cup shredded reduced-fat cheese
Fat-free sour cream (optional)

1. Sauté onions and garlic in oil in skillet. 2. Combine all ingredients except cheese and sour cream. 3. Cook on low 4 to 6 hours, or just until pasta is tender. 4. Add cheese and sour cream as desired when serving.

Tomato Beef Stew

Prep time: 15 minutes | Cook time: 8 hours | Serves 6 to 8

5 pounds (2.3 kg) stewing meat, cubed
2 onions, chopped
1 (14½-ounce / 411-g) can chopped tomatoes
1 (10¾-ounce / 305-g) can tomato soup
5 to 6 carrots, sliced
5 to 6 potatoes, peeled and cubed
1 cup sliced celery
1 bell pepper, sliced
2 teaspoons salt
½ teaspoon pepper
2 cloves minced garlic

1. Combine all ingredients in slow cooker. 2. Cover. Cook on low 8 hours. 3. Serve.

Potato Soup with Ground Beef

Prep time: 20 minutes | Cook time: 3½ to 4 hours | Serves 6 to 8

1 pound (454 g) ground beef
4 cups potatoes, peeled and cut into ½-inch cubes
1 small onion, chopped
3 (8-ounce / 227-g) cans tomato sauce
2 teaspoons salt
½ teaspoon pepper
4 cups water
½ teaspoon hot pepper sauce (optional)

1. Brown the ground beef in a nonstick skillet. Drain well. Place meat in slow cooker. 2. Add cubed potatoes, chopped onion, and tomato sauce. 3. Stir in salt, pepper, water, and hot pepper sauce, if you wish. 4. Cover and cook on high until mixture starts to simmer, about 1 hour. 5. Turn to low and continue cooking until potatoes are tender, about 2½ to 3 hours.

Cream Cheese Potato Soup

Prep time: 15 minutes | Cook time: 4 hours | Serves 6

3 cups water
1 cup ham, diced
5 medium potatoes, diced finely
1 (8-ounce / 227-g) package fat-free cream cheese, cubed
Half an onion, chopped
1 teaspoon garlic salt
½ teaspoon black pepper
½ teaspoon dill weed

1. Combine all ingredients in slow cooker. 2. Cover. Cook on high 4 hours, stirring occasionally. 3. Turn to low until ready to serve.

Curried Pork and Pea Soup

Prep time: 15 minutes | Cook time: 4 to 12 hours | Serves 6 to 8

1 (1½-pound / 680-g) boneless pork shoulder roast
1 cup yellow or green split peas, rinsed and drained
½ cup finely chopped carrots
½ cup finely chopped celery
½ cup finely chopped onions
6 cups chicken broth

2 teaspoons curry powder
½ teaspoon paprika
¼ teaspoon ground cumin
¼ teaspoon pepper
2 cups torn fresh spinach

1. Trim fat from pork and cut pork into ½-inch pieces. 2. Combine split peas, carrots, celery, and onions in slow cooker. 3. Stir in broth, curry powder, paprika, cumin, and pepper. Stir in pork. 4. Cover. Cook on low 10 to 12 hours, or on high 4 hours. 5. Stir in spinach. Serve immediately.

Tempting Beef Stew

Prep time: 10 minutes | Cook time: 10 to 12 hours | Serves 10 to 12

2 to 3 pounds (907 g to 1.4 kg) beef stewing meat
3 carrots, thinly sliced
1 (1-pound / 454-g) package frozen green peas with onions
1 (1-pound / 454-g) package frozen green beans
1 (16-ounce / 454-g) can whole or stewed tomatoes
½ cup beef broth
½ cup white wine
½ cup brown sugar
4 tablespoons tapioca
½ cup bread crumbs
2 teaspoons salt
1 bay leaf
Pepper to taste

1. Combine all ingredients in slow cooker. 2. Cover. Cook on low 10 to 12 hours. 3. Serve.

Vegetable Cheese Soup

Prep time: 15 minutes | Cook time: 4 to 10 hours | Serves 5

2 cups cream-style corn
1 cup peeled and chopped potatoes
1 cup peeled and chopped carrots
2 (14½-ounce / 411-g) cans vegetable or chicken broth
1 (16-ounce / 454-g) jar processed cheese

1. Combine all ingredients except cheese in the slow cooker. 2. Cover and cook on low 8 to 10 hours, or on high 4 to 5 hours. 3. Thirty to 60 minutes before serving, stir in the cheese. Then cook on high for 30 to 60 minutes to melt and blend the cheese.

Beef 'n Black Bean Soup

Prep time: 30 minutes | Cook time: 5 to 7 hours | Serves 10

1 pound (454 g) extra-lean ground beef
2 (14½-ounce / 411-g) cans fat-free, low-sodium chicken broth
1 (14½-ounce / 411-g) can low-sodium, diced tomatoes, undrained
8 green onions, thinly sliced
3 medium carrots, thinly sliced
2 celery ribs, thinly sliced
2 garlic cloves, minced
1 tablespoon sugar
1½ teaspoons dried basil
½ teaspoon salt
½ teaspoon dried oregano
½ teaspoon ground cumin
½ teaspoon chili powder
2 (15-ounce / 425-g) cans black beans, rinsed and drained
1½ cups rice, cooked

1. In a nonstick skillet over medium heat, cook beef until no longer pink. Drain. 2. Place beef in slow cooker. 3. Add remaining ingredients except black beans and rice. 4. Cover. Cook on high 1 hour. 5. Reduce to low. Cook 4 to 5 hours, or until vegetables are tender. 6. Add beans and rice. 7. Cook 1 hour longer on low, or until heated through.

Green Chili Stew

Prep time: 20 minutes | Cook time: 4 to 6 hours | Serves 6 to 8

3 tablespoons oil
2 garlic cloves, minced
1 large onion, diced
1 pound (454 g) ground sirloin
½ pound (227 g) ground pork
3 cups chicken broth
2 cups water
2 (4-ounce / 113-g) cans diced green chilies
4 large potatoes, diced
1 (10-ounce / 283-g) package frozen corn
1 teaspoon black pepper
1 teaspoon crushed dried oregano
½ teaspoon ground cumin
1 teaspoon salt

1. Brown onion, garlic, sirloin, and pork in oil in skillet. Cook until meat is no longer pink. 2. Combine all ingredients in slow cooker. 3. Cover. Cook on low 4 to 6 hours, or until potatoes are soft.

Pork-Veggie Stew

Prep time: 15 minutes | Cook time: 6 hours | Serves 8

2 pounds (907 g) boneless pork loin, cut into 1-inch cubes
8 medium potatoes, peeled and cut into 2-inch pieces
6 large carrots, peeled and cut into 2-inch pieces
1 cup ketchup
2¼ cups water, divided

1. Brown pork cubes in a large nonstick skillet. 2. Lightly spray slow cooker with nonstick cooking spray. 3. Place all ingredients except ketchup and ¼ cup water in slow cooker. 4. Cover and cook on high 5 hours. One hour before serving, combine ketchup with ¼ cup water. Pour over stew. Cook one more hour.

Taco Soup with Pizza Sauce

Prep time: 15 minutes | Cook time: 3 to 4 hours | Serves 8 to 10

2 pounds (907 g) ground beef, browned
1 small onion, chopped and sautéed in ground beef drippings
¾ teaspoon salt
½ teaspoon pepper
1½ packages dry taco seasoning
1 quart pizza sauce
1 quart water
Tortilla chips
Shredded Mozzarella cheese
Sour cream

1. Combine ground beef, onion, salt, pepper, taco seasoning, pizza sauce, and water in 5-quart, or larger, slow cooker. 2. Cover. Cook on low 3 to 4 hours. 3. Top individual servings with tortilla chips, cheese, and sour cream.

Delicious Sausage Soup

Prep time: 15 minutes | Cook time: 4 to 5 hours | Serves 4

5½ cups chicken broth
½ cup heavy cream
3 carrots, grated
4 potatoes, sliced or cubed
4 cups kale, chopped
1 pound (454 g) spicy Italian sausage, browned
½ teaspoon salt
½ teaspoon crushed red pepper flakes

1. Combine broth and cream in slow cooker. Turn on high. 2. Add carrots, potatoes, kale, and sausage. 3. Sprinkle spices over top. 4. Cover. Cook on high 4 to 5 hours, stirring occasionally.

Curried Carrot Soup

Prep time: 20 minutes | Cook time: 2 hours | Serves 6 to 8

1 garlic clove, minced
1 large onion, chopped
2 tablespoons oil
1 tablespoon butter
1 teaspoon curry powder
1 tablespoon flour
4 cups chicken or vegetable broth
6 large carrots, sliced
¼ teaspoon salt
¼ teaspoon ground red pepper (optional)
1½ cups plain yogurt, or light sour cream

1. In skillet cook minced garlic and onion in oil and butter until limp but not brown. 2. Add curry and flour. Cook 30 seconds. Pour into slow cooker. 3. Add chicken broth and carrots. 4. Cover. Cook on high for about 2 hours, or until carrots are soft. 5. Purée mixture in blender. Season with salt and pepper. Return to slow cooker and keep warm until ready to serve. 6. Add a dollop of yogurt or sour cream to each serving.

Joy's Brunswick Stew

Prep time: 10 minutes | Cook time: 4 hours | Serves 8

1 pound (454 g) skinless, boneless chicken breasts, cubed
2 potatoes, thinly sliced
1 (10¾-ounce / 305-g) can tomato soup
1 (16-ounce / 454-g) can stewed tomatoes
1 (10-ounce / 283-g) package frozen corn
1 (10-ounce / 283-g) package frozen lima beans
3 tablespoons onion flakes
¼ teaspoon salt
⅛ teaspoon pepper

Combine all ingredients in slow cooker. 2. Cover. Cook on high 2 hours. Reduce to low and cook 2 hours.

Lamb Stew

Prep time: 35 minutes | Cook time: 8 to 10 hours | Serves 6

2 pounds (907 g) lean lamb, cubed
½ teaspoon sugar
2 tablespoons canola oil
1½ teaspoons salt
¼ teaspoon black pepper
¼ cup flour
2 cups water
¾ cup red cooking wine
¼ teaspoon garlic powder
2 teaspoons Worcestershire sauce
6 to 8 carrots, sliced
4 small onions, quartered
4 ribs celery, sliced
3 medium potatoes, diced

1. Sprinkle lamb with sugar. Brown in oil in skillet. 2. Remove lamb and place in cooker, reserving drippings. Stir salt, pepper, and flour into drippings in skillet until smooth. Stir in water and wine until smooth, stirring loose the meat drippings. Continue cooking and stirring occasionally until broth simmers and thickens. 3. Pour into cooker. Add remaining ingredients and stir until well mixed. 4. Cover. Cook on low 8 to 10 hours.

Mountain Bike Soup

Prep time: 10 minutes | Cook time: 2 to 6 hours | Serves 4

1 (12-ounce / 340-g) can chicken broth
1 (12-ounce / 340-g) can V-8 juice, regular or spicy
⅓ cup barley, rice, or broken spaghetti noodles, uncooked
⅓ cup chopped pepperoni, ham, or bacon
1 (15-ounce / 425-g) can cut green beans with liquid

1. Dump it all in. Put on the lid. Turn it on low. 2. Go for a long ride on your bike, from 2 to 6 hours.

Chapter 5　Beans and Grains

Lotsa-Beans Pot

Prep time: 30 minutes | Cook time: 3 to 4 hours | Serves 15 to 20

8 bacon strips, diced
2 onions, thinly sliced
1 cup packed brown sugar
½ cup cider vinegar
1 teaspoon salt
1 teaspoon ground mustard
½ teaspoon garlic powder
1 (28-ounce / 794-g) can baked beans
1 (16-ounce / 454-g) can kidney beans, rinsed and drained
1 (15½-ounce / 439-g) can pinto beans, rinsed and drained
1 (15-ounce / 425-g) can lima beans, rinsed and drained
1 (15½-ounce / 439-g) can black-eyed peas, rinsed and drained

1. Cook bacon in skillet until crisp. Remove to paper towels. 2. Drain, reserving 2 tablespoons drippings. 3. Sauté onions in drippings until tender. 4. Add brown sugar, vinegar, salt, mustard, and garlic powder to skillet. Bring to boil. 5. Combine beans and peas in slow cooker. Add onion mixture and bacon. Mix well. 6. Cover. Cook on high 3 to 4 hours.

Easy Baked Beans

Prep time: 10 minutes | Cook time: 2 hours | Serves 8

2 (16-ounce / 454-g) cans baked beans
¼ cup brown sugar
½ teaspoon dried mustard
½ cup ketchup
2 small onions, chopped
1 teaspoon Worcestershire sauce

1. Combine all ingredients in slow cooker. 2. Cover. Cook on high 2 hours.

Hometown Spanish Rice

Prep time: 20 minutes | Cook time: 2 to 4 hours | Serves 6 to 8

1 large onion, chopped
1 bell pepper, chopped
1 pound (454 g) bacon, cooked, and broken into bite-size pieces
2 cups long-grain rice, cooked
1 (28-ounce / 794-g) can stewed tomatoes with juice
Grated Parmesan cheese (optional)
Nonstick cooking spray

1. Sauté onion and pepper in a small nonstick frying pan until tender. 2. Spray interior of slow cooker with nonstick cooking spray. 3. Combine all ingredients in the slow cooker. 4. Cover and cook on low 4 hours, or on high 2 hours, or until heated through. 5. Sprinkle with Parmesan cheese just before serving, if you wish.

Five Baked Beans

Prep time: 10 minutes | Cook time: 4 to 12 hours | Serves 12

6 slices turkey bacon
1 cup onions, chopped
1 clove garlic, minced
1 (16-ounce / 454-g) can low-sodium lima beans, drained
1 (16-ounce / 454-g) can low-sodium beans with tomato sauce, undrained
1 (15½-ounce / 439-g) can low-sodium red kidney beans, drained
1 (15-ounce / 425-g) can low-sodium butter beans, drained
1 (15-ounce / 425-g) can low-sodium garbanzo beans, drained
¾ cup ketchup
½ cup unsulphured molasses
¼ cup brown sugar
1 tablespoon prepared mustard
1 tablespoon Worcestershire sauce
1 onion sliced and cut into rings (optional)

1. In a nonstick skillet, cook bacon until browned. 2. Combine chopped onions, bacon, garlic, lima beans, beans with tomato sauce, kidney beans, butter beans, garbanzo beans, ketchup, molasses, brown sugar, mustard, and Worcestershire sauce in slow cooker. 3. Top with onions if desired. 4. Cover. Cook on low 10 to 12 hours, or on high 4 to 5 hours.

Four Zesty Beans

Prep time: 5 minutes | Cook time: 2 to 2½ hours | Serves 10

2 (15½-ounce / 439-g) cans Great Northern beans, rinsed and drained
2 (15-ounce / 425-g) cans black beans, rinsed and drained
1 (15-ounce / 425-g) can butter beans, rinsed and drained
1 (15-ounce / 425-g) can baked beans, undrained
2 cups salsa
½ cup brown sugar

1. In slow cooker combine Great Northern beans, black beans, butter beans, and baked beans. 2. Stir in salsa and brown sugar. 3. Cover. Cook on low 2 to 2½ hours.

Pizza Beans

Prep time: 30 minutes | Cook time: 7 to 9 hours | Serves 6

1 (16-ounce / 454-g) can pinto beans, drained
1 (16-ounce / 454-g) can kidney beans, drained
1 (2¼-ounce / 64-g) can ripe olives sliced, drained
1 (28-ounce / 794-g) can stewed or whole tomatoes
¾ pound (340 g) bulk Italian sausage
1 tablespoon oil
1 green pepper, chopped
1 medium onion, chopped
1 garlic clove, minced
1 teaspoon salt
1 teaspoon dried oregano
1 teaspoon dried basil
Parmesan cheese

1. Combine beans, olives, and tomatoes in slow cooker. 2. Brown sausage in oil in skillet. Drain, reserving drippings. Transfer sausage to slow cooker. 3. Sauté green pepper in drippings 1 minute, stirring constantly. Add onions and continue stirring until onions start to become translucent. Add garlic and cook 1 more minute. Transfer to slow cooker. 4. Stir in seasonings. 5. Cover. Cook on low 7 to 9 hours. 6. To serve, sprinkle with Parmesan cheese.

Cowboy Beans

Prep time: 20 minutes | Cook time: 3 to 7 hours | Serves 10 to 12

- 6 slices bacon, cut in pieces
- ½ cup onions, chopped
- 1 garlic clove, minced
- 1 (16-ounce / 454-g) can baked beans
- 1 (16-ounce / 454-g) can kidney beans, drained
- 1 (15-ounce / 425-g) can butter beans or pinto beans, drained
- 2 tablespoons dill pickle relish or chopped dill pickles
- ⅓ cup chili sauce or ketchup
- 2 teaspoons Worcestershire sauce
- ½ cup brown sugar
- ⅛ teaspoon hot pepper sauce (optional)

1. Lightly brown bacon, onions, and garlic in skillet. Drain. 2. Combine all ingredients in slow cooker. Mix well. 3. Cover. Cook on low 5 to 7 hours, or on high 3 to 4 hours.

Red Bean and Brown Rice Stew

Prep time: 15 minutes | Cook time: 6 hours | Serves 6

- 2 cups dried red beans
- Water
- ¾ cup brown rice, uncooked
- 4 cups water
- 6 carrots, peeled if you wish, and cut into chunks
- 1 large onion, cut into chunks
- 1 tablespoon cumin

1. Place dried beans in slow cooker and cover with water. Allow to soak for 8 hours or overnight. Drain. Discard soaking water. 2. Return soaked beans to cooker. Stir in all remaining ingredients. 3. Cover and cook on low 6 hours, or until all vegetables are tender.

Wild Rice

Prep time: 10 minutes | Cook time: 2½ to 3 hours | Serves 5

- 1 cup wild rice or wild rice mixture, uncooked
- ½ cup sliced fresh mushrooms
- ½ cup diced onions
- ½ cup diced green or red bell peppers
- 1 tablespoon oil
- ½ teaspoon salt
- ¼ teaspoon black pepper
- 2½ cups fat-free, low-sodium chicken broth

1. Layer rice and vegetables in slow cooker. Pour oil, salt, and pepper over vegetables. Stir. 2. Heat chicken broth. Pour over all ingredients in slow cooker. 3. Cover. Cook on high 2½ to 3 hours, or until rice is soft and liquid is absorbed.

Never Fail Rice

Prep time: 5 minutes | Cook time: 2 to 6 hours | Serves 6

- 1 cup long-grain rice, uncooked
- 2 cups water
- ½ teaspoon salt
- ½ tablespoon butter

1. Combine all ingredients in small slow cooker. 2. Cover. Cook on low 4 to 6 hours, or on high 2 to 3 hours, or until rice is just fully cooked. 3. Fluff with a fork. Serve.

No-Meat Baked Beans

Prep time: 10 minutes | Cook time: 6½ to 9½ hours | Serves 8 to 10

- 1 pound (454 g) dried navy beans
- 6 cups water
- 1 small onion, chopped
- ¾ cup ketchup
- ½ cup brown sugar
- ¾ cup water
- 1 teaspoon dry mustard
- 3 tablespoons dark molasses
- 1 teaspoon salt

1. Soak beans in water overnight in large soup kettle. Cook beans in water until soft, about 1½ hours. Drain, discarding bean water. 2. Stir together all ingredients in slow cooker. Mix well. 3. Cover. Cook on low 5 to 8 hours, or until beans are well flavored but not breaking down.

Flavorful Fruited Rice

Prep time: 10 minutes | Cook time: 2 hours | Serves 4

- ⅓ cup chopped onion
- 1 (6-ounce / 170-g) package long-grain and wild rice mix
- 2 cups chicken broth
- ¼ cup dried cranberries
- ¼ cup chopped dried apricots
- Nonstick cooking spray

1. Spray small frying pan with nonstick cooking spray. Add chopped onions and cook on medium heat about 5 minutes, or until onions begin to brown. 2. Place onions and remaining ingredients in the slow cooker, including the seasonings in the rice package. Stir well to dissolve seasonings. 3. Cover and cook on high 2 hours. Fluff with fork to serve.

Casey's Beans

Prep time: 20 minutes | Cook time: 5 to 6 hours | Serves 10 to 12

- ½ pound (227 g) ground beef
- 10 slices bacon, diced
- ½ cup chopped onions
- ⅓ cup brown sugar
- ⅓ cup sugar (optional)
- ¼ cup ketchup
- ¼ cup barbecue sauce
- 2 tablespoons prepared mustard
- 2 tablespoons molasses
- ½ teaspoon salt
- ½ teaspoon chili powder
- ½ teaspoon pepper
- 1 (1-pound / 454-g) can kidney beans, drained
- 1 (1-pound / 454-g) can butter beans, drained
- 1 (1-pound / 454-g) can black beans, drained
- 1 (1-pound / 454-g) can pork and beans

1. Brown ground beef, bacon, and onion in deep saucepan. Drain. 2. Stir in remaining ingredients, except beans. Mix well. Stir in beans. Pour into slow cooker. 3. Cover. Cook on low 5 to 6 hours.

"Lean" Cowboy Beans

Prep time: 15 minutes | Cook time: 1 to 2 hours | Serves 8

1 pound (454 g) ground turkey
1 (16-ounce / 454-g) can baked beans, undrained
1 (16-ounce / 454-g) can kidney beans, drained
2 cups onions, chopped
¾ cup brown sugar
1 cup ketchup
2 tablespoons dry mustard
¼ teaspoon salt
2 teaspoons cider vinegar

1. Brown turkey in nonstick skillet over medium heat. 2. Combine all ingredients in slow cooker sprayed with nonfat cooking spray. 3. Cover. Cook on high 1 to 2 hours.

Sweet-Sour Bean Trio

Prep time: 10 minutes | Cook time: 6 to 8 hours | Serves 8

4 slices lean bacon
1 onion, chopped
¼ cup brown sugar
1 teaspoon prepared mustard
1 clove garlic, crushed
½ teaspoon salt
¼ cup vinegar
1 (16-ounce / 454-g) can low-sodium lima beans, drained
1 (16-ounce / 454-g) can low-sodium baked beans, undrained
1 (16-ounce / 454-g) can low-sodium kidney beans, drained

1. Brown bacon in a nonstick skillet. Crumble. Combine bacon, 2 tablespoons drippings from bacon, onion, brown sugar, mustard, garlic, salt, and vinegar. 2. Mix with beans in slow cooker. 3. Cover. Cook on low 6 to 8 hours.

Barbecued Baked Beans

Prep time: 10 minutes | Cook time: 3 to 4 hours | Serves 8 to 10

2 (16-ounce / 454-g) cans baked beans, your choice of variety
2 (15-ounce / 425-g) cans kidney or pinto beans, or one of each, drained
½ cup brown sugar
1 cup ketchup
1 onion, chopped

1. Combine all ingredients in slow cooker. Mix well. 2. Cover and cook on low 3 to 4 hours, or until heated through.

Slow Cooker Kidney Beans

Prep time: 15 minutes | Cook time: 6 to 7 hours | Serves 12

2 (30-ounce / 850-g) cans kidney beans, rinsed and drained
1 (28-ounce / 794-g) can diced tomatoes, drained
2 medium red bell peppers, chopped
1 cup ketchup
½ cup brown sugar
¼ cup honey
¼ cup molasses
1 tablespoon Worcestershire sauce
1 teaspoon dry mustard
2 medium red apples, cored, cut into pieces

1. Combine all ingredients, except apples, in slow cooker. 2. Cover. Cook on low 4 to 5 hours. 3. Stir in apples. 4. Cover. Cook 2 more hours.

Arroz con Queso

Prep time: 15 minutes | Cook time: 6 to 9 hours | Serves 6 to 8

1 (14½-ounce / 411-g) can whole tomatoes, mashed
1 (15-ounce / 425-g) can Mexican style beans, undrained
1½ cups long-grain rice, uncooked
1 cup shredded Monterey Jack cheese
1 large onion, finely chopped
1 cup cottage cheese
1 (4¼-ounce / 120-g) can chopped green chili peppers, drained
1 tablespoon oil
3 garlic cloves, minced
1 teaspoon salt
1 cup shredded Monterey Jack cheese

1. Combine all ingredients except final cup of cheese. Pour into well greased slow cooker. 2. Cover. Cook on low 6 to 9 hours. 3. Sprinkle with remaining cheese before serving.

Chili Boston Baked Beans

Prep time: 15 minutes | Cook time: 6 to 8 hours | Serves 20

1 cup raisins
2 small onions, diced
2 tart apples, diced
1 cup chili sauce
1 cup chopped ham or crumbled bacon
2 (15-ounce / 425-g) cans baked beans
3 teaspoons dry mustard
½ cup sweet pickle relish

1. Mix together all ingredients. 2. Cover. Cook on low 6 to 8 hours.

Risi Bisi (Peas and Rice)

Prep time: 15 minutes | Cook time: 2½ to 3½ hours | Serves 6

1½ cups converted long-grain white rice, uncooked
¾ cup chopped onions
2 garlic cloves, minced
2 (14½-ounce / 411-g) cans reduced-sodium chicken broth
⅓ cup water
¾ teaspoon Italian seasoning
½ teaspoon dried basil leaves
½ cup frozen baby peas, thawed
¼ cup grated Parmesan cheese

1. Combine rice, onions, and garlic in slow cooker. 2. In saucepan, mix together chicken broth and water. Bring to boil. Add Italian seasoning and basil leaves. Stir into rice mixture. 3. Cover. Cook on low 2 to 3 hours, or until liquid is absorbed. 4. Stir in peas. Cover. Cook 30 minutes. Stir in cheese.

Herb Rice

Prep time: 5 minutes | Cook time: 4 to 6 hours | Serves 6

3 chicken bouillon cubes
3 cups water
1½ cups long-grain rice, uncooked
1 teaspoon dried rosemary
½ teaspoon dried marjoram
¼ cup dried parsley, chopped
1 tablespoon butter or margarine
¼ cup onions, diced
½ cup slivered almonds (optional)

1. Mix together chicken bouillon cubes and water. 2. Combine all ingredients in slow cooker. 3. Cook on low 4 to 6 hours, or until rice is fully cooked.

Rice 'n Beans 'n Salsa

Prep time: 10 minutes | Cook time: 4 to 10 hours | Serves 6 to 8

2 (16-ounce / 454-g) cans black or navy beans, drained
1 (14-ounce / 397-g) chicken broth
1 cup long-grain white or brown rice, uncooked
1 quart salsa, your choice of heat
1 cup water
½ teaspoon garlic powder

1. Combine all ingredients in slow cooker. Stir well. 2. Cover and cook on low 8 to 10 hours, or on high 4 hours.

Hearty Barbecued Beans

Prep time: 20 minutes | Cook time: 2 to 3 hours | Serves 10

1 pound (454 g) ground beef
½ cup chopped onions
½ teaspoon salt
¼ teaspoon pepper
1 (28-ounce / 794-g) can pork and beans (your favorite variety)
½ cup ketchup
1 tablespoon Worcestershire sauce
1 tablespoon vinegar
¼ teaspoon Tabasco sauce

1. Brown beef and onions together in skillet. Drain. 2. Combine all ingredients in slow cooker. 3. Cover. Cook on high 2 to 3 hours, stirring once or twice. 4. Serve.

Mixed Slow Cooker Beans

Prep time: 10 minutes | Cook time: 4 to 5 hours | Serves 6

1 (16-ounce / 454-g) can kidney beans, drained
1 (15½-ounce / 439-g) can baked beans, undrained
1 pint home-frozen, or 1 (1-pound / 454-g) package frozen, lima beans
1 pint home-frozen, or 1 (1-pound / 454-g) package frozen, green beans
4 slices lean turkey bacon, browned and crumbled
½ cup ketchup
⅓ cup sugar
⅓ cup brown sugar
2 tablespoons vinegar
½ teaspoon salt

1. Combine beans and bacon in slow cooker. 2. Stir together remaining ingredients. Add to beans and mix well. 3. Cover. Cook on low 4 to 5 hours.

Wild Rice Pilaf

Prep time: 10 minutes | Cook time: 3½ to 5 hours | Serves 6

1½ cups wild rice, uncooked
½ cup finely chopped onion
1 (14-ounce / 397-g) chicken broth
2 cups water
1 (4-ounce / 113-g) can sliced mushrooms, drained
½ teaspoon dried thyme leaves
Nonstick cooking spray

1. Spray slow cooker with nonstick cooking spray. 2. Rinse rice and drain well. 3. Combine rice, onion, chicken broth, and water in slow cooker. Mix well. 4. Cover and cook on high 3 to 4 hours. 5. Add mushrooms and thyme and stir gently. 6. Cover and cook on low 30 to 60 minutes longer, or until wild rice pops and is tender.

Football Bean Serve

Prep time: 20 minutes | Cook time: 6 to 8 hours | Serves 12

1 cup minced onions
2 cups diced celery
2 cups diced carrots
2 (15-ounce / 425-g) cans kidney beans, drained and rinsed
2 (15-ounce / 425-g) cans pinto beans, drained and rinsed
2 (15-ounce / 425-g) cans diced tomatoes
2 cups water
1 tablespoon garlic powder
1 tablespoon parsley flakes
1 tablespoon dried oregano
1 tablespoon ground cumin
1 tablespoon salt

1. Brown turkey with onions in a nonstick skillet over medium heat. Add celery and carrots and cook until just wilted. Place in slow cooker. 2. Add remaining ingredients. Stir to combine. 3. Cover. Cook on low 6 to 8 hours. 4. Serve.

"Famous" Baked Beans

Prep time: 20 minutes | Cook time: 3 to 6 hours | Serves 10

1 pound (454 g) ground beef
¼ cup minced onions
1 cup ketchup
4 (15-ounce / 425-g) cans pork and beans
1 cup brown sugar
2 tablespoons liquid smoke
1 tablespoon Worcestershire sauce

1. Brown beef and onions in skillet. Drain. Spoon meat and onions into slow cooker. 2. Add remaining ingredients and stir well. 3. Cover. Cook on high 3 hours, or on low 5 to 6 hours.

Creole Black Beans

Prep time: 15 minutes | Cook time: 8 hours | Serves 6 to 8

¾ pound (340 g) lean smoked sausage, sliced in ¼-inch pieces and browned
3 (15-ounce / 425-g) cans black beans, drained
1½ cups chopped onions
1½ cups chopped green bell peppers
1½ cups chopped celery
4 garlic cloves, minced
2 teaspoons dried thyme
1½ teaspoons dried oregano
1½ teaspoons black pepper
1 chicken bouillon cube
3 bay leaves
1 (8-ounce / 227-g) can tomato sauce
1 cup water

1. Combine all ingredients in slow cooker. 2. Cover. Cook on low 8 hours, or on high 4 hours. 3. Remove bay leaves before serving.

Cheddar Rice

Prep time: 15 minutes | Cook time: 2 to 3 hours | Serves 8 to 10

2 cups brown rice, uncooked
3 tablespoons butter
½ cup thinly sliced green onions or shallots
1 teaspoon salt
5 cups water
½ teaspoon pepper
2 cups shredded Cheddar cheese
1 cup slivered almonds (optional)

1. Combine rice, butter, green onion, and salt in slow cooker. 2. Bring water to boil and pour over rice mixture. 3. Cover and cook on high 2 to 3 hours, or until rice is tender and liquid is absorbed. 4. Five minutes before serving stir in pepper and cheese. 5. Garnish with slivered almonds, if you wish.

Hot Bean Dish without Meat

Prep time: 10 minutes | Cook time: 3 to 4 hours | Serves 8 to 10

1 (16-ounce / 454-g) can kidney beans, drained
1 (15-ounce / 425-g) can lima beans, drained
¼ cup vinegar
2 tablespoons molasses
2 heaping tablespoons brown sugar
2 tablespoons minced onion
Mustard to taste
Tabasco sauce to taste

1. Place beans in slow cooker. 2. Combine remaining ingredients. Pour over beans. 3. Cover. Cook on low 3 to 4 hours.

# Chapter 6: Beef, Pork, and Lamb

Lamb Tagine

Prep time: 15 minutes | Cook time: 7 hours | Serves 6

1 navel orange
2 tablespoons all-purpose flour
2 pounds (907 g) boneless leg of lamb, trimmed and cut into 1½-inch cubes
½ cup chicken stock
2 large white onions, chopped
1 teaspoon pumpkin pie spice
1 teaspoon ground cumin
½ teaspoon sea salt
¼ teaspoon saffron threads, crushed in your palm
¼ teaspoon ground red pepper
1 cup pitted dates
2 tablespoons honey
3 cups hot cooked couscous, for serving
2 tablespoons toasted slivered almonds, for serving

1. Grate 2 teaspoons of zest from the orange into a small bowl. Squeeze ¼ cup juice from the orange into another small bowl. 2. Add the flour to the orange juice, stirring with a whisk until smooth. Stir in the orange zest. 3. Heat a large nonstick skillet over medium-high heat. Add the lamb and sauté 7 minutes or until browned. Stir in the stock, scraping the bottom of the pan with a wooden spoon to loosen the flavorful brown bits. Stir in the orange juice mixture. 4. Stir the onions into the lamb mixture. Add the pumpkin pie spice, cumin, salt, saffron, and ground red pepper. 5. Pour the lamb mixture into the crock pot. Cover and cook on low for 6 hours or until the lamb is tender. 6. Stir the dates and honey into the lamb mixture. Cover and cook on low for 1 hour or until thoroughly heated. 7. Serve the lamb tagine over the couscous and sprinkle with the almonds.

Spanish Meatballs

Prep time: 10 minutes | Cook time: 5 hours 10 minutes | Serves 8

2 pounds (907 g) ground pork
1 medium yellow onion, finely chopped
1½ teaspoons ground cumin
1½ teaspoons hot smoked paprika
5 tablespoons plain dried bread crumbs
2 large eggs, lightly beaten
3 tablespoons chopped fresh parsley
Coarse sea salt
Black pepper
3 tablespoons extra-virgin olive oil
1 (28-ounce / 794-g) can diced tomatoes, with the juice
Rustic bread, for serving (optional)

1. In a large bowl, combine the pork, ¼ cup of the onion, cumin, ½ teaspoon of the paprika, bread crumbs, eggs, and parsley. Season with the salt and pepper. Mix thoroughly to combine. 2. Roll the meat mixture into 25 meatballs (each about 1½ inches), and put on a plate. 3. In a large nonstick skillet, heat 1½ tablespoons of the olive oil over medium-high heat. In two batches, brown the meatballs on all sides, 8 minutes per batch. Transfer the browned meatballs to the crock pot. 4. Add the remaining onion to the skillet, and cook until fragrant, stirring often, about 2 minutes. Transfer the onion to the crock pot, sprinkle in the remaining 1 teaspoon paprika, and add the tomatoes. Season with salt and pepper. 5. Cover and cook on low until the meatballs are tender, 5 hours. Serve with slices of rustic bread, if desired.

Tarragon Lamb Shanks with Cannellini Beans

Prep time: 20 minutes | Cook time: 10 hours | Serves 12

four 1½-pound lamb shanks
one 19-ounce can cannellini or other white beans, rinsed and drained
2 medium-sized carrots, diced
1 large yellow onion, chopped
1 large stalk celery, chopped
2 cloves garlic, thinly sliced
2 teaspoons tarragon
½ teaspoon sea salt
¼ teaspoon black pepper
one 28-ounce can diced tomatoes, with the juice

1. Trim the fat from the lamb shanks. 2. Put the beans, carrots, onion, celery, and garlic in the crock pot and stir to combine. 3. Place lamb shanks on the bean mixture, and sprinkle with the tarragon, salt, and pepper. 4. Pour the tomatoes over the lamb. Cover and cook on high for 1 hour. 5. Reduce heat to low, and cook 9 hours or until the lamb is very tender. Remove the lamb shanks from crock pot and place on a plate. 6. Pour the bean mixture through a colander or sieve over a bowl, reserving the liquid. Let the liquid stand for 5 minutes. Skim the fat from the surface of the liquid. Return the bean mixture to the liquid. Return to the crock pot. 7. Remove the lamb from the bones. Discard the bones. Return the lamb to the crock pot. Cover and cook to reheat, about 15 minutes. 8. Serve the lamb hot with the bean mixture.

Lamb with Olives and Potatoes

Prep time: 20 minutes | Cook time: 4 hours | Serves 4

1¼ pounds (567 g) small potatoes, halved
4 large shallots, cut into ½-inch wedges
3 cloves garlic, minced
1 tablespoon lemon zest
3 sprigs fresh rosemary
Coarse sea salt
Black pepper
4 tablespoons all-purpose flour
¾ cup chicken stock
3½ pounds (1.6 kg) lamb shanks, cut crosswise into 1½-inch pieces and fat trimmed
2 tablespoons extra-virgin olive oil
½ cup dry white wine
1 cup pitted green olives, halved
2 tablespoons lemon juice

1. Combine the potatoes, shallots, garlic, lemon zest, and rosemary sprigs in the crock pot. Season with salt and pepper. 2. In a small bowl, whisk together 1 tablespoon of the flour and the stock. Add to the crock pot. 3. Place the remaining 3 tablespoons flour on a plate. Season the lamb with salt and pepper; then coat in the flour, shaking off any excess. 4. In a large skillet over medium-high, heat the olive oil. In batches, cook the lamb until browned on all sides, about 10 minutes. Transfer to the crock pot. 5. Add the wine to the skillet and cook, stirring with a wooden spoon and scraping up the flavorful browned bits from the bottom of the pan, until reduced by half, about 2 minutes. Then add to the crock pot. 6. Cover and cook until the lamb is tender, on high for about 3½ hours, or on low for 7 hours. 7. Stir in olive halves, then cover, and cook 20 additional minutes. 8. To serve, transfer the lamb and vegetables to warm plates. 9. Skim the fat from the cooking liquid, then stir in the lemon juice, and season the sauce with salt and pepper. 10. Serve the sauce with the lamb and vegetables.

Lamb Shanks and Potatoes

Prep time: 10 minutes | Cook time: 8 hours | Serves 6

1 (15-ounce/ 425-g) can crushed tomatoes in purée
3 tablespoons tomato paste
2 tablespoons apricot jam
6 cloves garlic, thinly sliced
3 strips orange zest
¾ teaspoon crushed dried rosemary
½ teaspoon ground ginger
½ teaspoon ground cinnamon
Coarse sea salt
Black pepper
3½ pounds (1.6 kg) lamb shanks, trimmed of excess fat and cut into 1½-inch slices
1¼ pounds (567 g) small new potatoes, halved (or quartered, if large)

1. Stir together the tomatoes and purée, tomato paste, jam, garlic, orange zest, rosemary, ginger, and cinnamon in the crock pot. Season with salt and pepper. 2. Add the lamb and potatoes, and spoon the tomato mixture over the lamb to coat. 3. Cover and cook until the lamb and potatoes are tender, on low for 8 hours or on high for 5 hours. Season again with salt and pepper, if desired. 4. Serve hot.

Braised Pork Loin with Port and Dried Plums

Prep time: 20 minutes | Cook time: 6 hours 25 minutes | Serves 10

1 (3¼-pound / 1.5-kg) boneless pork loin roast, trimmed
1½ teaspoons black pepper
1 teaspoon sea salt
1 teaspoon dry mustard
1 teaspoon dried sage
½ teaspoon dried thyme
1 tablespoon olive oil
2 large yellow onions, sliced
1 cup finely chopped leek, white and light green parts, rinsed
1 large carrot, finely chopped
½ cup port or other sweet red wine
⅔ cup chicken stock
1 cup pitted dried plums (about 20)
2 bay leaves
2 tablespoons cornstarch
2 tablespoons water

1. Cut the pork roast in half crosswise. 2. Combine the pepper, salt, dry mustard, sage, and thyme in a small bowl. Rub the seasoning mixture over the surface of the roast halves. 3. Heat a Dutch oven over medium-high heat. Add the olive oil to pan and swirl to coat. Add the pork and brown on all sides, about 4 minutes. Place the pork in the crock pot. 4. Add the onions, leek, and carrot to the Dutch oven, and sauté for 5 minutes or until vegetables are golden. 5. Stir in the wine and stock, and cook for about 1 minute, scraping the bottom of the pan with a wooden spoon to loosen up the flavorful browned bits. 6. Pour the wine-vegetable mixture over the pork in crock pot. Add the plums and bay leaves. 7. Cover and cook on high for 1 hour. Reduce the heat to low, and cook for 5 to 6 hours, or until the pork is tender. 8. Remove the pork from the crock pot, set aside on a platter, and keep warm. Increase the heat to high. 9. Combine the cornstarch and 2 tablespoons water in a small bowl. Whisk to combine, and then whisk into the cooking liquid in the crock pot. 10. Cook, uncovered, for 15 minutes or until the sauce is thick, stirring frequently. 11. Discard the bay leaves. Slice the pork, and serve hot with the sauce.

Italian Braised Pork

Prep time: 10 minutes | Cook time: 4⅓ hours | Serves 4

2½ pounds (1.1 kg) boneless pork shoulder
Coarse sea salt
Black pepper
2 tablespoons olive oil
1 large yellow onion, finely diced
3 cloves garlic, minced
1 stalk celery, finely diced
¾ teaspoon fennel seeds
½ cup dry red wine
1 (28-ounce / 794-g) can crushed tomatoes
4 cups prepared hot couscous, for serving

1. Season the pork with salt and pepper. 2. In a large skillet, heat the olive oil over medium-high heat. Cook the pork, turning occasionally, until browned on all sides, about 8 minutes. Transfer the pork to the crock pot. 3. Reduce the heat under the skillet to medium, and add the onion, garlic, celery, and fennel seeds. Cook, stirring often, until the onion is softened, about 4 minutes. 4. Add the wine and cook, stirring with a wooden spoon and scraping up the flavorful browned bits from the bottom of the pan, until the liquid is reduced by half, about 2 minutes. Add the wine mixture to the crock pot, and stir in the tomatoes. 5. Cover and cook on high for 4 hours, or until the pork is very tender, or on low for 8 hours. 6. Transfer the pork to a cutting board. Shred the meat into bite-size pieces. Discard any pieces of fat. 7. Skim the fat off the sauce in the crock pot and discard. Return the shredded pork to the crock pot and stir to combine. Cook the pork and sauce for 5 minutes to reheat. 8. Serve hot over the couscous.

Beef Meatballs in Garlic Cream Sauce

Prep time: 15 minutes | Cook time: 6 to 8 hours | Serves 4

For the Sauce:
1 cup low-sodium vegetable broth or low-sodium chicken broth
1 tablespoon extra-virgin olive oil
2 garlic cloves, minced
1 tablespoon dried onion flakes
1 teaspoon dried rosemary
2 tablespoons freshly squeezed lemon juice
Pinch sea salt
Pinch freshly ground black pepper

For the Meatballs:
1 pound (454 g) raw ground beef
1 large egg
2 tablespoons bread crumbs
1 teaspoon ground cumin
1 teaspoon salt
½ teaspoon freshly ground black pepper
TO FINISH
2 cups plain Greek yogurt
2 tablespoons chopped fresh parsley

Make the Sauce: In a medium bowl, whisk together the vegetable broth, olive oil, garlic, onion flakes, rosemary, lemon juice, salt, and pepper until combined. Make the Meatballs: In a large bowl, mix together the ground beef, egg, bread crumbs, cumin, salt, and pepper until combined. Shape the meat mixture into 10 to 12 (2½-inch) meatballs. 1. Pour the sauce into the crock pot. 2. Add the meatballs to the crock pot. 3. Cover the cooker and cook for 6 to 8 hours on Low heat. 4. Stir in the yogurt. Replace the cover on the cooker and cook for 15 to 30 minutes on Low heat, or until the sauce has thickened. 5. Garnish with fresh parsley for serving.

Beef Bourguignon with Egg Noodles

Prep time: 15 minutes | Cook time: 8 hours | Serves 8

2 pounds (907 g) lean beef stew meat
6 tablespoons all-purpose flour
2 large carrots, cut into 1-inch slices
16 ounces (454 g) pearl onions, peeled fresh or frozen, thawed
8 ounces (227 g) mushrooms, stems removed
2 garlic cloves, minced
¾ cup beef stock
½ cup dry red wine
¼ cup tomato paste
1½ teaspoons sea salt
½ teaspoon dried rosemary
¼ teaspoon dried thyme
½ teaspoon black pepper
8 ounces (227 g) uncooked egg noodles
¼ cup chopped fresh thyme leaves

1. Place the beef in a medium bowl, sprinkle with the flour, and toss well to coat. 2. Place the beef mixture, carrots, onions, mushrooms, and garlic in the crock pot. 3. Combine the stock, wine, tomato paste, salt, rosemary, thyme, and black pepper in a small bowl. Stir into the beef mixture. 4. Cover and cook on low for 8 hours. 5. Cook the noodles according to package directions, omitting any salt. 6. Serve the beef mixture over the noodles, sprinkled with the thyme.

Beef Ragù

Prep time: 15 minutes | Cook time: 4½ hours | Serves 6

1 medium yellow onion, diced small
3 cloves garlic, minced
6 tablespoons tomato paste
3 tablespoons chopped fresh oregano leaves (or 3 teaspoons dried oregano)
1 (4-pound / 1.8-kg) beef chuck roast, halved
Coarse sea salt
Black pepper
2 cups beef stock
2 tablespoons red wine vinegar

1. Combine the onion, garlic, tomato paste, and oregano in the crock pot. 2. Season the roast halves with salt and pepper and place on top of the onion mixture in the crock pot. Add the beef stock. 3. Cover and cook until meat is tender and can easily be pulled apart with a fork, on high for 4½ hours, or on low for 9 hours. Let cool 10 minutes. 4. Shred the meat while it is still in the crock pot using two forks. Stir the vinegar into the sauce. Serve hot, over pasta.

Beef Brisket with Onions

Prep time: 10 minutes | Cook time: 6 hours | Serves 6

1 large yellow onion, thinly sliced
2 garlic cloves, smashed and peeled
1 first cut of beef brisket (4 pounds / 1.8 kg), trimmed of excess fat
Coarse sea salt
Black pepper
2 cups chicken broth
2 tablespoons chopped fresh parsley leaves, for serving

1. Combine the onion and garlic in the crock pot. 2. Season the brisket with salt and pepper, and place, fat-side up, in the crock pot. 3. Add the broth to the crock pot. Cover and cook until the brisket is fork-tender, on high for about 6 hours. 4. Remove the brisket to a cutting board and thinly slice across the grain. 5. Serve with the onion and some cooking liquid, sprinkled with parsley.

Italian Pot Roast

Prep time: 15 minutes | Cook time: 6 hours | Serves 8

1 (3-pound / 1.4-kg) beef chuck roast, trimmed and halved crosswise
4 cloves garlic, halved lengthwise
1½ teaspoons coarse sea salt
1 teaspoon black pepper
1 tablespoon olive oil
1 large yellow onion, cut into 8 wedges
1¼ pounds (567 g) small white potatoes
1 (28-ounce / 794-g) can whole tomatoes in purée
1 tablespoon chopped fresh rosemary leaves (or 1 teaspoon dried and crumbled rosemary)

1. With a sharp paring knife, cut four slits in each of the beef roast halves, and stuff the slits with one-half of the garlic halves. Generously season the beef with the salt and pepper. 2. In a large skillet, heat the olive oil over medium-high heat, swirling to coat the bottom of the pan. Cook the beef until browned on all sides, about 5 minutes. 3. Combine the beef, onion, potatoes, tomatoes, rosemary, and the remaining garlic in the crock pot. 4. Cover and cook until the meat is fork-tender, on high for about 6 hours. 5. Transfer the meat to a cutting board. Thinly slice, and discard any fat or gristle. 6. Skim the fat from the top of the sauce in the crock pot. 7. Serve hot, dividing the beef and vegetables among the eight bowls, and generously spooning the sauce over the top.

Slow-Cooked Steak Fajitas

Prep time: 25 minutes | Cook time: 8½ to 9½ hours | Serves 12

1½ pounds (680 g) beef flank steak
1 (15-ounce / 425-g) can low-sodium diced tomatoes with garlic and onion, undrained
1 jalapeño pepper, seeded and chopped
2 garlic cloves, minced
1 teaspoon ground coriander
1 teaspoon ground cumin
1 teaspoon chili powder
½ teaspoon salt
2 medium onions, sliced
2 medium green bell peppers, julienned
2 medium sweet red bell peppers, julienned
1 tablespoon minced fresh parsley
2 teaspoons cornstarch
1 tablespoon water
12 (6-inch) flour tortillas, warmed
¾ cup fat-free sour cream
¾ cup low-sodium salsa

1. Slice steak thinly into strips across grain. Place in slow cooker. 2. Add tomatoes, jalapeño, garlic, coriander, cumin, chili powder, and salt. 3. Cover. Cook on low 7 hours. 4. Add onions, peppers, and parsley. 5. Cover. Cook 1 to 2 hours longer, or until meat is tender. 6. Combine cornstarch and water until smooth. Gradually stir into slow cooker. 7. Cover. Cook on high 30 minutes, or until slightly thickened. 8. Using a slotted spoon, spoon about ½ cup of meat mixture down the center of each tortilla. 9. Add 1 tablespoon sour cream and 1 tablespoon salsa to each. 10. Fold bottom of tortilla over filling and roll up.

Herbed Lamb Meatballs

Prep time: 10 minutes | Cook time: 6 to 8 hours | Serves 4

- 1 (28-ounce / 794-g) can no-salt-added diced tomatoes
- 2 garlic cloves, minced, divided
- 1 pound (454 g) raw ground lamb
- 1 small onion, finely diced, or 1 tablespoon dried onion flakes
- 1 large egg
- 2 tablespoons bread crumbs
- 1 teaspoon dried basil
- 1 teaspoon dried oregano
- 1 teaspoon dried rosemary
- 1 teaspoon dried thyme
- 1 teaspoon sea salt
- ½ teaspoon freshly ground black pepper

1. In a crock pot, combine the tomatoes and 1 clove of garlic. Stir to mix well. 2. In a large bowl, mix together the ground lamb, onion, egg, bread crumbs, basil, oregano, rosemary, thyme, salt, pepper, and the remaining 1 garlic clove until all of the ingredients are well-blended. Shape the meat mixture into 10 to 12 (2½-inch) meatballs. Put the meatballs in the crock pot. 3. Cover the cooker and cook for 6 to 8 hours on Low heat.

Moroccan Lamb Roast

Prep time: 15 minutes | Cook time: 6 to 8 hours | Serves 6

- ¼ cup low-sodium beef broth or low-sodium chicken broth
- 1 teaspoon dried ginger
- 1 teaspoon dried cumin
- 1 teaspoon ground turmeric
- 1 teaspoon paprika
- 1 teaspoon garlic powder
- 1 teaspoon red pepper flakes
- ½ teaspoon ground cinnamon
- ½ teaspoon ground coriander
- ½ teaspoon ground nutmeg
- ½ teaspoon ground cloves
- ½ teaspoon sea salt
- ½ teaspoon freshly ground black pepper
- 1 (3-pound/ 1.4-kg) lamb roast
- 4 ounces (113 g) carrots, chopped
- ¼ cup sliced onion
- ¼ cup chopped fresh mint

1. Pour the broth into a crock pot. 2. In a small bowl, stir together the ginger, cumin, turmeric, paprika, garlic powder, red pepper flakes, cinnamon, coriander, nutmeg, cloves, salt, and black pepper. Rub the spice mix firmly all over the lamb roast. Put the lamb in the crock pot and add the carrots and onion. 3. Top everything with the mint. 4. Cover the cooker and cook for 6 to 8 hours on Low heat.

Greek Lamb Chops

Prep time: 10 minutes | Cook time: 6 to 8 hours | Serves 6

- 3 pounds (1.4 kg) lamb chops
- ½ cup low-sodium beef broth
- Juice of 1 lemon
- 1 tablespoon extra-virgin olive oil
- 2 garlic cloves, minced
- 1 teaspoon dried oregano
- 1 teaspoon sea salt
- ½ teaspoon freshly ground black pepper

1. Put the lamb chops in a crock pot. 2. In a small bowl, whisk together the beef broth, lemon juice, olive oil, garlic, oregano, salt, and pepper until blended. Pour the sauce over the lamb chops. 3. Cover the cooker and cook for 6 to 8 hours on Low heat.

Osso Buco

Prep time: 10 minutes | Cook time: 8 to 10 hours | Serves 4

- 1 (15-ounce) can no-salt-added diced tomatoes
- 1 cup low-sodium beef broth
- 2 carrots, diced
- 1 small onion, diced
- 1 celery stalk, diced
- 2 garlic cloves, minced
- 1 teaspoon sea salt
- 2 to 3 pounds bone-in beef shanks
- 2 tablespoons Italian seasoning
- Handful fresh parsley

1. In a crock pot, combine the tomatoes, beef broth, carrots, onion, celery, garlic, and salt. Stir to mix well. 2. Generously season the beef shanks with the Italian seasoning. Nestle the shanks into the vegetable mixture. 3. Cover the cooker and cook for 8 to 10 hours on Low heat. 4. Garnish with fresh parsley for serving.

Kofta with Vegetables in Tomato Sauce

Prep time: 15 minutes | Cook time: 6 to 8 hours | Serves 4

- 1 pound (454 g) raw ground beef
- 1 small white or yellow onion, finely diced
- 2 garlic cloves, minced
- 1 tablespoon dried parsley
- 2 teaspoons ground coriander
- 1 teaspoon ground cumin
- ½ teaspoon sea salt
- ½ teaspoon freshly ground black pepper
- ¼ teaspoon ground nutmeg
- ¼ teaspoon dried mint
- ¼ teaspoon paprika
- 1 (28-ounce/ 794-g) can no-salt-added diced tomatoes
- 2 or 3 zucchini, cut into 1½-inch-thick rounds
- 4 ounces (113 g) mushrooms
- 1 large red onion, chopped
- 1 green bell pepper, seeded and chopped

1. In large bowl, mix together the ground beef, white or yellow onion, garlic, parsley, coriander, cumin, salt, pepper, nutmeg, mint, and paprika until well combined and all of the spices and onion are well blended into the meat. Form the meat mixture into 10 to 12 oval patties. Set aside. 2. In a crock pot, combine the tomatoes, zucchini, mushrooms, red onion, and bell pepper. Stir to mix well. 3. Place the kofta patties on top of the tomato mixture. 4. Cover the cooker and cook for 6 to 8 hours on Low heat.

Barbecued Ribs and Sauce

Prep time: 5 minutes | Cook time: 8 to 10 hours | Serves 10

- 3 pounds (1.4 kg) lean country-style pork ribs
- 2½ pounds (1.1 kg) sauerkraut, rinsed
- 2 cups low-sodium barbecue sauce
- 1 cup water

1. Place ribs on bottom of cooker. 2. Layer sauerkraut over ribs. 3. Mix barbecue sauce and water together. Pour over meat and kraut. 4. Cover. Cook on low 8 to 10 hours.

Mediterranean Pork with Olives

Prep time: 10 minutes | Cook time: 6 to 8 hours | Serves 4

1 cup low-sodium chicken broth
Juice of 1 lemon
2 garlic cloves, minced
1 teaspoon sea salt
1 teaspoon dried oregano
1 teaspoon dried parsley
½ teaspoon freshly ground black pepper
2 cups whole green olives, pitted
1 pint cherry tomatoes

1. Put the onion in a crock pot and arrange the pork chops on top. 2. In a small bowl, whisk together the chicken broth, lemon juice, garlic, salt, oregano, parsley, and pepper. Pour the sauce over the pork chops. Top with the olives and tomatoes. 3. Cover the cooker and cook for 6 to 8 hours on Low heat.

Balsamic Pork Tenderloin

Prep time: 10 minutes | Cook time: 6 to 8 hours | Serves 6

1 small onion, sliced
1 (3-pound/ 1.4-kg) pork tenderloin
1 cup balsamic vinegar
½ cup low-sodium beef broth
3 garlic cloves, crushed
2 tablespoons capers, undrained
1½ teaspoons olive oil
1 teaspoon dried rosemary
1 teaspoon sea salt
½ teaspoon freshly ground black pepper

1. Put the onion in a crock pot and arrange the pork tenderloin on top. 2. In a small bowl, whisk together the vinegar, beef broth, garlic, capers, olive oil, rosemary, salt, and pepper until combined. Pour the sauce over the pork. 3. Cover the cooker and cook for 6 to 8 hours on Low heat.

Pork Casserole with Fennel and Potatoes

Prep time: 20 minutes | Cook time: 6 to 8 hours | Serves 6

2 large fennel bulbs
3 pounds (1.4 kg) pork tenderloin, cut into 1½-inch pieces
2 pounds (907 g) red potatoes, quartered
1 cup low-sodium chicken broth
4 garlic cloves, minced
1½ teaspoons dried thyme
1 teaspoon dried parsley
1 teaspoon sea salt
Freshly ground black pepper
⅓ cup shredded Parmesan cheese

1. Cut the stalks off the fennel bulbs. Trim a little piece from the bottom of the bulbs to make them stable, then cut straight down through the bulbs to halve them. Cut the halves into quarters. Peel off and discard any wilted outer layers. Cut the fennel pieces crosswise into slices. 2. In a crock pot, combine the fennel, pork, and potatoes. Stir to mix well. 3. In a small bowl, whisk together the chicken broth, garlic, thyme, parsley, and salt until combined. Season with pepper and whisk again. Pour the sauce over the pork. 4. Cover the cooker and cook for 6 to 8 hours on Low heat. 5. Top with Parmesan cheese for serving.

Curried Beef

Prep time: 10 minutes | Cook time: 8 hours | Serves 6

1 pound (454 g) stew beef, trimmed and cut into 1-inch pieces
2 (15-ounce / 425-g) cans diced tomatoes, with their juice
1 pound (454 g) red potatoes, scrubbed and cut into 1-inch pieces
1 onion, sliced
4 large carrots, peeled and cut into 1-inch pieces
1 tablespoon grated fresh ginger
2 tablespoons curry powder
1 teaspoon ground cumin
1 teaspoon garlic powder
½ teaspoon sea salt

1. In your crock pot, combine all the ingredients. 2. Cover and cook on low for 8 hours. 3. Using a large spoon, skim the fat from the surface of the curry and discard.

Korean Barbecue Beef Sandwiches

Prep time: 10 minutes | Cook time: 8 hours | Serves 8

2 pounds (907 g) boneless chuck roast, trimmed of excess fat
½ cup rice vinegar
¼ cup olive oil
2 tablespoons Sriracha sauce
2 tablespoons low-sodium soy sauce
2 tablespoons honey
½ teaspoon toasted sesame oil
2 tablespoons grated fresh ginger
2 teaspoons garlic powder
8 whole-wheat hamburger buns

1. Put the chuck roast whole in the crock pot. 2. In a blender, blend the vinegar, olive oil, Sriracha, soy sauce, honey, sesame oil, ginger, and garlic powder until well mixed. Pour the mixture over the beef. 3. Cover and cook on low for 8 hours. 4. Transfer the roast to a cutting board and shred the meat with two forks. Skim the fat from the sauce and discard. Return the beef to the sauce and toss to coat. Serve on the buns.

Hungarian Beef

Prep time: 10 minutes | Cook time: 8¼ hours | Serves 5 to 6

2 pounds (907 g) beef chuck, cubed
1 onion, sliced
½ teaspoon garlic powder
½ cup ketchup
2 tablespoons Worcestershire sauce
1 tablespoon brown sugar
½ teaspoon salt
2 teaspoons paprika
½ teaspoon dry mustard
1 cup cold water
¼ cup flour
½ cup water

1. Place meat in slow cooker. Add onion. 2. Combine garlic powder, ketchup, Worcestershire sauce, brown sugar, salt, paprika, mustard, and 1 cup water. Pour over meat. 3. Cover. Cook on low 8 hours. 4. Dissolve flour in ½ cup water. Stir into meat mixture. Cook on high until thickened, about 10 minutes. 5. Serve.

Easy Crock Taco Filling

Prep time: 20 minutes | Cook time: 6 to 8 hours | Serves 4 to 6

1 large onion, chopped
1 pound (454 g) ground beef
2 (15-ounce / 425-g) cans chili beans
1 (15-ounce / 425-g) can Santa Fe, or Mexican, or Fiesta corn
¾ cup water
¼ teaspoon cayenne pepper (optional)
½ teaspoon garlic powder (optional)

1. Brown ground beef and chopped onion in a nonstick skillet. Drain. 2. Mix all ingredients together in the slow cooker, blending well. 3. Cover and cook on low for 6 to 8 hours.

Scalloped Potatoes and Ham

Prep time: 20 minutes | Cook time: 6 to 8 hours | Serves 4 to 6

2 to 3 pounds (907 g to 1.4 kg) potatoes, peeled, sliced, divided
1 (12-ounce / 340-g) package, or 1 pound (454 g), cooked ham, cubed, divided
1 small onion, chopped, divided
2 cups shredded Cheddar cheese, divided
1 (10¾-ounce / 305-g) can cream of celery or mushroom soup
Nonstick cooking spray

1. Spray the interior of the cooker with nonstick cooking spray. 2. Layer ⅓ each of the potatoes, ham, onion, and cheese into the cooker. 3. Repeat twice. 4. Spread soup on top. 5. Cover and cook on low 6 to 8 hours, or until potatoes are tender.

Frankfurter Succotash

Prep time: 10 minutes | Cook time: 4 to 6 hours | Serves 4 to 6

1 pound (454 g) hot dogs, cut into ½-inch slices
2 (10-ounce / 283-g) packages frozen succotash, thawed and drained
1 (10¾-ounce / 305-g) can Cheddar cheese soup

1. Stir all ingredients together in slow cooker. 2. Cover and cook on low 4 to 6 hours, or until vegetables are tender.

Good-Time Beef Brisket

Prep time: 10 minutes | Cook time: 8 to 10 hours | Serves 6 to 8

1 (3½- to 4-pound / 1.6- to 1.8-kg) beef brisket
1 can beer
2 cups tomato sauce
2 teaspoons prepared mustard
2 tablespoons balsamic vinegar
2 tablespoons Worcestershire sauce
1 teaspoon garlic powder
½ teaspoon ground allspice
2 tablespoons brown sugar
1 small green or red bell pepper, chopped
1 medium onion, chopped
1 teaspoon salt
½ teaspoon pepper

1. Place brisket in slow cooker. 2. Combine remaining ingredients. Pour over meat. 3. Cover. Cook on low 8 to 10 hours. 4. Remove meat from sauce. Slice very thinly. 5. Serve.

Pasta Bolognese

Prep time: 15 minutes | Cook time: 8 hours | Serves 6

1 pound (454 g) ground veal
3 carrots, peeled and finely chopped
2 onions, finely chopped
1 cup dry red wine
1 cup skim milk
2 tablespoons tomato paste
2 teaspoons garlic powder
2 teaspoons Italian seasoning
½ teaspoon sea salt
¼ teaspoon freshly ground black pepper
3 cups cooked whole-wheat pasta

1. Crumble the ground veal into your crock pot. 2. Add the carrots, onions, wine, skim milk, tomato paste, garlic powder, Italian seasoning, salt, and pepper. 3. Cover and cook on low for 8 hours. 4. Serve on top of the hot, cooked pasta.

Tortilla Casserole

Prep time: 20 minutes | Cook time: 3¼ to 4¼ hours | Serves 4

4 to 6 white or whole wheat tortillas, divided
1 pound (454 g) ground beef
1 envelope dry taco seasoning
1 (16-ounce / 454-g) can fat-free refried beans
1½ cups shredded low-fat cheese of your choice, divided
3 to 4 tablespoons sour cream (optional)
Nonstick cooking spray

1. Spray the inside of the cooker with nonstick cooking spray. Tear about ¾ of the tortillas into pieces and line the sides and bottom of the slow cooker. 2. Brown the ground beef in a nonstick skillet. Drain. Return to skillet and mix in taco seasoning. 3. Layer refried beans, browned and seasoned meat, 1 cup cheese, and sour cream if you wish, over tortilla pieces. 4. Place remaining tortilla pieces on top. 5. Sprinkle with remaining cheese. Cover and cook on low 3 to 4 hours.

German Pot Roast

Prep time: 15 minutes | Cook time: 4 to 8 hours | Serves 12

2 pounds (907 g) boneless, lean pork roast
1 teaspoon garlic salt
½ teaspoon black pepper
4 large sweet potatoes, peeled and diced
2 medium onions, sliced
½ teaspoon dried oregano
1 (14½-ounce / 411-g) can low-sodium tomatoes

1. Place pork roast in slow cooker. 2. Sprinkle with garlic salt and pepper. 3. Add remaining ingredients. 4. Cover. Cook on low 7 to 8 hours, or on high 4 to 5 hours.

Meal-in-One-Casserole

Prep time: 20 minutes | Cook time: 4 hours | Serves 4 to 6

- 1 pound (454 g) ground beef
- 1 medium onion, chopped
- 1 medium green pepper, chopped
- 1 (15¼-ounce / 432-g) can whole-kernel corn, drained
- 1 (4-ounce / 113-g) can mushrooms, drained
- 1 teaspoon salt
- ¼ teaspoon pepper
- 1 (11-ounce / 312-g) jar salsa
- 5 cups medium egg noodles, uncooked
- 1 (28-ounce / 794-g) can diced tomatoes, undrained
- 1 cup shredded Cheddar cheese

1. Cook beef and onion in saucepan over medium heat until meat is no longer pink. Drain. Transfer to slow cooker. 2. Top with green pepper, corn, and mushrooms. Sprinkle with salt and pepper. Pour salsa over mushrooms. Cover and cook on low 3 hours. 3. Cook noodles according to package in separate pan. Drain and add to slow cooker after mixture in cooker has cooked for 3 hours. Top with tomatoes. Sprinkle with cheese. 4. Cover. Cook on low 1 more hour.

Ed's Chili

Prep time: 15 minutes | Cook time: 2 to 2½ hours | Serves 4 to 6

- 1 pound (454 g) ground beef
- 1 package dry taco seasoning mix
- Half a 1 (12-ounce / 340-g) jar salsa
- 1 (16-ounce / 454-g) can kidney beans, undrained
- 1 (15-ounce / 425-g) can black beans, undrained
- 1 (14½-ounce / 411-g) can diced tomatoes, undrained
- Pinch of sugar
- Shredded cheese
- Chopped onions
- Sour cream
- Diced fresh tomatoes
- Guacamole
- Sliced black olives

1. Brown ground beef in skillet. Drain. 2. Combine first 7 ingredients in slow cooker. 3. Cover. Heat on high until mixture comes to boil. Reduce heat to low. Simmer 1½ hours. 4. To reduce liquids, continue cooking uncovered. 5. Top individual servings with choice of shredded cheese, onions, a dollop of sour cream, fresh diced tomatoes, guacamole, and sliced olives.

Shepherd's Pie

Prep time: 40 minutes | Cook time: 3 hours | Serves 3 to 4

- 1 pound (454 g) ground pork
- 1 tablespoon vinegar
- 1¼ teaspoons salt, divided
- ¼ teaspoon hot pepper
- 1 teaspoon paprika
- ¼ teaspoon dried oregano
- ¼ teaspoon black pepper
- 1 teaspoon chili powder
- 1 small onion, chopped
- 1 (15-ounce / 425-g) can corn, drained
- 3 large potatoes
- ¼ cup milk
- 1 teaspoon butter
- Dash of pepper
- Shredded cheese

1. Combine pork, vinegar, and spices except ¼ teaspoon salt. Cook in skillet until brown. Add onion and cook until onions begin to glaze. Spread in bottom of slow cooker. 2. Spread corn over meat. 3. Boil potatoes until soft. Mash with milk, butter, ¼ teaspoon salt, and dash of pepper. Spread over meat and corn. 4. Cover. Cook on low 3 hours. Sprinkle top with cheese a few minutes before serving.

Sweet and Sour Sausage Dish

Prep time: 15 minutes | Cook time: 3 to 6 hours | Serves 8 to 10

- 2 (20-ounce / 567-g) cans pineapple chunks, drained
- 2 large green peppers, sliced into bite-sized strips
- 3 (16-ounce / 454-g) packages smoked sausage, cut into 1-inch chunks
- 1 (18-ounce / 510-g) bottle honey barbecue sauce

1. Combine pineapples, peppers, and sausage chunks in slow cooker. 2. Pour barbecue sauce over mixture and stir. 3. Cover and cook on high 3 hours, or on low 6 hours, or until dish is heated through.

Barbecued Spareribs

Prep time: 5 minutes | Cook time: 6 to 8 hours | Serves 4

- 1 (4-pound / 1.8-kg) country-style spareribs, cut into serving-size pieces
- 1 (10¾-ounce / 305-g) can tomato soup
- ½ cup cider vinegar
- ½ cup brown sugar
- 1 tablespoon soy sauce
- 1 teaspoon celery seed
- 1 teaspoon salt
- 1 teaspoon chili powder
- Dash cayenne pepper

1. Place ribs in slow cooker. 2. Combine remaining ingredients and pour over ribs. 3. Cover. Cook on low 6 to 8 hours. 4. Skim fat from juices before serving.

Slow Cooker Chili

Prep time: 25 minutes | Cook time: 6 to 12 hours | Serves 8 to 10

- 3 pounds (1.4 kg) beef stewing meat, browned
- 2 cloves garlic, minced
- ¼ teaspoon pepper
- ½ teaspoon cumin
- ¼ teaspoon dry mustard
- 1 (7½-ounce / 213-g) can jalapeño relish
- 1 cup beef broth
- 1 to 1½ onions, chopped, according to your taste preference
- ½ teaspoon salt
- ½ teaspoon dried oregano
- 1 tablespoon chili powder
- 1 (7-ounce / 198-g) can green chilies, chopped
- 1 (14½-ounce / 411-g) can stewed tomatoes, chopped
- 1 (15-ounce / 425-g) can tomato sauce
- 2 (15-ounce / 425-g) cans red kidney beans, rinsed and drained
- 2 (15-ounce / 425-g) cans pinto beans, rinsed and drained

1. Combine all ingredients except kidney and pinto beans in slow cooker. 2. Cover. Cook on low 10 to 12 hours, or on high 6 to 7 hours. Add beans halfway through cooking time. 3. Serve.

Apple-Raisin Ham

Prep time: 15 minutes | Cook time: 4 to 5 hours | Serves 6

1½ pounds (680 g) fully cooked ham
1 (21-ounce / 595-g) can apple pie filling
⅓ cup golden raisins
⅓ cup orange juice
¼ teaspoon ground cinnamon
2 tablespoons water

1. Cut ham slices into six equal pieces. 2. In a mixing bowl, combine pie filling, raisins, orange juice, cinnamon, and water. 3. Place 1 slice of ham in your slow cooker. Spread ⅙ of the apple mixture over top. 4. Repeat layers until you have used all the ham and apple mixture. 5. Cover and cook on low 4 to 5 hours.

Chili con Carne

Prep time: 15 minutes | Cook time: 5 to 6 hours | Serves 8

1 pound (454 g) ground beef
1 cup chopped onions
¾ cup chopped green peppers
1 garlic clove, minced
1 (14½-ounce / 411-g) can tomatoes, cut up
1 (16-ounce / 454-g) can kidney beans, drained
1 (8-ounce / 227-g) can tomato sauce
2 teaspoons chili powder
½ teaspoon dried basil

1. Brown beef, onion, green pepper, and garlic in saucepan. Drain. 2. Combine all ingredients in slow cooker. 3. Cover. Cook on low 5 to 6 hours. 4. Serve.

Fajita Steak

Prep time: 10 minutes | Cook time: 6 to 8 hours | Serves 6

1 (15-ounce / 425-g) can tomatoes with green chilies
¼ cup salsa, your choice of heat
1 (8-ounce / 227-g) can tomato sauce
2 pounds (907 g) round steak, cut in 2-inch × 4-inch strips
1 envelope dry Fajita spice mix
1 cup water (optional)

1. Combine all ingredients—except water—in your slow cooker. 2. Cover and cook on low 6 to 8 hours, or until meat is tender but not overcooked. 3. Check meat occasionally to make sure it isn't cooking dry. If it begins to look dry, stir in water, up to 1 cup.

Amazing Meat Loaf

Prep time: 15 minutes | Cook time: 2 to 8 hours | Serves 8

½ cup ketchup, divided
2 pounds (907 g) ground beef
2 eggs
⅔ cup dry quick oats
1 envelope dry onion soup mix

1. Reserve 2 tablespoons ketchup. Combine ground beef, eggs, dry oats, soup mix, and remaining ketchup. Shape into loaf. Place in slow cooker. 2. Top with remaining ketchup. 3. Cover and cook on low for 6 to 8 hours, or on high for 2 to 4 hours.

Chili and Cheese on Rice

Prep time: 15 minutes | Cook time: 4 hours | Serves 6

1 pound (454 g) ground beef
1 onion, diced
1 teaspoon dried basil
1 teaspoon dried oregano
1 (16-ounce / 454-g) can light red kidney beans
1 (15½-ounce / 439-g) can chili beans
1 pint stewed tomatoes, drained
Rice, cooked
Shredded Cheddar cheese

1. Brown ground beef and onion in skillet. Season with basil and oregano. 2. Combine all ingredients except rice and cheese in slow cooker. 3. Cover. Cook on low 4 hours. 4. Serve over cooked rice. Top with cheese.

Beef a la Mode

Prep time: 10 minutes | Cook time: 6 to 8 hours | Serves 6

1 (2-pound / 907-g) boneless beef roast, cut into 6 serving-size pieces
½ pound (227 g) salt pork or bacon, cut up
3 onions, chopped
Pepper to taste
Water

1. Place beef and pork in slow cooker. 2. Sprinkle onions over top of meat. 3. Add pepper to taste. 4. Pour water in alongside meat, about 1-inch deep. 5. Cook on low 6 to 8 hours. 6. Serve.

Cabbage and Corned Beef

Prep time: 15 minutes | Cook time: 5 to 10 hours | Serves 12

3 large carrots, cut into chunks
1 cup chopped celery
1 teaspoon salt
½ teaspoon black pepper
1 cup water
1 (4-pound / 1.8-kg) corned beef
1 large onion, cut into pieces
4 potatoes, peeled and chunked
Half a small head of cabbage, cut in wedges

1. Place carrots, celery, seasonings, and water in slow cooker. 2. Add beef. Cover with onions. 3. Cover. Cook on low 8 to 10 hours, or on high 5 to 6 hours. (If your schedule allows, this dish has especially good taste and texture if you begin it on high for 1 hour, and then turn it to low for 5 to 6 hours, before going on to Step 4.) 4. Lift corned beef out of cooker and add potatoes, pushing them to bottom of slow cooker. Return beef to cooker. 5. Cover. Cook on low 1 hour. 6. Lift corned beef out of cooker and add cabbage, pushing the wedges down into the broth. Return beef to cooker. 7. Cover. Cook on low 1 more hour. 8. Remove corned beef. Cool and slice on the diagonal. Serve surrounded by vegetables.

Shredded Pork

Prep time: 10 minutes | Cook time: 4 to 10 hours | Serves 8 to 12

1 (3- to 4-pound / 1.4- to 1.8-kg) pork butt roast
1½ envelopes taco seasoning
3 to 5 cloves garlic, sliced, according to your taste preference
1 large onion, quartered
1 (4-ounce / 113-g) can whole green chilies, drained
1 cup water

1. Place roast in slow cooker. 2. In a bowl, mix all remaining ingredients together. Spoon over meat in cooker. 3. Cover and cook on low 8 to 10 hours, or on high 4 to 6 hours, or until meat is tender but not dry. 4. Place pork on a platter and shred with 2 forks. Stir shredded meat back into sauce. 5. Serve.

Barbecued Bacon and Beans

Prep time: 20 minutes | Cook time: 3 to 8 hours | Serves 4 to 6

1 pound (454 g) bacon
¼ cup chopped onions
¾ cup ketchup
½ cup brown sugar
3 teaspoons Worcestershire sauce
¾ teaspoon salt
4 cups green beans

1. Brown bacon in skillet until crisp and then break into pieces. Reserve 2 tablespoons bacon drippings. 2. Sauté onions in bacon drippings. 3. Combine ketchup, brown sugar, Worcestershire sauce, and salt. Stir into bacon and onions. 4. Pour mixture over green beans and mix lightly. 5. Pour into slow cooker and cook on high 3 to 4 hours, or on low 6 to 8 hours.

Onion-Mushroom Pot Roast

Prep time: 10 minutes | Cook time: 5 to 12 hours | Serves 6

1 (3- to 4-pound / 1.4- to 1.8-kg) pot roast or chuck roast
1 (4-ounce / 113-g) can sliced mushrooms, drained
1 teaspoon salt
¼ teaspoon pepper
½ cup beef broth
1 envelope dry onion soup mix

1. Place pot roast in your slow cooker. 2. Add mushrooms, salt, and pepper. 3. In a small bowl, mix beef broth with the onion soup mix. Spoon over the roast. Cover and cook on high 5 to 6 hours, or on 4. Low 10 to 12 hours, or until meat is tender but not dry.

Pot-Luck Wiener Bake

Prep time: 8 minutes | Cook time: 3 hours | Serves 6

4 cups cooked potatoes, peeled and diced
1 (10¾-ounce / 305-g) can cream of mushroom soup
1 cup mayonnaise
1 cup sauerkraut, drained
1 pound (454 g) wieners, sliced

1. Mix all ingredients in slow cooker. 2. Cover and cook on low 3 hours.

Dilled Pot Roast

Prep time: 5 minutes | Cook time: 7¼ to 9¼ hours | Serves 8

1 (2¾-pound / 1.3-kg) beef pot roast
1 teaspoon salt
¼ teaspoon black pepper
2 teaspoons dried dill weed, divided
¼ cup water
2 tablespoons wine vinegar
4 tablespoons flour
½ cup water
2 cups fat-free sour cream

1. Sprinkle both sides of beef with salt, pepper, and 1 teaspoon dill weed. Place in slow cooker. 2. Add ¼ cup water and vinegar. 3. Cover. Cook on low 7 to 9 hours. 4. Remove meat from pot. Turn cooker to high. 5. Stir flour into ½ cup water. Stir into meat drippings. 6. Stir in additional 1 teaspoon dill weed if you wish. 7. Cover. Cook on high 5 minutes. 8. Stir in sour cream. 9. Cover. Cook on high another 5 minutes. 10. Slice beef and serve.

Pork Chops and Stuffing with Curry

Prep time: 10 minutes | Cook time: 6 to 7 hours | Serves 3 to 4

1 box stuffing mix
1 cup water
1 (10¾-ounce / 305-g) can cream of mushroom soup
1 teaspoon, or more, curry powder, according to your taste preference
3 to 4 pork chops

1. Combine stuffing mix and water. Place half in bottom of slow cooker. 2. Combine soup and curry powder. Pour half over stuffing. Place pork chops on top. 3. Spread remaining stuffing over pork chops. Pour rest of soup on top. 4. Cover. Cook on low 6 to 7 hours. 5. Serve.

Perfect Pork Chops

Prep time: 15 minutes | Cook time: 3 to 4 hours | Serves 2

2 small onions
2 (¾-inch thick) boneless, center loin pork chops, frozen
Fresh ground pepper to taste
1 chicken bouillon cube
¼ cup hot water
2 tablespoons prepared mustard with white wine
Fresh parsley sprigs or lemon slices (optional)

1. Cut off ends of onions and peel. Cut onions in half crosswise to make 4 thick "wheels." Place in bottom of slow cooker. 2. Sear both sides of frozen chops in heavy skillet. Place in cooker on top of onions. Sprinkle with pepper. 3. Dissolve bouillon cube in hot water. Stir in mustard. Pour into slow cooker. 4. Cover. Cook on high 3 to 4 hours. 5. Serve topped with fresh parsley sprigs or lemon slices, if desired.

Easy Company Beef

Prep time: 5 minutes | Cook time: 10 hours | Serves 8

3 pounds (1.4 kg) stewing beef, cubed
1 (10¾-ounce / 305-g) can cream of mushroom soup
1 (7-ounce / 198-g) jar mushrooms, undrained
½ cup red wine
1 envelope dry onion soup mix

1. Combine all ingredients in slow cooker. 2. Cover. Cook on low 10 hours. 3. Serve.

Machaca Beef

Prep time: 5 minutes | Cook time: 10 to 12 hours | Serves 12

1 (1½-pound / 680-g) lean beef roast
1 large onion, sliced
1 (4-ounce / 113-g) can chopped green chilies
2 low-sodium beef bouillon cubes
1½ teaspoons dry mustard
½ teaspoon garlic powder
¾ teaspoon seasoned salt
½ teaspoon black pepper
1 cup low-sodium salsa

1. Combine all ingredients except salsa in slow cooker. Add just enough water to cover. 2. Cover cooker and cook on low 10 to 12 hours, or until beef is tender. Drain and reserve liquid. 3. Shred beef using two forks to pull it apart. 4. Combine beef, salsa, and enough of the reserved liquid to make a desired consistency. 5. Serve.

Turkey-Beef Loaf

Prep time: 10 minutes | Cook time: 4 to 10 hours | Serves 8

½ pound (227 g) extra-lean ground beef
1 pound (454 g) lean ground turkey
1 medium onion, chopped
2 eggs
⅔ cup dry quick oats
1 envelope dry onion soup mix
½ to 1 teaspoon liquid smoke
1 teaspoon dry mustard
1 cup ketchup, divided
Nonfat cooking spray

1. Mix beef, turkey, and chopped onion thoroughly. 2. Combine with eggs, oats, dry soup mix, liquid smoke, mustard, and all but 2 tablespoons of ketchup. 3. Shape into loaf and place in slow cooker sprayed with nonfat cooking spray. Top with remaining ketchup. 4. Cover. Cook on low 8 to 10 hours, or on high 4 to 6 hours.

Spicy Pork Chops

Prep time: 5 minutes | Cook time: 6 to 8 hours | Serves 4

4 frozen pork chops
1 cup Italian salad dressing
½ cup brown sugar
⅓ cup prepared spicy mustard

Beef and Noodle Casserole

Prep time: 20 minutes | Cook time: 4 hours | Serves 10

1 pound (454 g) extra-lean ground beef
1 medium onion, chopped
1 medium green bell pepper, chopped
1 (17-ounce / 482-g) can whole-kernel corn, drained
1 (4-ounce / 113-g) can mushroom stems and pieces, drained
1 teaspoon salt
¼ teaspoon black pepper
1 (11-ounce / 312-g) jar salsa
5 cups dry medium egg noodles, cooked
1 (28-ounce / 794-g) can low-sodium diced tomatoes, undrained
1 cup low-fat shredded Cheddar cheese

1. Brown ground beef and onion in nonstick skillet over medium heat. Transfer to slow cooker. 2. Top with remaining ingredients in order listed. 3. Cover. Cook on low 4 hours.

Barbecued Hamburgers

Prep time: 20 minutes | Cook time: 3 to 6 hours | Makes 4 sandwiches

1 pound (454 g) ground beef
¼ cup chopped onions
3 tablespoons ketchup
1 teaspoon salt
1 egg, beaten
¼ cup seasoned bread crumbs
1 (18-ounce / 510-g) bottle of your favorite barbecue sauce

1. Combine beef, onions, ketchup, salt, egg, and bread crumbs. Form into 4 patties. Brown both sides lightly in skillet. Place in slow cooker. 2. Cover with barbecue sauce. 3. Cover. Cook on high 3 hours, or on low 6 hours.

Carolina Pot Roast

Prep time: 20 minutes | Cook time: 3 hours | Serves 3 to 4

3 medium-large sweet potatoes, peeled and cut into 1-inch chunks
½ cup brown sugar
1 (1-pound / 454-g) pork roast
Scant ¼ teaspoon cumin
Salt to taste
Water

1. Place sweet potatoes in bottom of slow cooker. Sprinkle brown sugar over potatoes. 2. Heat nonstick skillet over medium-high heat. Add roast and brown on all sides. Sprinkle meat with cumin and salt while browning. Place pork on top of potatoes. 3. Add an inch of water to the cooker, being careful not to wash the seasoning off the meat. 4. Cover and cook on low 3 hours, or until meat and potatoes are tender but not dry or mushy.

1. Place pork chops in slow cooker. 2. Mix remaining 3 ingredients together in a bowl. Pour over chops. 3. Cover and cook on low 6 to 8 hours, or until meat is tender but not dry.

Tender Pork Roast

Prep time: 10 minutes | Cook time: 3 to 8 hours | Serves 8

1 (3-pound / 1.4-kg) boneless pork roast, cut in half
1 (8-ounce / 227-g) can tomato sauce
¾ cup soy sauce
½ cup sugar
2 teaspoons dry mustard

1. Place roast in slow cooker. 2. Combine remaining ingredients in a bowl. Pour over roast. 3. Cover and cook on low 6 to 8 hours, or on high 3 to 4 hours, or until meat is tender but not dry. 4. Remove roast from slow cooker to a serving platter. Discard juices or thicken for gravy.

Roast Beef with Ginger Ale

Prep time: 15 minutes | Cook time: 8 to 10 hours | Serves 6 to 8

1 (3-pound / 1.4-kg) beef roast
½ cup flour
1 envelope dry onion soup mix
1 envelope dry brown gravy mix
2 cups ginger ale

1. Coat the roast with flour. Reserve any flour that doesn't stick to the roast. Place roast in your slow cooker. 2. Combine the dry soup mix, gravy mix, remaining flour, and ginger ale in a bowl. Mix well. 3. Pour sauce over the roast. 4. Cover and cook on low 8 to 10 hours or until the roast is tender. 5. Serve.

Sausage in Spaghetti Sauce

Prep time: 15 minutes | Cook time: 3 to 6 hours | Serves 10 to 12

4 pounds (1.8 kg) sausage of your choice
1 red bell pepper
1 green bell pepper
1 large onion
1 (26-ounce / 737-g) jar spaghetti sauce

1. Heat nonstick skillet over medium-high heat. Brown sausage in nonstick skillet in batches. As a batch is finished browning on all sides, cut into 1½-inch chunks. Then place in slow cooker. 2. Slice or chop peppers and onion and put on top of sausage. 3. Add spaghetti sauce over all. 4. Cover and cook on low 6 hours, or on high 3 hours.

Golden Autumn Stew

Prep time: 40 minutes | Cook time: 2 to 4 hours | Serves 8 to 10

2 cups cubed Yukon gold potatoes
2 cups cubed, peeled sweet potatoes
2 cups cubed, peeled butternut squash
1 cup cubed, peeled rutabaga
1 cup diced carrots
1 cup sliced celery
1 pound (454 g) smoked sausage
2 cups apple juice or cider
1 tart apple, thinly sliced
Salt to taste
Pepper to taste
1 tablespoon sugar or honey

1. Combine vegetables in slow cooker. 2. Place ring of sausage on top. 3. Add apple juice and apple slices. 4. Cover. Cook on high 2 hours and on low 4 hours, or until vegetables are tender. Do not stir. 5. To serve, remove sausage ring. Season with salt, pepper, and sugar as desired. Place vegetables in bowl. Slice meat into rings and place on top. 6. Serve.

Potatoes and Green Beans with Ham

Prep time: 5 minutes | Cook time: 6 to 8 hours | Serves 4

1 (1-pound / 454-g) ham slice, cut in chunks
2 cups green beans, frozen or fresh
2 cups red-skinned potatoes, quartered, but not peeled
½ cup water
½ cup chopped onion
4 slices American cheese

1. Place all ingredients, except cheese, in slow cooker. Gently mix together. 2. Cover and cook on low 6 to 8 hours, or until vegetables are tender. 3. One hour before the end of the cooking time, lay cheese slices over top.

Noodle Hamburger Dish

Prep time: 20 minutes | Cook time: 3 to 4 hours | Serves 10

1½ pounds (680 g) ground beef, browned and drained
1 green pepper, diced
1 quart whole tomatoes
1 (10¾-ounce / 305-g) can cream of mushroom soup
1 large onion, diced
1½ tablespoons Worcestershire sauce
1 (8-ounce / 227-g) package noodles, uncooked
1 teaspoon salt
¼ teaspoon pepper
1 cup shredded cheese

1. Combine all ingredients except cheese in slow cooker. 2. Cover. Cook on high 3 to 4 hours. 3. Sprinkle with cheese before serving.

Hot Dogs and Noodles

Prep time: 25 minutes | Cook time: 5 to 6 hours | Serves 6

1 (8-ounce / 227-g) package medium egg noodles, cooked and drained
1¼ cups grated Parmesan cheese
1 cup milk
¼ cup butter or margarine, melted
1 tablespoon flour
¼ teaspoon salt
1 (1-pound / 454-g) package hot dogs, sliced
¼ cup packed brown sugar
¼ cup mayonnaise
2 tablespoons prepared mustard

1. Place noodles, cheese, milk, butter, flour, and salt in slow cooker. Mix well. 2. Combine hot dogs with remaining ingredients. Spoon evenly over noodles. 3. Cover. Cook on low 5 to 6 hours.

Saucy Pork Chops

Prep time: 15 minutes | Cook time: 6 to 8 hours | Serves 5

5 to 6 center-cut loin pork chops
3 tablespoons oil
1 onion, sliced
1 green pepper, cut in strips
1 (8-ounce / 227-g) can tomato sauce
3 to 4 tablespoons brown sugar
1 tablespoon vinegar
1½ teaspoons salt
1 to 2 teaspoons Worcestershire sauce

1. Brown chops in oil in skillet. Transfer to slow cooker. 2. Add remaining ingredients to cooker. 3. Cover. Cook on low 6 to 8 hours. 4. Serve.

Sausage-Sauerkraut Supper

Prep time: 20 minutes | Cook time: 8 to 9 hours | Serves 10 to 12

4 cups cubed carrots
4 cups cubed red potatoes
2 (14-ounce / 397-g) cans sauerkraut, rinsed and drained
2½ pounds (1.1 kg) fresh Polish sausage, cut into 3-inch pieces
1 medium onion, thinly sliced
3 garlic cloves, minced
1½ cups dry white wine or chicken broth
½ teaspoon pepper
1 teaspoon caraway seeds

1. Layer carrots, potatoes, and sauerkraut in slow cooker. 2. Brown sausage in skillet. Transfer to slow cooker. Reserve 1 tablespoon drippings in skillet. 3. Sauté onion and garlic in drippings until tender. Stir in wine. Bring to boil. Stir to loosen brown bits. Stir in pepper and caraway seeds. Pour over sausage. 4. Cover. Cook on low 8 to 9 hours.

8-Hour Tangy Beef

Prep time: 5 minutes | Cook time: 8 to 9 hours | Serves 6 to 8

1 (3½- to 4-pound / 1.6- to 1.8-kg) beef roast
1 (12-ounce / 340-g) can ginger ale
1½ cups ketchup

1. Put beef in slow cooker. 2. Pour ginger ale and ketchup over roast. 3. Cover. Cook on low 8 to 9 hours. 4. Shred with 2 forks and serve.

Beef Roulades

Prep time: 20 minutes | Cook time: 4 to 6 hours | Serves 12

4 pounds (1.8 kg) round steak
4 cups prepared packaged herb-seasoned stuffing mix
2 (10¾-ounce / 305-g) cans cream of mushroom soup
1 to 2 cups water

1. Cut steak into 12 long pieces. Pound each piece until thin and flattened. 2. Place ⅓ cup prepared stuffing on each slice of meat. Roll up and fasten with toothpick. Place in slow cooker. 3. In a bowl, mix soup and water together and then pour over steak. 4. Cover and cook on high 4 to 6 hours, or until meat is tender but not overcooked.

Italian Spaghetti Sauce

Prep time: 20 minutes | Cook time: 8 to 9 hours | Serves 8 to 10

2 pounds (907 g) sausage or ground beef
3 medium onions, chopped (about 2¼ cups)
2 cups sliced mushrooms
6 garlic cloves, minced
2 (14½-ounce / 411-g) cans diced tomatoes, undrained
1 (29-ounce / 822-g) can tomato sauce
1 (12-ounce / 340-g) can tomato paste
2 tablespoons dried basil
1 tablespoon dried oregano
1 tablespoon sugar
1 teaspoon salt
½ teaspoon crushed red pepper flakes

1. Cook sausage, onions, mushrooms, and garlic in skillet over medium heat for 10 minutes. Drain. Transfer to slow cooker. 2. Stir in remaining ingredients. 3. Cover. Cook on low 8 to 9 hours.

Beef Stew with Shiitake Mushrooms

Prep time: 10 minutes | Cook time: 8 to 9 hours | Serves 4 to 6

12 new potatoes, cut into quarters
½ cup chopped onions
1 (8-ounce / 227-g) package baby carrots
1 (3.4-ounce / 96-g) package fresh shiitake mushrooms, sliced, or 2 cups regular white mushrooms, sliced
1 (16-ounce / 454-g) can whole tomatoes
1 (14½-ounce / 411-g) can beef broth
½ cup flour
1 tablespoon Worcestershire sauce
1 teaspoon salt
1 teaspoon sugar
1 teaspoon dried marjoram leaves
¼ teaspoon pepper
1 pound (454 g) beef stewing meat, cubed

1. Combine all ingredients except beef in slow cooker. Add beef. 2. Cover. Cook on low 8 to 9 hours. Stir well before serving.

Holiday Meatballs

Prep time: 10 minutes | Cook time: 3 to 6 hours | Serves 15

2 (15-ounce / 425-g) bottles hot ketchup
2 cups blackberry wine
2 (12-ounce / 340-g) jars apple jelly
2 pounds (907 g) frozen, precooked meatballs, or your own favorite meatballs, cooked

1. Heat ketchup, wine, and jelly in slow cooker on high. 2. Add frozen meatballs. 3. Cover. Cook on high 4 to 6 hours.

Italian Beef au Jus

Prep time: 10 minutes | Cook time: 8 hours | Serves 8

1 (3- to 5-pound / 1.4- to 2.3-kg) boneless beef roast
1 (10-ounce / 283-g) package dry au jus mix
1 package dry Italian salad dressing mix
1 (14½-ounce / 411-g) can beef broth
Half a soup can water

1. Place beef in slow cooker. 2. Combine remaining ingredients. Pour over roast. 3. Cover. Cook on low 8 hours. 4. Slice meat before serving.

Sausage and Scalloped Potatoes

Prep time: 20 minutes | Cook time: 4 to 10 hours | Serves 8

2 pounds (907 g) potatoes, sliced ¼-inch thick, divided
1 pound (454 g) fully cooked smoked sausage link, sliced ½-inch thick, divided
2 medium-sized onions, chopped, divided
1 (10¾-ounce / 305-g) can condensed Cheddar cheese soup, divided
1 (10¾-ounce / 305-g) can condensed cream of celery soup
1 (10-ounce / 283-g) package frozen peas, thawed (optional)
Nonstick cooking spray

1. Spray interior of cooker with nonstick cooking spray. 2. Layer into the cooker one-third of the potatoes, one-third of the sausage, one-third of the onion, and one-third of the Cheddar cheese soup. 3. Repeat layers two more times. 4. Top with cream of celery soup. 5. Cover and cook on low 8 to 10 hours, or on high 4 to 5 hours, or until vegetables are tender. 6. If you wish, stir in peas. Cover and let stand 5 minutes. (If you forgot to thaw the peas, stir them in but let stand 10 minutes.)

Magic Meat Loaf

Prep time: 20 minutes | Cook time: 9 to 11 hours | Serves 6

1 egg, beaten
¼ cup milk
1½ teaspoons salt
2 slices bread, crumbled
1½ pounds (680 g) ground beef
Half a small onion, chopped
2 tablespoons chopped green peppers
2 tablespoons chopped celery
Ketchup
Green pepper rings
4 to 6 potatoes, cubed
3 tablespoons butter, melted

1. Combine egg, milk, salt, and bread crumbs in large bowl. 2. Allow bread crumbs to soften. Add meat, onions, green peppers, and celery. Shape into loaf and place off to the side in slow cooker. 3. Top with ketchup and green pepper rings. 4. Toss potatoes with melted butter. Spoon into cooker alongside meat loaf. 5. Cover. Cook on high 1 hour, then on low 8 to 10 hours.

Party Meatball Subs

Prep time: 15 minutes | Cook time: 8 to 10 hours | Serves 30

1 (10-pound / 4.5-kg) bag prepared meatballs
1 large onion, sliced
10 good-sized fresh mushrooms, sliced
2 (26-ounce / 737-g) jars spaghetti sauce, your choice of flavors
2 cloves garlic, minced
1 pound (454 g) Mozzarella cheese, shredded (optional)

1. Combine all ingredients except the cheese in your slow cooker. Stir well to coat the meatballs with sauce. 2. Cover and cook on low 8 to 10 hours, stirring occasionally throughout cooking time to mix juices. 3. Sprinkle Mozzarella cheese and serve, if you wish.

Ground Beef Pizza Fondue

Prep time: 10 minutes | Cook time: 2 to 3 hours | Serves 8 to 12

1 pound (454 g) ground beef
2 cans pizza sauce with cheese
8 ounces (227 g) Cheddar cheese, shredded
8 ounces (227 g) Mozzarella cheese, shredded
1 teaspoon dried oregano
½ teaspoon fennel seed (optional)
1 tablespoon cornstarch

1. Brown beef, crumble fine, and drain. 2. Combine all ingredients in slow cooker. 3. Cover. Heat on low 2 to 3 hours. 4. Serve.

Mushrooms and Cheese Meatballs

Prep time: 10 minutes | Cook time: 6 to 8 hours | Serves 12 to 15

1 (3- to 4-pound / 1.4- to 1.8-kg) bag prepared meatballs
3 (10¾-ounce / 305-g) cans cream of mushroom or cream of celery, soup
1 (4-ounce / 113-g) can button mushrooms
1 (16-ounce / 454-g) jar Cheese Whiz
1 medium onion, diced

1. Combine all ingredients in slow cooker. 2. Cover. Cook on low 6 to 8 hours. 3. Serve.

Pork and Beef Barbecue

Prep time: 15 minutes | Cook time: 6 to 8 hours | Serves 14

1 (8-ounce / 227-g) can tomato sauce
½ cup brown sugar, packed
¼ cup chili powder, or less
¼ cup cider vinegar
2 teaspoons Worcestershire sauce
1 teaspoon salt
1 pound (454 g) lean beef stewing meat, cut into ¾-inch cubes
1 pound (454 g) lean pork tenderloin, cut into ¾-inch cubes
3 green bell peppers, chopped
3 large onions, chopped

1. Combine tomato sauce, brown sugar, chili powder, cider vinegar, Worcestershire sauce, and salt in slow cooker. 2. Stir in meats, green peppers, and onions. 3. Cover. Cook on high 6 to 8 hours. 4. Shred meat with two forks. Stir all ingredients together well. 5. Serve.

Our Favorite Chili

Prep time: 20 minutes | Cook time: 4 to 10 hours | Serves 10 to 12

1½ pounds (680 g) ground beef
¼ cup chopped onions
1 rib celery, chopped
1 (29-ounce / 822-g) can stewed tomatoes
2 (15½-ounce / 439-g) cans red kidney beans, undrained
2 (16-ounce / 454-g) cans chili beans, undrained
½ cup ketchup
1½ teaspoons lemon juice
2 teaspoons vinegar
1½ teaspoons brown sugar
1½ teaspoons salt
1 teaspoon Worcestershire sauce
½ teaspoon garlic powder
½ teaspoon dry mustard powder
1 tablespoon chili powder
2 (6-ounce / 170-g) cans tomato paste

1. Brown ground beef, onions, and celery in skillet. Drain. Place in slow cooker. 2. Add remaining ingredients. Mix well. 3. Cover. Cook on low 8 to 10 hours, or on high 4 to 5 hours. 4. Serve.

Tiajuana Tacos

Prep time: 20 minutes | Cook time: 2 hours | Serves 6

3 cups cooked chopped beef
1 (1-pound / 454-g) can refried beans
½ cup chopped onions
½ cup chopped green peppers
½ cup chopped ripe olives
1 (8-ounce / 227-g) can tomato sauce
3 teaspoons chili powder
1 tablespoon Worcestershire sauce
½ teaspoon garlic powder
¼ teaspoon pepper
¼ teaspoon paprika
⅛ teaspoon celery salt
⅛ teaspoon ground nutmeg
¾ cup water
1 teaspoon salt
1 cup crushed corn chips
6 taco shells
Shredded lettuce
Chopped tomatoes
Shredded Cheddar cheese

1. Combine first 15 ingredients in slow cooker. 2. Cover. Cook on high 2 hours. 3. Just before serving, fold in corn chips. 4. Spoon mixture into taco shells. Top with lettuce, tomatoes, and cheese.

Barbecued Roast Beef

Prep time: 15 minutes | Cook time: 6 to 7 hours | Serves 8

1 (4-pound / 1.8-kg) beef roast
1 cup ketchup
1 onion, chopped
¾ cup water
3 tablespoons Worcestershire sauce
¾ cup brown sugar

1. Place roast in slow cooker. 2. In a small bowl, mix together all remaining ingredients except the brown sugar. Pour over roast. 3. Cover and cook on low 6 to 7 hours. Approximately 1 hour before serving, sprinkle with ¾ cup brown sugar.

North Carolina Barbecue

Prep time: 15 minutes | Cook time: 5 to 8 hours | Serves 8 to 12

1 (3- to 4-pound / 1.4- to 1.8-kg) pork loin, roast or shoulder
1 cup apple cider vinegar
¼ cup, plus 1 tablespoon, prepared mustard
¼ cup, plus 1 tablespoon, Worcestershire sauce
2 teaspoons red pepper flakes

1. Trim fat from pork. Place in slow cooker. 2. In a bowl, mix remaining ingredients together. Spoon over meat. 3. Cover and cook on high 5 hours, or on low 8 hours, or until meat is tender but not dry. 4. Slice, or break meat apart, and serve drizzled with the cooking juices.

Flavor-Filled Pork and Sauerkraut

Prep time: 30 minutes | Cook time: 10 to 11 hours | Serves 10 to 15

1 (4- to 5-pound / 1.8- to 2.3-kg) lean pork loin roast
1 (1- to 2-pound / 454 to 907-g) bag sauerkraut, divided
Half a small head of cabbage, thinly sliced, divided
1 large onion, thinly sliced, divided
1 apple, quartered, cored, and sliced, divided
1 teaspoon dill weed (optional)
½ cup brown sugar (optional)
1 cup water

1. Brown roast for 10 minutes in a heavy nonstick skillet. Place roast in slow cooker. 2. Cover with a layer of half the sauerkraut, then a layer of half the cabbage, a layer of half the onion, and a layer of half the apple. 3. Repeat the layers. 4. If you wish to use the dill weed and brown sugar, mix them and the water together in a bowl. Pour over layers. or simply pour water over top. 5. Cover and cook on high 1 hour. Turn to low and cook until meat is tender, about 9 to 10 hours.

1-2 to 3-4 Casserole

Prep time: 35 minutes | Cook time: 7 to 9 hours | Serves 8

1 pound (454 g) ground beef
2 onions, sliced
3 carrots, thinly sliced
4 potatoes, thinly sliced
½ teaspoon salt
⅛ teaspoon pepper
1 cup cold water
½ teaspoon cream of tartar
1 (10¾-ounce / 305-g) can cream of mushroom soup
¼ cup milk
½ teaspoon salt
⅛ teaspoon pepper

1. Layer in greased slow cooker: ground beef, onions, carrots, ½ teaspoon salt, and ⅛ teaspoon pepper. 2. Dissolve cream of tartar in water in bowl. Toss sliced potatoes with water. 3. Drain. Combine soup and milk. Toss with potatoes. Add remaining salt and pepper. Arrange potatoes in slow cooker. 4. Cover. Cook on low 7 to 9 hours.

Meatball-Barley Casserole

Prep time: 40 minutes | Cook time: 4 to 8 hours | Serves 6

⅔ cup pearl barley
1 pound (454 g) ground beef
½ cup soft bread crumbs
1 small onion, chopped
¼ cup milk
¼ teaspoon pepper
1 teaspoon salt
Oil
½ cup thinly sliced celery
½ cup finely chopped sweet peppers
1 (10¾-ounce / 305-g) can cream of celery soup
⅓ cup water
Paprika

1. Cook barley as directed on package. Set aside. 2. Combine beef, bread crumbs, onion, milk, pepper, and salt. Shape into 20 balls. Brown on all sides in oil in skillet. Drain and place in slow cooker. 3. Add barley, celery, and peppers. 4. Combine soup and water. Pour into slow cooker. Mix all together gently. 5. Sprinkle with paprika. 6. Cover. Cook on low 6 to 8 hours, or on high 4 hours.

Spanish Rice

Prep time: 15 minutes | Cook time: 6 to 10 hours | Serves 8

2 pounds (907 g) ground beef, browned
2 medium onions, chopped
2 green peppers, chopped
1 (28-ounce / 794-g) can tomatoes
1 (8-ounce / 227-g) can tomato sauce
1½ cups water
2½ teaspoons chili powder
2 teaspoons salt
2 teaspoons Worcestershire sauce
1½ cups rice, uncooked

1. Combine all ingredients in slow cooker. 2. Cover. Cook on low 8 to 10 hours, or on high 6 hours.

Burgundy Roast

Prep time: 10 minutes | Cook time: 5 hours | Serves 6 to 8

1 (4-pound / 1.8-kg) venison or beef roast
1 (10¾-ounce / 305-g) can cream of mushroom soup
1 cup burgundy wine
1 large onion, finely chopped
2 tablespoons chopped parsley

1. Place meat in slow cooker. 2. Blend soup and wine together in a mixing bowl. Pour over meat. 3. Top with onion and parsley. 4. Cover and cook on low 5 hours, or until meat is tender but not dry. 5. Serve.

Grandma's Chili

Prep time: 20 minutes | Cook time: 4 hours | Serves 8

1 large onion, chopped
2 pounds (907 g) ground beef
1 (28-ounce / 794-g) can stewed tomatoes
1 (16-ounce / 454-g) can dark kidney beans, undrained
1 (15-ounce / 425-g) can Hormel chili with beans
1 (10¾-ounce / 305-g) can tomato soup
1 teaspoon K.C. Masterpiece BBQ sauce
¼ teaspoon garlic salt
¼ teaspoon garlic powder
¼ teaspoon onion salt
¼ teaspoon chili powder
Pinch of sugar

1. Brown onion and beef in skillet, leaving meat in larger chunks. Place in slow cooker. 2. Add remaining ingredients. Stir. 3. Cover. Cook on high 4 hours. 4. Serve.

Chili Hot Dogs

Prep time: 10 minutes | Cook time: 2 to 3 hours | Serves 4 to 5

1 package hot dogs, cut into ¾-inch slices
1 (28-ounce / 794-g) can baked beans
1 teaspoon prepared mustard
1 teaspoon instant minced onion
⅓ cup chili sauce

1. In slow cooker, combine all ingredients. 2. Cover and cook on low 2 to 3 hours. 3. Serve.

Stuffed Peppers with Beef

Prep time: 15 minutes | Cook time: 4 to 12 hours | Serves 6 to 8

6 to 8 green peppers
1 to 2 pounds (454 to 907 g) ground beef
1 onion, chopped
¼ teaspoon salt
¼ teaspoon pepper
1 egg
1 slice white bread
1 (28-ounce / 794-g) can whole or stewed tomatoes

1. Cut peppers in half and remove seeds. 2. Combine ground beef, onion, salt, pepper, and egg. Tear bread into small pieces. Add to ground beef mixture. Stuff into peppers. 3. Form remaining meat into oblong shape. Place meatloaf and peppers into slow cooker. Pour in tomatoes. 4. Cover. Cook on low 6 to 12 hours, or on high 4 to 5 hours.

New Mexico Steak

Prep time: 10 minutes | Cook time: 4 hours | Serves 4 to 6

1 large onion, sliced
1 (2-pound / 907-g) round steak, cut into serving size pieces
Salt and pepper to taste
2 (7-ounce / 198-g) cans green chili salsa

1. Place onion slices in bottom of slow cooker. 2. Sprinkle steak with salt and pepper. Add steak pieces to cooker. 3. Spoon chili salsa over all, being careful not to wash off the seasonings. 4. Cover and cook on high 1 hour. Turn to low and cook 3 hours, or until steak is tender but not overcooked.

Zippy Beef Roast

Prep time: 15 minutes | Cook time: 5 to 10 hours | Serves 6 to 8

3 to 4 pounds (1.4 to 1.8 kg) beef roast
1 (12-ounce / 340-g) can cola
1 (10¾-ounce / 305-g) can cream of mushroom soup
1 envelope dry onion soup mix

1. Place beef in slow cooker. 2. In a small bowl, blend cola and mushroom soup together. Pour over roast. 3. Sprinkle with dry onion soup mix. 4. Cover and cook on low for 10 hours, or on high for 5 hours, or until meat is tender but not dry.

Slow-Cooked Round Steak

Prep time: 15 minutes | Cook time: 4 to 5 hours | Serves 4 to 6

1 (1¾-pound / 794-g) round steak
¼ cup flour
2 onions, sliced thickly
1 green pepper, sliced in strips
1 (10¾-ounce / 305-g) can cream of mushroom soup

1. Cut steak into serving-size pieces. Dredge in flour. Brown in a nonstick skillet. 2. Place browned steak in slow cooker. Top with onion and pepper slices. 3. Pour soup over all, making sure steak pieces are covered. 4. Cover and cook on low 4 to 5 hours.

Three-Ingredient Sauerkraut Meal

Prep time: 5 minutes | Cook time: 8 to 10 hours | Serves 8

2 cups low-sodium barbecue sauce
1 cup water
2 pounds (907 g) thinly sliced lean pork chops, trimmed of fat
2 pounds (907 g) sauerkraut, rinsed

1. Mix together barbecue sauce and water. 2. Combine barbecue sauce, pork chops, and sauerkraut in slow cooker. 3. Cover. Cook on low 8 to 10 hours

Meatballs and Spaghetti Sauce

Prep time: 35 minutes | Cook time: 6 to 8 hours | Serves 6 to 8

Meatballs:
1½ pounds (680 g) ground beef
2 eggs
1 cup bread crumbs
Oil
Sauce:
1 (28-ounce / 794-g) can tomato purée
1 (6-ounce / 170-g) can tomato paste
1 (10¾-ounce / 305-g) can tomato soup
¼ to ½ cup grated Romano or Parmesan cheese
1 teaspoon oil
1 garlic clove, minced
Sliced mushrooms (either canned or fresh) (optional)

1. Combine ground beef, eggs, and bread crumbs. Form into 16 meatballs. Brown in oil in skillet. 2. Combine sauce ingredients in slow cooker. Add meatballs. Stir together gently. 3. Cover. Cook on low 6 to 8 hours. Add mushrooms 1 to 2 hours before sauce is finished. 4. Serve.

Ham and Cheese Casserole

Prep time: 30 minutes | Cook time: 2 to 4 hours | Serves 8 to 10

1 (16-ounce / 454-g) package medium egg noodles, divided
1 (10¾-ounce / 305-g) can condensed cream of celery soup
1 pint sour cream
2 cups fully cooked ham, cubed, divided
2 cups shredded cheese, your choice, divided

1. Prepare noodles according to package instructions. Drain. 2. In a small bowl combine soup and sour cream until smooth. Set aside. 3. In a greased slow cooker, layer one-third of the cooked noodles, one-third of the ham, and one-third of the cheese. 4. Top with one-fourth of soup mixture. 5. Repeat steps 3 and 4 twice until all ingredients are used. The final layer should be the soup-sour cream mixture. 6. Cook 2 to 4 hours on low, or until heated through.

Taters 'n Beef

Prep time: 20 minutes | Cook time: 4¼ to 6¼ hours | Serves 6 to 8

2 pounds (907 g) ground beef, browned
1 teaspoon salt
½ teaspoon pepper
¼ cup chopped onions
1 cup canned tomato soup
6 potatoes, sliced
1 cup milk

1. Combined beef, salt, pepper, onions, and soup. 2. Place a layer of potatoes in bottom of slow cooker. Cover with a portion of the meat mixture. Repeat layers until ingredients are used. 3. Cover. Cook on low 4 to 6 hours. Add milk and cook on high 15 to 20 minutes.

Mexican Casserole

Prep time: 15 minutes | Cook time: 8 to 9 hours | Serves 8

1 pound (454 g) extra-lean ground beef
1 medium onion, chopped
1 small green bell pepper, chopped
1 (16-ounce / 454-g) can kidney beans, rinsed and drained
1 (14½-ounce / 411-g) can diced tomatoes, undrained
1 (8-ounce / 227-g) can tomato sauce
¼ cup water
1 envelope reduced-sodium taco seasoning
1 tablespoon chili powder
1⅓ cups instant rice, uncooked
1 cup low-fat Cheddar cheese

1. Brown ground beef and onion in nonstick skillet. 2. Combine all ingredients in slow cooker except rice and cheese. 3. Cook on low 8 to 9 hours. 4. Stir in rice, cover, and cook until tender. 5. Sprinkle with cheese. Cover and cook until cheese is melted. Serve.

Veggies and Beef Pot Roast

Prep time: 15 minutes | Cook time: 10 to 12 hours | Serves 8 to 10

12 ounces (340 g) whole tiny new potatoes, or 2 medium potatoes, cubed, or 2 medium sweet potatoes, cubed
8 small carrots, cut in small chunks
2 small onions, cut in wedges
2 ribs celery, cut up
2½ to 3 pounds (1.1 to 1.4 kg) beef chuck or pot roast
2 tablespoons cooking oil
¾ cup water, dry wine, or tomato juice
1 tablespoon Worcestershire sauce
1 teaspoon instant beef bouillon granules
1 teaspoon dried basil

1. Place vegetables in bottom of slow cooker. 2. Brown roast in oil in skillet. Place on top of vegetables. 3. Combine water, Worcestershire sauce, bouillon, and basil. Pour over meat and vegetables. 4. Cover. Cook on low 10 to 12 hours.

Cranberry Ham

Prep time: 10 minutes | Cook time: 4½ hours | Serves 4

1 (1- to 2-pound / 454 to 907-g) fully cooked ham, or 2-inch-thick slice of fully cooked ham
1 cup whole cranberry sauce
2 tablespoons brown sugar

1. Place ham in slow cooker. Cover with cranberry sauce. Sprinkle brown sugar over top. 2. Cook on low 4½ hours, or until meat is heated through but not drying out.

Stuffed Cabbage

Prep time: 25 minutes | Cook time: 8 to 10 hours | Serves 8

4 cups water
12 large cabbage leaves, cut from head at base and washed
1 pound (454 g) lean ground beef or lamb
½ cup rice, cooked
½ teaspoon salt
¼ teaspoon black pepper
¼ teaspoon dried thyme
¼ teaspoon nutmeg
¼ teaspoon cinnamon
1 (6-ounce / 170-g) can tomato paste
¾ cup water

1. Boil 4 cups water in saucepan. Turn off heat. Soak cabbage leaves in water for 5 minutes. Remove. Drain. Cool. 2. Combine ground beef, rice, salt, pepper, thyme, nutmeg, and cinnamon. 3. Place 2 tablespoons of mixture on each cabbage leaf. Roll firmly. Stack in slow cooker. 4. Combine tomato paste and ¾ cup water. 5. Pour over stuffed cabbage. Cover. Cook on low 8 to 10 hours.

Chili Spaghetti

Prep time: 25 minutes | Cook time: 4 hours | Serves 8 to 10

½ cup diced onions
2 cups tomato juice
2 teaspoons chili powder
1 teaspoon salt
¾ cup shredded mild cheese
1½ pounds (680 g) ground beef, browned
12 ounces (340 g) dry spaghetti, cooked

1. Combine all ingredients in slow cooker. 2. Cover. Cook on low 4 hours. Check mixture about halfway through the cooking time. If it's becoming dry, stir in an additional cup of tomato juice.

Lotsa-Beans Chili

Prep time: 25 minutes | Cook time: 8 to 9 hours | Serves 12 to 15

1 pound (454 g) ground beef
1 pound (454 g) bacon, diced
½ cup chopped onions
½ cup brown sugar
½ cup sugar
½ cup ketchup
2 teaspoons dry mustard
1 teaspoon salt
½ teaspoon pepper
2 (15-ounce / 425-g) cans green beans, drained
2 (14½-ounce / 411-g) cans baked beans
2 (15-ounce / 425-g) cans butter beans, drained
2 (16-ounce / 454-g) cans kidney beans, rinsed and drained

1. Brown ground beef and bacon in slow cooker. Drain. 2. Combine all ingredients in slow cooker. 3. Cover. Cook on high 1 hour. Reduce heat to low and cook 7 to 8 hours.

CC Roast (Company's Coming)

Prep time: 15 minutes | Cook time: 10 to 12 hours | Serves 8

1 (3-pound / 1.4-kg) boneless pot roast
2 tablespoons flour
1 tablespoon prepared mustard
1 tablespoon chili sauce
1 tablespoon Worcestershire sauce
1 teaspoon red cider vinegar
1 teaspoon sugar
4 potatoes, sliced
2 onions, sliced

1. Place pot roast in slow cooker. 2. Make a paste with the flour, mustard, chili sauce, Worcestershire sauce, vinegar, and sugar. Spread over the roast. 3. Top with potatoes and then the onions. 4. Cover. Cook on low 10 to 12 hours.

Mexicali Round Steak

Prep time: 10 minutes | Cook time: 8 to 9 hours | Serves 6

1½ pounds (680 g) round steak, trimmed of fat
1 cup frozen corn, thawed
½ to 1 cup fresh cilantro, chopped, according to your taste preference
½ cup low-sodium, fat-free beef broth
3 ribs celery, sliced
1 large onion, sliced
1 (20-ounce / 567-g) jar salsa
1 (15-ounce / 425-g) can black beans or pinto beans, rinsed and drained
1 cup fat-free Cheddar cheese

1. Cut beef into 6 pieces. Place in slow cooker. 2. Combine remaining ingredients, except cheese, and pour over beef. 3. Cover. Cook on low 8 to 9 hours. 4. Sprinkle with cheese before serving.

Stuffed "Baked" Topping

Prep time: 35 minutes | Cook time: 1 hour | Serves 12

3 pounds (1.4 kg) ground beef
1 cup chopped green peppers
½ cup chopped onions
6 tablespoons butter
¼ cup flour
3 cups milk
½ cup pimento or chopped sweet red peppers
¾ pound (340 g) Cheddar cheese
¾ pound (340 g) your favorite mild cheese
½ teaspoon hot pepper sauce
¼ teaspoon dry mustard
Salt to taste
12 baked potatoes

1. Brown ground beef, green peppers, and onions in butter. Transfer mixture to slow cooker, reserving drippings. 2. Stir flour into drippings. Slowly add milk. Cook until thickened. 3. Add pimento, cheeses, and seasonings. Pour over ingredients in slow cooker. 4. Cover. Heat on low. 5. Serve over baked potatoes, each one split open on an individual dinner plate.

Ground Beef 'n Biscuits

Prep time: 20 minutes | Cook time: 1 to 1½ hours | Serves 8

1½ pounds (680 g) extra-lean ground beef
½ cup chopped celery
½ cup chopped onions
2 tablespoons flour
1 teaspoon salt
¼ teaspoon black pepper
½ teaspoon dried oregano
2 (8-ounce / 227-g) cans tomato sauce
1 (10-ounce / 283-g) package frozen peas, thawed
2 (7½-ounce / 213-g) cans refrigerated buttermilk biscuits
2 cups fat-free shredded Cheddar cheese

1. Brown ground beef, celery, and onions in nonstick skillet. 2. Stir in flour, salt, pepper, and oregano. 3. Add tomato sauce and peas. 4. Pour into slow cooker. (A large oval cooker allows the biscuits to be arranged over top. You can also divide the mixture between two round slow cookers and accommodate the biscuits in that way.) 5. Arrange biscuits over top and sprinkle with cheese. 6. Cook uncovered on high for 1 to 1½ hours.

Beef in Onion Gravy

Prep time: 20 minutes | Cook time: 6 to 8 hours | Serves 3

1 (10¾-ounce / 305-g) can cream of mushroom soup
1 tablespoon dry onion soup mix
2 tablespoons beef bouillon granules
1 tablespoon quick-cooking tapioca
1 pound (454 g) beef stew meat, cut into 1-inch cubes
Cooking spray

1. Spray the interior of the cooker with cooking spray. 2. In the slow cooker, combine soup, soup mix, bouillon, and tapioca. Let stand 15 minutes. 3. Stir in beef. 4. Cover and cook on low 6 to 8 hours, or until meat is tender but not dry.

Old World Sauerbraten

Prep time: 10 minutes | Cook time: 16 to 22 hours | Serves 8

1 (3½- to 4-pound / 1.6- to 1.8-kg) beef rump roast
1 cup water
1 cup vinegar
1 lemon, sliced but unpeeled
10 whole cloves
1 large onion, sliced
4 bay leaves
6 whole peppercorns
2 tablespoons salt
2 tablespoons sugar
12 gingersnaps, crumbled

1. Place meat in deep ceramic or glass bowl. 2. Combine water, vinegar, lemon, cloves, onion, bay leaves, peppercorns, salt, and sugar. Pour over meat. Cover and refrigerate 24 to 36 hours. Turn meat several times during marinating. 3. Place beef in slow cooker. Pour 1 cup marinade over meat. 4. Cover. Cook on low 6 to 8 hours. Remove meat. 5. Strain meat juices and return to pot. Turn to high. Stir in gingersnaps. Cover and cook on high 10 to 14 minutes. Slice meat. Pour finished sauce over meat.

Ham-Yam-Apple

Prep time: 10 minutes | Cook time: 4 to 5 hours | Serves 4

1 slice fully cooked ham (about 1 pound / 454 g)
1 (29-ounce / 822-g) can sweet potatoes or yams, drained
2 apples, thinly sliced
¼ cup light brown sugar
2 tablespoons orange juice

1. Cube ham. 2. Combine all ingredients in slow cooker. 3. Cook on low 4 to 5 hours, or until apples are tender.

Slow-Cooked Pork Stew

Prep time: 20 minutes | Cook time: 4 to 6 hours | Serves 8

2 pounds (907 g) lean pork loin, cut into 1-inch cubes
½ pound (227 g) baby carrots
3 large potatoes, cut into 1-inch cubes
2 parsnips, cut into 1-inch cubes
2 onions, cut into wedges, slices, or chopped coarsely
3 garlic cloves, minced
1 to 2 teaspoons ground black pepper, depending on your taste preferences
1 teaspoon dried thyme
1 teaspoon salt
2½ cups low-sodium canned vegetable juice
2 tablespoons brown sugar
1 tablespoon prepared mustard
4 teaspoons tapioca

1. Place pork in slow cooker. 2. Add carrots, potatoes, parsnips, onions, garlic, pepper, thyme, and salt. Mix together well. 3. In a medium bowl, combine vegetable juice, brown sugar, mustard, and tapioca. Pour over meat and vegetables. 4. Cover. Cook on low 6 hours, or on high 4 hours.

Easy Sweet and Sour Pork Chops

Prep time: 5 minutes | Cook time: 5 to 8 hours | Serves 6

1 (16-ounce / 454-g) bag frozen Asian vegetables
6 pork chops
1 (12-ounce / 340-g) bottle sweet and sour sauce
½ cup water
1 cup frozen pea pods

1. Place partially thawed Asian vegetables in slow cooker. Arrange chops on top. 2. Combine sauce and water. Pour over chops. 3. Cover. Cook on low 7 to 8 hours. 4. Turn to high and add pea pods. 5. Cover. Cook on high 5 minutes.

Extra Easy Chili

Prep time: 10 minutes | Cook time: 4 to 8 hours | Serves 4 to 6

1 pound (454 g) ground beef or turkey, uncooked
1 envelope dry chili seasoning mix
1 (16-ounce / 454-g) can chili beans in sauce
2 (28-ounce / 794-g) cans crushed or diced tomatoes seasoned with garlic and onion

1. Crumble meat in bottom of slow cooker. 2. Add remaining ingredients. Stir. 3. Cover. Cook on high 4 to 6 hours, or on low 6 to 8 hours. Stir halfway through cooking time. 4. Serve.

Unforgettable Sloppy Joes

Prep time: 10 minutes | Cook time: 4 to 5 hours | Makes 4 to 6 sandwiches

1 pound (454 g) ground beef
1 onion, chopped
¾ cup ketchup
2 tablespoons chili sauce
1 tablespoon Worcestershire sauce
1 tablespoon prepared mustard
1 tablespoon vinegar
1 tablespoon sugar

1. Brown beef and onion in saucepan. Drain. 2. Combine all ingredients in slow cooker. 3. Cover. Cook on low 4 to 5 hours. 4. Serve

Corned Beef Dinner

Prep time: 10 minutes | Cook time: 10 to 11 hours | Serves 6

2 onions, sliced
2 garlic cloves, minced
3 potatoes, pared and quartered
3 carrots, sliced
2 bay leaves
1 small head cabbage, cut into 4 wedges
1 (3- to 4-pound / 1.4- to 1.8-kg) corned beef brisket
1 cup water
½ cup brown sugar
1 tablespoon prepared mustard
Dash of ground cloves

1. Layer onions, garlic, potatoes, carrots, bay leaves, and cabbage in slow cooker. 2. Place brisket on top. 3. Add water. 4. Cover. Cook on low 10 to 11 hours. 5. During last hour of cooking, combine brown sugar, mustard, and cloves. Spread over beef. 6. Discard bay leaves. Slice meat and arrange on platter of vegetables.

Beef Stew Bourguignonne

Prep time: 15 minutes | Cook time: 10¼ to 12¼ hours | Serves 6

2 pounds (907 g) stewing beef, cut in 1-inch cubes
2 tablespoons cooking oil
1 (10¾-ounce / 305-g) can condensed golden cream of mushroom soup
1 teaspoon Worcestershire sauce
⅓ cup dry red wine
½ teaspoon dried oregano
2 teaspoons salt
½ teaspoon pepper
½ cup chopped onions
½ cup chopped carrots
1 (4-ounce / 113-g) can mushroom pieces, drained
½ cup cold water
¼ cup flour
Noodles, cooked

1. Brown meat in oil in saucepan. Transfer to slow cooker. 2. Mix together soup, Worcestershire sauce, wine, oregano, salt and pepper, onions, carrots, and mushrooms. Pour over meat. 3. Cover. Cook on low 10 to 12 hours. 4. Combine water and flour. Stir into beef mixture. Turn cooker to high. 5. Cook and stir until thickened and bubbly. 6. Serve over noodles.

Beef-Vegetable Casserole

Prep time: 20 minutes | Cook time: 4 to 5 hours | Serves 8

1 pound (454 g) extra-lean ground beef or turkey
1 medium onion, chopped
½ cup chopped celery
4 cups chopped cabbage
2½ cups canned stewed tomatoes, slightly mashed
1 tablespoon flour
1 teaspoon salt
1 tablespoon sugar
¼ to ½ teaspoon black pepper, according to your taste preference

1. Sauté meat, onion, and celery in nonstick skillet until meat is browned. 2. Pour into slow cooker. 3. Top with layers of cabbage, tomatoes, flour, salt, sugar, and pepper. 4. Cover. Cook on high 4 to 5 hours.

Taco Casserole

Prep time: 25 minutes | Cook time: 7 to 8 hours | Serves 6

1½ pounds (680 g) ground beef, browned
1 (14½-ounce / 411-g) can diced tomatoes with chilies
1 (10¾-ounce / 305-g) can cream of onion soup
1 package dry taco seasoning mix
¼ cup water
6 corn tortillas, cut in ½-inch strips
½ cup sour cream
1 cup shredded Cheddar cheese
2 green onions, sliced

(optional)

1. Combine beef, tomatoes, soup, seasoning mix, and water in slow cooker. 2. Stir in tortilla strips. 3. Cover. Cook on low 7 to 8 hours. 4. Spread sour cream over casserole. Sprinkle with cheese. 5. Cover. Let stand 5 minutes until cheese melts. 6. Remove cover. Garnish with green onions. Allow to stand for 15 more minutes before serving.

Barbecued Hot Dogs

Prep time: 5 minutes | Cook time: 4½ hours | Serves 8

1 cup apricot preserves
4 ounces (113 g) tomato sauce
⅓ cup vinegar
2 tablespoons soy sauce
2 tablespoons honey
1 tablespoon oil
1 teaspoon salt
¼ teaspoon ground ginger
2 pounds (907 g) hot dogs, cut into 1-inch pieces

1. Combine all ingredients except hot dogs in slow cooker. 2. Cover. Cook on high 30 minutes. Add hot dog pieces. Cook on low 4 hours. 3. Serve as an appetizer.

African Beef Curry

Prep time: 20 minutes | Cook time: 6 to 8 hours | Serves 6

1 pound (454 g) extra-lean ground beef, browned
1 large onion, thinly sliced
1 green bell pepper, diced
1 tomato, peeled and diced
1 apple, peeled, cored, and diced
1 to 2 teaspoons curry (or more to taste)
4 cups prepared rice

1. Spray slow cooker with fat-free cooking spray. 2. Add all ingredients except rice in slow cooker and mix well. 3. Cover and cook on high 6 to 8 hours. 4. Serve over hot rice.

Slow-Cooked Short Ribs

Prep time: 35 minutes | Cook time: 9 to 10 hours | Serves 12

⅔ cup flour
2 teaspoons salt
½ teaspoon pepper
4 pounds (1.8 kg) boneless beef short ribs
Oil or ⅓ cup butter
1 large onion, chopped
1½ cups beef broth
¾ cup wine or cider vinegar
½ to ¾ cup packed brown sugar, according to your taste preference
½ cup chili sauce
⅓ cup ketchup
⅓ cup Worcestershire sauce
5 garlic cloves, minced
1½ teaspoons chili powder

1. Combine flour, salt, and pepper in plastic bag. Add ribs and shake to coat. 2. Brown meat in small amount of oil, or in butter, in batches in skillet. Transfer to slow cooker. 3. Combine remaining ingredients in saucepan. Cook, stirring up browned drippings, until mixture comes to boil. Pour over ribs. 4. Cover. Cook on low 9 to 10 hours. 5. Serve.

Beef and Beans over Rice

Prep time: 15 minutes | Cook time: 5½ to 7½ hours | Serves 8

1½ pounds (680 g) boneless round steak
1 tablespoon prepared mustard
1 tablespoon chili powder
½ teaspoon salt (optional)
¼ teaspoon black pepper
1 garlic clove, minced
2 (14½-ounce / 411-g) cans low-sodium diced tomatoes
1 medium onion, chopped
1 beef bouillon cube, crushed
1 (16-ounce / 454-g) can kidney beans, rinsed and drained

1. Cut steak into thin strips. 2. Combine mustard, chili powder, salt (if desired), pepper, and garlic in a bowl. 3. Add steak. Toss to coat. 4. Transfer to slow cooker. Add tomatoes, onion, and bouillon. 5. Cover. Cook on low 5 to 7 hours. 6. Stir in beans. Cook 30 minutes longer. 7. Serve.

Italian Beef

Prep time: 20 minutes | Cook time: 8 hours | Serves 6

1 (4- to 5-pound / 1.8- to 2.3-kg) beef roast, cut into 1 to 1½-inch cubes
2 or 3 beef bouillon cubes
1 teaspoon garlic salt
2 tablespoons Italian salad dressing

1. Place roast, bouillon cubes, garlic salt, and dressing in slow cooker. Stir. 2. Add 1 to 1½-inch water around the beef, being careful not to disturb the seasoning on the top of the meat. 3. Cover and cook on low 8 hours, or until tender but not overcooked. 4. Remove beef from cooker and shred with 2 forks. Return shredded meat to cooker and stir into broth. 5. Serve.

Pork Chops on Rice

Prep time: 30 minutes | Cook time: 4 to 9 hours | Serves 4

½ cup brown rice
⅔ cup converted white rice
¼ cup butter
½ cup chopped onions
1 (4-ounce / 113-g) can sliced mushrooms, drained
½ teaspoon dried thyme
½ teaspoon sage
½ teaspoon salt
¼ teaspoon black pepper
4 (¾- to 1-inch thick) boneless pork chops
1 (10½-ounce / 298-g) can beef consomme
2 tablespoons Worcestershire sauce
½ teaspoon dried thyme
½ teaspoon paprika
¼ teaspoon ground nutmeg

1. Sauté white and brown rice in butter in skillet until rice is golden brown. 2. Remove from heat and stir in onions, mushrooms, thyme, sage, salt, and pepper. Pour into greased slow cooker. 3. Arrange chops over rice. 4. Combine consomme and Worcestershire sauce. Pour over chops. 5. Combine thyme, paprika, and nutmeg. Sprinkle over chops. 6. Cover. Cook on low 7 to 9 hours, or on high 4 to 5 hours.

Powerhouse Beef Roast with Tomatoes, Onions, and Peppers

Prep time: 15 minutes | Cook time: 8 to 10 hours | Serves 5 to 6

1 (3-pound / 1.4-kg) boneless chuck roast
1 garlic clove, minced
1 tablespoon oil
2 to 3 onions, sliced
2 to 3 sweet green and red peppers, sliced
1 (16-ounce / 454-g) jar salsa
2 (14½-ounce / 411-g) cans Mexican-style stewed tomatoes

1. Brown roast and garlic in oil in skillet. Place in slow cooker. 2. Add onions and peppers. 3. Combine salsa and tomatoes and pour over ingredients in slow cooker. 4. Cover. Cook on low 8 to 10 hours. 5. Slice meat to serve.

No-Fuss Sauerkraut

Prep time: 7 minutes | Cook time: 4 to 5 hours | Serves 12

1 (3-pound / 1.4-kg) pork roast
3 (2-pound / 907-g) packages sauerkraut (drain and discard juice from 1 package)
2 apples, peeled and sliced
½ cup brown sugar
1 cup apple juice

1. Place meat in large slow cooker. 2. Place sauerkraut on top of meat. 3. Add apples and brown sugar. Add apple juice. 4. Cover. Cook on high 4 to 5 hours. 5. Serve.

Sweet-Sour Beef and Vegetables

Prep time: 10 minutes | Cook time: 4 to 6 hours | Serves 6

2 pounds (907 g) round steak, cut in 1-inch cubes
2 tablespoons oil
2 (8-ounce / 227-g) cans tomato sauce
2 teaspoons chili powder
2 cups sliced carrots
2 cups small white onions
1 teaspoon paprika
¼ cup sugar
1 teaspoon salt
⅓ cup vinegar
½ cup light molasses
1 large green pepper, cut in 1-inch pieces

1. Brown steak in oil in saucepan. 2. Combine all ingredients in slow cooker. 3. Cover. Cook on high 4 to 6 hours.

Ham and Cabbage

Prep time: 30 minutes | Cook time: 6 to 7 hours | Serves 4

2 pounds (907 g) uncooked ham
12 whole cloves
8 medium red potatoes
1 medium head green cabbage
Water

1. Rinse ham, then stick cloves evenly into ham. Place in center of slow cooker. 2. Cut potatoes in half. Add to slow cooker around the ham. 3. Quarter cabbage and remove center stem. Add to cooker, again surrounding the ham. 4. Fill with water to cover. 5. Cover and cook on high 6 to 7 hours, or until vegetables and meat are tender, but not dry or mushy. 6. Serve.

Italian Sausage Dinner

Prep time: 10 minutes | Cook time: 5 to 10 hours | Serves 6

1½ pounds (680 g) Italian sausage, cut in ¾-inch slices
2 tablespoons A-1 steak sauce
1 (28-ounce / 794-g) can diced Italian-style tomatoes, with juice
2 chopped green peppers
½ teaspoon red pepper flakes (optional)
2 cups minute rice, uncooked

1. Place all ingredients, except rice, in slow cooker. 2. Cover and cook on low 7½ to 9½ hours, or on high 4½ hours. 3. Stir in uncooked rice. Cover and cook an additional 20 minutes on high or low.

Beef Pot Roast

Prep time: 10 minutes | Cook time: 6 to 7 hours | Serves 6 to 8

1 (4- to 5-pound / 1.8- to 2.3-kg) beef chuck roast
1 garlic clove, cut in half
Salt to taste
Pepper to taste
1 carrot, chopped
1 rib celery, chopped
1 small onion, sliced
¾ cup sour cream
3 tablespoons flour
½ cup dry white wine

1. Rub roast with garlic. Season with salt and pepper. Place in slow cooker. 2. Add carrots, celery, and onion. 3. Combine sour cream, flour, and wine. Pour into slow cooker. 4. Cover. Cook on low 6 to 7 hours.

Easy Meatballs for a Group

Prep time: 5 minutes | Cook time: 4 hours | Serves 10 to 12

80 to 100 frozen small meatballs
1 (16-ounce / 454-g) jar barbecue sauce
1 (16-ounce / 454-g) jar apricot jam

1. Fill slow cooker with meatballs. 2. Combine sauce and jam. Pour over meatballs. 3. Cover. Cook on low 4 hours, stirring occasionally. 4. Serve as an appetizer, or as a main dish.

Smothered Lentils

Prep time: 10 minutes | Cook time: 8 hours | Serves 6

2 cups dry lentils, rinsed and sorted
1 medium onion, chopped
½ cup chopped celery

2 garlic cloves, minced
1 cup ham, cooked and chopped
½ cup chopped carrots
1 cup diced tomatoes
1 teaspoon dried marjoram
1 teaspoon ground coriander
Salt to taste
Pepper to taste
3 cups water

1. Combine all ingredients in slow cooker. 2. Cover. Cook on low 8 hours. (Check lentils after 5 hours of cooking. If they've absorbed all the water, stir in 1 more cup water.)

Veal and Peppers

Prep time: 10 minutes | Cook time: 4 to 7 hours | Serves 4

1½ pounds (680 g) boneless veal, cubed
3 green peppers, quartered
2 onions, thinly sliced
½ pound (227 g) fresh mushrooms, sliced
1 teaspoon salt
½ teaspoon dried basil
2 cloves garlic, minced
1 (28-ounce / 794-g) can tomatoes

1. Combine all ingredients in slow cooker. 2. Cover. Cook on low 7 hours, or on high 4 hours. 3. Serve.

Tomato Mexican Pot Roast

Prep time: 5 minutes | Cook time: 8 to 10 hours | Serves 8

1½ cups chunky salsa
1 (6-ounce / 170-g) can tomato paste
1 envelope dry taco seasoning mix
1 cup water
1 (3-pound / 1.4-kg) beef chuck roast
½ cup chopped cilantro

1. In a mixing bowl, combine first four ingredients. 2. Place roast in slow cooker and pour salsa mixture over top. 3. Cover and cook on low 8 to 10 hours, or until beef is tender but not dry. Remove to a platter. 4. Stir cilantro into sauce before serving with beef.

Meal-in-One

Prep time: 25 minutes | Cook time: 4 hours | Serves 6 to 8

2 pounds (907 g) ground beef
1 onion, diced
1 green bell pepper, diced
1 teaspoon salt
¼ teaspoon pepper
1 large bag frozen hash brown potatoes
1 (16-ounce / 454-g) container sour cream
1 (24-ounce / 680-g) container cottage cheese
1 cup Monterey Jack cheese, shredded

1. Brown ground beef, onion, and green pepper in skillet. Drain. Season with salt and pepper. 2. In slow cooker, layer one-third of the potatoes, meat, sour cream, and cottage cheese. Repeat twice. 3. Cover. Cook on low 4 hours, sprinkling Monterey Jack cheese over top during last hour. 4. Serve.

Veal Hawaiian

Prep time: 20 minutes | Cook time: 6 hours | Serves 4

1½ pounds (680 g) boneless veal shoulder, trimmed of all fat and cut into 1-inch cubes
1 cup water
¼ cup sherry
2 tablespoons low-sodium soy sauce
1 teaspoon ground ginger
1 teaspoon artificial sweetener

1. Lightly brown veal in a nonstick skillet. 2. Combine remaining ingredients in slow cooker. Stir in veal. 3. Cover. Cook on low 6 hours.

German Dinner

Prep time: 10 minutes | Cook time: 9 to 11 hours | Serves 6

1 (32-ounce / 907-g) bag sauerkraut, drained
1 pound (454 g) extra-lean ground beef
1 small green bell pepper, grated
2 (11½-ounce / 326-g) cans V-8 juice
½ cup chopped celery (optional)

1. Combine all ingredients in slow cooker. 2. Cook for 1 hour on high, and then on low 8 to 10 hours.

A-Touch-of-Asia Ribs

Prep time: 10 minutes | Cook time: 4 to 8 hours | Serves 8 to 10

6 pounds (2.7 kg) country-style pork ribs, cut into serving-size pieces
¼ cup teriyaki sauce
¼ cup cornstarch
1 (27-ounce / 765-g) jar duck sauce
2 tablespoons minced garlic (optional)

1. Place ribs in the bottom of your slow cooker. 2. In a large bowl, stir together teriyaki sauce and cornstarch. Blend in duck sauce and garlic if you wish. 3. Pour the sauce over the ribs, making sure that each layer is well covered. 4. Cover and cook on low 8 hours, or on high 4 to 5 hours.

Yum-Yums

Prep time: 35 minutes | Cook time: 4 to 6 hours | Makes 12 sandwiches

3 pounds (1.4 kg) ground beef
2 onions, chopped
1 (10¾-ounce / 305-g) can cream of chicken soup
1½ cups tomato juice
1 teaspoon prepared mustard
1 teaspoon Worcestershire sauce
1 teaspoon salt
¼ teaspoon pepper

1. Brown beef and onions in skillet. Drain. 2. Add remaining ingredients. Pour into slow cooker. 3. Cover. Cook on low 4 to 6 hours. 4. Serve.

Saucy Italian Roast

Prep time: 10 minutes | Cook time: 8 to 9 hours | Serves 8 to 10

1 (3- to 3½-pound / 1.4- to 1.6-kg) boneless rump roast
½ teaspoon salt
½ teaspoon garlic powder
¼ teaspoon pepper
¼ to ½ cup beef broth

1 (4½-ounce / 128-g) jar mushroom pieces, drained
1 medium onion, diced
1 (14-ounce / 397-g) jar spaghetti sauce

Cut roast in half. 2. Combine salt, garlic powder, and pepper. Rub over both halves of the roast. Place in slow cooker. 3. Top with mushrooms and onions. 4. Combine spaghetti sauce and broth. Pour over roast. 5. Cover. Cook on low 8 to 9 hours. 6. Slice roast. Serve.

Beef and Ham Meatballs

Prep time: 20 minutes | Cook time: 2¾ to 3¾ hours | Serves 5 to 7

1½ pounds (680 g) ground beef
1 (4½-ounce / 128-g) can deviled ham
⅔ cup evaporated milk
2 eggs, beaten slightly
1 tablespoon grated onion
2 cups soft bread crumbs
1 teaspoon salt

¼ teaspoon allspice
¼ teaspoon pepper
¼ cup flour
¼ cup water
1 tablespoon ketchup
2 teaspoons dill weed
1 cup sour cream

1. Combine beef, ham, milk, eggs, onion, bread crumbs, salt, allspice, and pepper. Shape into 2-inch meatballs. Arrange in slow cooker. 2. Cover. Cook on low 2½ to 3½ hours. Turn control to high. 3. Dissolve flour in water until smooth. Stir in ketchup and dill weed. Add to meatballs, stirring gently. 4. Cook on high 15 to 20 minutes, or until slightly thickened. 5. Turn off heat. Stir in sour cream. 6. Serve.

Chapter 7 Pizzas, Wraps, and Sandwiches

Herby Beef Sandwiches

Prep time: 5 minutes | Cook time: 7 to 8 hours | Makes 10 to 12 sandwiches

1 (3- to 4-pound / 1.4- to 1.8-kg) boneless beef chuck roast
3 tablespoons fresh basil, or 1 tablespoon dried basil
3 tablespoons fresh oregano, or 1 tablespoon dried oregano
1½ cups water
1 package dry onion soup mix
10 to 12 Italian rolls

1. Place roast in slow cooker. 2. Combine basil, oregano, and water. Pour over roast. 3. Sprinkle with onion soup mix. 4. Cover. Cook on low 7 to 8 hours. Shred meat with fork. 5. Serve on Italian rolls.

Herby French Sandwiches

Prep time: 5 minutes | Cook time: 5 to 6 hours | Makes 6 to 8 sandwiches

1 (3-pound / 1.4-kg) chuck roast
2 cups water
½ cup soy sauce
1 teaspoon garlic powder
1 bay leaf
3 to 4 whole peppercorns
1 teaspoon dried rosemary (optional)
1 teaspoon dried thyme (optional)
6 to 8 French rolls

1. Place roast in slow cooker. 2. Combine remaining ingredients in a mixing bowl. Pour over meat. 3. Cover and cook on high 5 to 6 hours, or until meat is tender but not dry. 4. Remove meat from broth and shred with fork. Stir back into sauce. 5. Remove meat from the cooker by large forkfuls and place on French rolls.

Middle-Eastern Sandwiches (for a crowd)

Prep time: 50 minutes | Cook time: 6 to 8 hours | Makes 10 to 16 sandwiches

4 pounds (1.8 kg) boneless beef or venison, cut in ½-inch cubes
4 tablespoons cooking oil
2 cups chopped onions
2 garlic cloves, minced
1 cup dry red wine
1 (6-ounce / 170-g) can tomato paste
1 teaspoon dried oregano
1 teaspoon dried basil
½ teaspoon dried rosemary
2 teaspoons salt
Dash of pepper
¼ cup cold water
¼ cup cornstarch
Pita pocket breads
2 cups shredded lettuce
1 large tomato, seeded and diced
1 large cucumber, seeded and diced
8 ounces (227 g) plain yogurt

1. Brown meat, 1 pound (454 g) at a time, in skillet in 1 tablespoon oil. Reserve drippings and transfer meat to slow cooker. 2. Sauté onion and garlic in drippings until tender. Add to meat. 3. Add wine, tomato paste, oregano, basil, rosemary, salt, and pepper. 4. Cover. Cook on low 6 to 8 hours. 5. Turn cooker to high. Combine cornstarch and water in small bowl until smooth. Stir into meat mixture. Cook until bubbly and thickened, stirring occasionally. 6. Split pita breads to make pockets. Fill each with meat mixture, lettuce, tomato, cucumber, and yogurt. 7. Serve.

Wash-Day Sandwiches

Prep time: 10 minutes | Cook time: 6 to 7 hours | Makes 8 to 10 sandwiches

1½ to 2 pounds (680 to 907 g) lean lamb or beef, cubed
2 (15-ounce / 425-g) cans garbanzo beans, drained
2 (15-ounce / 425-g) cans white beans, drained
2 medium onions, peeled and quartered
1 quart water
1 teaspoon salt
1 tomato, peeled and quartered
1 teaspoon turmeric
3 tablespoons fresh lemon juice
8 to 10 pita bread pockets

1. Combine ingredients in slow cooker. 2. Cover. Cook on high 6 to 7 hours. 3. Lift stew from cooker with a strainer spoon and stuff in pita bread pockets.

Barbecued Beef Sandwiches

Prep time: 10 minutes | Cook time: 10 to 12 hours | Makes 18 to 20 sandwiches

1 (3½- to 4-pound / 1.6- to 1.8-kg) beef round steak, cubed
1 cup finely chopped onions
½ cup firmly packed brown sugar
1 tablespoon chili powder
½ cup ketchup
⅓ cup cider vinegar
1 (12-ounce / 340-g) can beer
1 (6-ounce / 170-g) can tomato paste
Buns

1. Combine all ingredients except buns in slow cooker. 2. Cover. Cook on low 10 to 12 hours. 3. Remove beef from sauce with slotted spoon. 4. Place in large bowl. Shred with 2 forks. Add 2 cups sauce from slow cooker to shredded beef. Mix well. 5. Pile into buns and serve immediately.

Barbecued Ham Sandwiches

Prep time: 7 minutes | Cook time: 5 hours | Makes 4 to 6 sandwiches

1 pound (454 g) chipped turkey ham or chipped honey-glazed ham
1 small onion, finely diced
½ cup ketchup
1 tablespoon vinegar
3 tablespoons brown sugar
Buns, for serving

1. Place half of meat in greased slow cooker. 2. Combine other ingredients. Pour half of mixture over meat. Repeat layers. 3. Cover. Cook on low 5 hours. 4. Fill buns and serve.

Beach Boy's Pot Roast

Prep time: 10 minutes | Cook time: 8 to 12 hours | Makes 6 to 8 sandwiches

1 (3- to 4-pound / 1.4- to 1.8-kg) chuck or top round roast
8 to 12 slivers of garlic
1 (32-ounce / 907-g) jar pepperoncini peppers, undrained
6 to 8 large hoagie rolls
12 to 16 slices of your favorite

86 | Chapter 7 Pizzas, Wraps, and Sandwiches

cheese

1. Cut slits into roast with a sharp knife and insert garlic slivers. 2. Place beef in slow cooker. Spoon peppers and all of their juice over top. 3. Cover and cook on low 8 to 12 hours, or until meat is tender but not dry. 4. Remove meat from cooker and allow to cool. Then use 2 forks to shred the beef. 5. Spread on hoagie rolls and top with cheese.

Hot Beef Sandwiches

Prep time: 10 minutes | Cook time: 8 to 10 hours | Makes 10 sandwiches

3 pounds (1.4 kg) beef chuck roast
1 large onion, chopped
¼ cup vinegar
1 clove garlic, minced
1 to 1½ teaspoons salt
¼ to ½ teaspoon pepper
Hamburger buns, for serving

1. Place meat in slow cooker. Top with onions. 2. Combine vinegar, garlic, salt, and pepper. Pour over meat. 3. Cover. Cook on low 8 to 10 hours. 4. Drain broth but save for dipping. 5. Shred meat. 6. Serve on hamburger buns with broth on side.

Tangy Barbecue Sandwiches

Prep time: 20 minutes | Cook time: 7 to 9 hours | Makes 14 to 18 sandwiches

3 cups chopped celery
1 cup chopped onions
1 cup ketchup
1 cup barbecue sauce
1 cup water
2 tablespoons vinegar
2 tablespoons Worcestershire sauce
2 tablespoons brown sugar
1 teaspoon chili powder
1 teaspoon salt
½ teaspoon pepper
½ teaspoon garlic powder
1 (3- to 4-pound / 1.4- to 1.8-kg) boneless chuck roast
14 to 18 hamburger buns

1. Combine all ingredients except roast and buns in slow cooker. When well mixed, add roast. 2. Cover. Cook on high 6 to 7 hours. 3. Remove roast. Cool and shred meat. Return to sauce. Heat well. 4. Serve on buns.

Tangy Sloppy Joes

Prep time: 15 minutes | Cook time: 3 to 10 hours | Makes 12 sandwiches

3 pounds (1.4 kg) ground beef, browned and drained
1 onion, finely chopped
1 green pepper, chopped
2 (8-ounce / 227-g) cans tomato sauce
¾ cup ketchup
1 tablespoon Worcestershire sauce
1 teaspoon chili powder
¼ teaspoon pepper
¼ teaspoon garlic powder
Rolls, for serving

1. Combine all ingredients except rolls in slow cooker. 2. Cover. Cook on low 8 to 10 hours, or on high 3 to 4 hours. 3. Serve.

Chapter 8 Poultry

Sausage, Fennel and Chicken

Prep time: 10 minutes | Cook time: 8 hours | Serves 2

½ fennel bulb, cored and sliced thin
½ red onion, halved and sliced thin
1 teaspoon extra-virgin olive oil
2 bone-in, skinless chicken thighs, about 8 ounces (227 g) each
⅛ teaspoon sea salt
1 hot Italian sausage link, casing removed

1. Put the fennel, onion, and olive oil in the crock pot. Gently stir to combine. 2. Season the chicken with the salt and set it atop the fennel and onion. 3. Crumble the sausage around the chicken. 4. Cover and cook on low for 8 hours.

Roasted Red Pepper and Mozzarella Stuffed Chicken Breasts

Prep time: 15 minutes | Cook time: 6 to 8 hours | Serves 2

1 teaspoon extra-virgin olive oil
2 boneless, skinless chicken breasts
⅛ teaspoon sea salt
Freshly ground black pepper
2 roasted red bell peppers, cut into thin strips
2 ounces (57 g) sliced mozzarella cheese
¼ cup roughly chopped fresh basil

1. Grease the inside of the crock pot with the olive oil. 2. Slice the chicken breasts through the center horizontally until nearly sliced in half. Open as if opening a book. Season all sides of the chicken with the salt and pepper. 3. Place a layer of the roasted peppers on one inside half of each chicken breast. Top the peppers with the mozzarella slices. Then sprinkle the cheese with the fresh basil. Fold the other half of the chicken over the filling. 4. Carefully place the stuffed chicken breasts into the crock pot, making sure the filling does not escape. Cover and cook on low for 6 to 8 hours, or until the chicken is cooked through.

Chicken with Mushrooms and Shallots

Prep time: 15 minutes | Cook time: 6 to 8 hours | Serves 2

1 teaspoon unsalted butter, at room temperature, or extra-virgin olive oil
2 cups thinly sliced cremini mushrooms
1 teaspoon fresh thyme
2 garlic cloves, minced
1 shallot, minced
3 tablespoons dry sherry
2 bone-in, skinless chicken thighs, about 6 ounces (170 g) each
⅛ teaspoon sea salt
Freshly ground black pepper

1. Grease the inside of the crock pot with the butter. 2. Put the mushrooms, thyme, garlic, and shallot into the crock pot, tossing them gently to combine. Pour in the sherry. 3. Season the chicken with the salt and pepper and place the thighs on top of the mushroom mixture. 4. Cover and cook on low for 6 to 8 hours.

Shredded Chicken Souvlaki

Prep time: 10 minutes | Cook time: 6 to 8 hours | Serves 6

3 pounds (1.4 kg) boneless, skinless chicken thighs
⅓ cup water
⅓ cup freshly squeezed lemon juice
¼ cup red wine vinegar
4 garlic cloves, minced
2 tablespoons extra-virgin olive oil
2 teaspoons dried oregano
¼ teaspoon sea salt
¼ teaspoon freshly ground black pepper

1. In a crock pot, combine the chicken, water, lemon juice, vinegar, garlic, olive oil, oregano, salt, and pepper. Stir to mix well. 2. Cover the cooker and cook for 6 to 8 hours on Low heat. 3. Transfer the chicken from the crock pot to a work surface. Using 2 forks, shred the chicken, return it to the crock pot, mix it with the sauce, and keep it warm until ready to serve.

Szechwan-Style Chicken and Broccoli

Prep time: 20 minutes | Cook time: 1 to 3 hours | Serves 4

2 whole boneless, skinless chicken or turkey breasts
Oil
½ cup picante sauce
2 tablespoons soy sauce
½ teaspoon sugar
½ tablespoon quick-cooking tapioca
1 medium onion, chopped
2 garlic cloves, minced
½ teaspoon ground ginger
2 cups broccoli florets
1 medium red pepper, cut into pieces

1. Cut chicken into 1-inch cubes and brown lightly in oil in skillet. Place in slow cooker. 2. Stir in remaining ingredients. 3. Cover. Cook on high 1 to 1½ hours, or on low 2 to 3 hours.

Chicken Enchilada Casserole

Prep time: 30 minutes | Cook time: 6 to 8 hours | Serves 4 to 6

1 onion, chopped
1 garlic clove, minced
1 tablespoon oil
1 (10-ounce / 283-g) can enchilada sauce
1 (8-ounce / 227-g) can tomato sauce
Salt to taste
Pepper to taste
8 corn tortillas
3 boneless chicken breast halves, cooked and cubed
1 (15-ounce / 425-g) can ranch-style beans, drained
1 (11-ounce / 312-g) can Mexicorn, drained
1 (¾-pound / 340-g) Cheddar cheese, shredded
1 (2¼-ounce / 64-g) can sliced black olives, drained

1. Sauté onion and garlic in oil in saucepan. Stir in enchilada sauce and tomato sauce. Season with salt and pepper. 2. Place two tortillas in bottom of slow cooker. Layer one-third chicken on top. Top with one-third sauce mixture, one-third beans, one-third corn, one-third cheese, and one-third black olives. Repeat layers 2 more times. Top with 2 tortillas. 3. Cover. Cook on low 6 to 8 hours.

Coconut Curry Chicken

Prep time: 15 minutes | Cook time: 3 to 4 hours | Serves 6

1 tablespoon coconut oil
1 teaspoon cumin seeds
2 medium onions, grated
7 to 8 ounces (198 to 227 g) canned plum tomatoes
1 teaspoon salt
1 teaspoon turmeric
½ to 1 teaspoon Kashmiri chili powder (optional)
2 to 3 fresh green chiles, chopped
1 cup coconut cream
12 chicken thighs, skinned, trimmed, and cut into bite-size chunks
1 teaspoon garam masala
Handful fresh coriander leaves, chopped

1. Heat the oil in a frying pan (or in the crock pot if you have a sear setting). Add the cumin seeds. When sizzling and aromatic, add the onions and cook until they are browning, about 5 to 7 minutes. 2. In a blender, purée the tomatoes and add them to the pan with the salt, turmeric, chili powder (if using), and fresh green chiles. 3. Stir together and put everything in the crock pot. Pour in the coconut cream. Add the meat and stir to coat with the sauce. 4. Cover and cook on low for 4 hours, or on high for 3 hours. 5. Taste the sauce and adjust the seasoning. If the sauce is very liquidy, turn the cooker to high and cook for 30 minutes more with the lid off. 6. Add the garam masala and throw in the fresh coriander leaves to serve.

Turkey Sausage and Egg Breakfast Casserole

Prep time: 15 minutes | Cook time: 8 hours | Serves 6

Nonstick cooking spray
12 ounces (340 g) cooked turkey breakfast sausage
2 red bell peppers, seeded and chopped
1 onion, chopped
8 ounces (227 g) fresh mushrooms, chopped
6 eggs
6 egg whites
½ cup skim milk
¼ teaspoon freshly ground black pepper
¼ cup low-fat grated Parmesan cheese

1. Spray the crock of your crock pot with nonstick cooking spray. 2. In a large bowl, combine the cooked sausage, bell pepper, onion, and mushrooms. 3. In a medium bowl, whisk together the eggs, egg whites, milk, and pepper. 4. Pour the eggs over the sausage mixture and mix well. 5. Fold in the cheese. 6. Pour the mixture into the crock pot. Cook on low for 8 hours. 7. Cut into wedges to serve.

Turkey Kofta Casserole

Prep time: 20 minutes | Cook time: 6 to 8 hours | Serves 4

For the Kofta:
2 pounds (907 g) raw ground turkey
1 small onion, diced
3 garlic cloves, minced
2 tablespoons chopped fresh parsley
1 tablespoon ground coriander
2 teaspoons ground cumin
1 teaspoon sea salt
1 teaspoon freshly ground black pepper
½ teaspoon ground nutmeg
½ teaspoon dried mint
½ teaspoon paprika
For the Casserole:
Nonstick cooking spray
4 large (about 2½ pounds / 1.1 kg) potatoes, peeled and cut into ¼-inch-thick rounds
4 large (about 3 pounds / 1.4 kg) tomatoes, cut into ¼-inch-thick rounds
Salt
Freshly ground black pepper
1 (8-ounce / 227-g) can no-salt-added, no-sugar-added tomato sauce

Make the Kofta: 1. In a large bowl, mix together the turkey, onion, garlic, parsley, coriander, cumin, salt, pepper, nutmeg, mint, and paprika until combined. 2. Form the kofta mixture into 13 to 15 equal patties, using about 2 to 3 tablespoons of the meat mixture per patty. Make the Casserole: 1. Coat a slow-cooker insert with cooking spray. 2. Layer the kofta patties, potatoes, and tomatoes in the prepared crock pot, alternating the ingredients as you go, like a ratatouille. Season with salt and pepper. 3. Spread the tomato sauce over the ingredients. 4. Cover the cooker and cook for 6 to 8 hours on Low heat, or until the potatoes are tender.

Bell Pepper and Tomato Chicken

Prep time: 15 minutes | Cook time: 5 hours | Serves 6 to 8

1 medium yellow onion, sliced thickly
1 bell pepper, any color, cored, seeded, and sliced thickly
4 cloves garlic, minced
6 ounces (170 g) pitted black olives, drained
1 (28-ounce / 794-g) can stewed tomatoes
1 (15-ounce / 425-g) can stewed tomatoes
1 (6-ounce / 170-g) can tomato paste
1 cup red or white wine
2 tablespoons lemon juice
4 to 6 boneless, skinless chicken breasts, cut in half
¼ cup chopped fresh parsley, or 2 tablespoons dried parsley
1 tablespoon dried basil
½ teaspoon ground nutmeg
Sea salt
Black pepper
1 tablespoon red pepper flakes (optional)

1. Place the onion, bell pepper, garlic, and olives in crock pot. 2. Add the stewed tomatoes, tomato paste, wine, and lemon juice. Stir to combine. 3. Place the chicken pieces in the crock pot. Make sure all the pieces are covered with the liquid. 4. Sprinkle with the parsley, basil, and nutmeg. Season with salt and black pepper, and add the red pepper flakes, if using. Cover and cook on high for 5 hours or on low for 8 hours. Make sure the chicken is cooked thoroughly. 5. Serve hot over cooked pasta of your choice or cooked spaghetti squash.

Mediterranean Roasted Turkey Breast

Prep time: 15 minutes | Cook time: 6 to 8 hours | Serves 4

3 garlic cloves, minced
1 teaspoon sea salt
1 teaspoon dried oregano
½ teaspoon freshly ground black pepper
½ teaspoon dried basil
½ teaspoon dried parsley
½ teaspoon dried rosemary
½ teaspoon dried thyme
¼ teaspoon dried dill

¼ teaspoon ground nutmeg
2 tablespoons extra-virgin olive oil
2 tablespoons freshly squeezed lemon juice
1 (4- to 6-pound / 1.8- to 2.7-kg) boneless or bone-in turkey breast
1 onion, chopped
½ cup low-sodium chicken broth
4 ounces (113 g) whole Kalamata olives, pitted
1 cup sun-dried tomatoes (packaged, not packed in oil), chopped

1. In a small bowl, stir together the garlic, salt, oregano, pepper, basil, parsley, rosemary, thyme, dill, and nutmeg. 2. Drizzle the olive oil and lemon juice all over the turkey breast and generously season it with the garlic-spice mix. 3. In a crock pot, combine the onion and chicken broth. Place the seasoned turkey breast on top of the onion. Top the turkey with the olives and sun-dried tomatoes. 4. Cover the cooker and cook for 6 to 8 hours on Low heat. 5. Slice or shred the turkey for serving.

Chicken Caprese Casserole

Prep time: 10 minutes | Cook time: 6 to 8 hours | Serves 4

2 pounds (907 g) boneless, skinless chicken thighs, cut into 1-inch cubes
1 (15-ounce / 425-g) can no-salt-added diced tomatoes
2 cups fresh basil leaves (about 1 large bunch)
¼ cup extra-virgin olive oil
2½ tablespoons balsamic vinegar
½ teaspoon sea salt
⅛ teaspoon freshly ground black pepper
2 cups shredded mozzarella cheese

1. In a crock pot, layer the chicken, tomatoes, and basil. 2. In a small bowl, whisk together the olive oil, vinegar, salt, and pepper until blended. Pour the dressing into the crock pot. Stir to mix well. 3. Cover the cooker and cook for 6 to 8 hours on Low heat. 4. Sprinkle the mozzarella cheese on top. Replace the cover on the cooker and cook for 10 to 20 minutes on Low heat, or until the cheese melts.

Turkey Tenderloins with Raisin Stuffing

Prep time: 15 minutes | Cook time: 7 hours | Serves 2

5 slices oatmeal bread, cubed
1 small onion, chopped
2 garlic cloves, minced
½ cup raisins
1 egg
2 tablespoons butter, melted
½ teaspoon salt
⅛ teaspoon freshly ground black pepper
½ cup chicken stock
2 (1-pound / 454-g) turkey tenderloins
2 tablespoons Dijon mustard
2 tablespoons honey
1 teaspoon poultry seasoning

1. In the crock pot, combine the bread, onion, garlic, raisins, egg, butter, salt, and pepper, and mix. Drizzle the stock over everything and stir gently to coat. 2. On a platter, rub the turkey tenderloins with the Dijon mustard and honey, and then sprinkle with the poultry seasoning. Place the tenderloins over the bread mixture in the crock pot. 3. Cover and cook on low for 6 to 7 hours, until the turkey registers 160ºF (71ºC) on a meat thermometer. 4. Slice the turkey and serve it with the stuffing.

Pesto Chicken and Potatoes

Prep time: 15 minutes | Cook time: 6 to 8 hours | Serves 6

For the Pesto:
1 cup fresh basil leaves
1 garlic clove, crushed
¼ cup pine nuts
¼ cup grated Parmesan cheese
2 tablespoons extra-virgin olive oil, plus more as needed
1 teaspoon sea salt
½ teaspoon freshly ground black pepper

For the Chicken:
Nonstick cooking spray
2 pounds (907 g) red potatoes, quartered
3 pounds (1.4 kg) boneless, skinless chicken thighs
½ cup low-sodium chicken broth

Make the Pesto: In a food processor, combine the basil, garlic, pine nuts, Parmesan cheese, olive oil, salt, and pepper. Pulse until smooth, adding more olive oil ½ teaspoon at a time if needed until any clumps are gone. Set aside. Make the Chicken: 1. Coat a slow-cooker insert with cooking spray and put the potatoes into the prepared crock pot. 2. Place the chicken on top of the potatoes. 3. In a medium bowl, whisk together the pesto and broth until combined and pour the mixture over the chicken. 4. Cover the cooker and cook for 6 to 8 hours on Low heat.

Chicken, Sweet Chicken

Prep time: 15 minutes | Cook time: 5 to 6 hours | Serves 6 to 8

2 medium raw sweet potatoes, peeled and cut into ¼-inch thick slices
8 boneless, skinless chicken thighs
1 (8-ounce / 227-g) jar orange marmalade
¼ cup water
¼ to ½ teaspoon salt
½ teaspoon pepper

1. Place sweet potato slices in slow cooker. 2. Rinse and dry chicken pieces. Arrange on top of the potatoes. 3. Spoon marmalade over the chicken and potatoes. 4. Pour water over all. Season with salt and pepper. 5. Cover and cook on high 1 hour, and then turn to low and cook 4 to 5 hours, or until potatoes and chicken are both tender.

Scalloped Chicken with Potatoes

Prep time: 5 minutes | Cook time: 4 to 10 hours | Serves 4

1 (5-ounce / 142-g) package scalloped potatoes
Scalloped potatoes dry seasoning pack
4 chicken breast halves or 8 legs
1 (10-ounce / 283-g) package frozen peas
2 cups water

1. Put potatoes, seasoning pack, chicken, and peas in slow cooker. Pour water over all. 2. Cover. Cook on low 8 to 10 hours, or on high 4 hours.

Tuscan Turkey

Prep time: 15 minutes | Cook time: 6 to 8 hours | Serves 4

- 1 pound (454 g) new potatoes, halved
- 1 red bell pepper, seeded and sliced
- 1 small onion, sliced
- 4 boneless, skinless turkey breast fillets (about 2 pounds / 907 g)
- 1 cup low-sodium chicken broth
- ½ cup grated Parmesan cheese
- 3 garlic cloves, minced
- 1 teaspoon dried oregano
- 1 teaspoon dried rosemary
- ½ teaspoon sea salt
- ½ teaspoon freshly ground black pepper
- ½ teaspoon dried thyme
- ¼ cup chopped fresh basil

1. In a crock pot, combine the potatoes, bell pepper, and onion. Stir to mix well. 2. Place the turkey on top of the vegetables. 3. In a small bowl, whisk together the chicken broth, Parmesan cheese, garlic, oregano, rosemary, salt, black pepper, and thyme until blended. Pour the sauce over the turkey. 4. Cover the cooker and cook for 6 to 8 hours on Low heat. 5. Garnish with fresh basil for serving.

Chicken with Dates and Almonds

Prep time: 15 minutes | Cook time: 6 to 8 hours | Serves 4

- 1 onion, sliced
- 1 (15-ounce / 425-g) can reduced-sodium chickpeas, drained and rinsed
- 2½ pounds (1.1 kg) bone-in, skin-on chicken thighs
- ½ cup low-sodium chicken broth
- 2 garlic cloves, minced
- 1 teaspoon sea salt
- 1 teaspoon ground cumin
- ½ teaspoon ground ginger
- ½ teaspoon ground coriander
- ¼ teaspoon ground cinnamon
- ¼ teaspoon freshly ground black pepper
- ½ cup dried dates
- ¼ cup sliced almonds

1. In a crock pot, gently toss together the onion and chickpeas. 2. Place the chicken on top of the chickpea mixture and pour the chicken broth over the chicken. 3. In a small bowl, stir together the garlic, salt, cumin, ginger, coriander, cinnamon, and pepper. Sprinkle the spice mix over everything. 4. Top with the dates and almonds. 5. Cover the cooker and cook for 6 to 8 hours on Low heat.

Chicken and Cornbread Stuffing

Prep time: 20 minutes | Cook time: 7 hours | Serves 2

- Nonstick cooking spray
- 3 cups cubed cornbread
- 1 onion, chopped
- ⅓ cup dried cranberries
- ⅓ cup golden raisins
- 3 tablespoons dark raisins
- ¼ cup whole milk
- ¼ cup sour cream
- ¼ cup chicken stock
- 2 tablespoons butter, melted
- ¾ teaspoon salt, divided
- ½ teaspoon dried sage leaves
- ⅛ teaspoon freshly ground black pepper
- 2 boneless, skinless chicken breasts
- ½ teaspoon ground sweet paprika

1. Spray the crock pot with the nonstick cooking spray. 2. In the crock pot, combine the cornbread cubes, onion, cranberries, and golden and dark raisins. 3. In a small bowl, mix the milk, sour cream, stock, butter, ½ teaspoon of salt, sage, and pepper, combining well. Pour this mixture over the stuffing mixture and stir to coat. 4. On a platter, sprinkle the chicken with the paprika and the remaining ¼ teaspoon of salt, and place it on top of the stuffing. 5. Cover and cook on low for 6 to 7 hours, or until the chicken registers 160°F (71°C) on a meat thermometer, and serve.

Gingery Quinoa Chicken

Prep time: 15 minutes | Cook time: 6 to 8 hours | Serves 2

- 1 teaspoon extra-virgin olive oil
- ½ cup quinoa
- ½ cup low-sodium chicken broth
- ½ cup coconut milk
- 1 teaspoon minced fresh ginger
- 1 teaspoon minced garlic
- Zest of 1 lime
- ½ teaspoon ground coriander
- 2 bone-in, skinless chicken thighs
- ⅛ teaspoon sea salt
- Freshly ground black pepper
- Juice of 1 lime, for garnish

1. Grease the inside of the crock pot with the olive oil. 2. Put the quinoa, broth, coconut milk, ginger, garlic, zest, and coriander in the crock. Stir thoroughly. 3. Season the chicken thighs with the salt and a few grinds of the black pepper. Place them on top of the quinoa. 4. Cover and cook for 6 to 8 hours, until the quinoa has absorbed all the liquid and the chicken is cooked through. 5. Drizzle each portion with lime juice just before serving.

Catalonian Chicken with Spiced Lemon Rice

Prep time: 10 minutes | Cook time: 4 hours 10 minutes | Serves 4

- 3 tablespoons all-purpose flour
- 2 tablespoons paprika
- 1 tablespoon garlic powder
- Sea salt
- Black pepper
- 6 chicken thighs
- ¼ cup olive oil
- 1 (15-ounce / 425-g) can diced tomatoes, with the juice
- 2 green bell peppers, diced into 2-inch pieces
- 1 large yellow onion, sliced into thick pieces
- 2 tablespoons tomato paste
- 4 cups chicken stock
- 1 cup uncooked brown rice
- ½ teaspoon red pepper flakes
- Zest and juice from 1 lemon
- ½ cup pitted green olives

1. In a large resealable bag, mix together the flour, paprika, and garlic powder and season with salt and pepper. Add the chicken, reseal the bag, and toss to coat. 2. In a large skillet over medium heat, heat the olive oil. Add the chicken and brown on both sides, 3 to 4 minutes per side. 3. While the chicken is cooking, add the tomatoes, bell peppers, and onion to the crock pot. 4. Place the browned chicken thighs in the crock pot. 5. In same skillet used to brown the chicken, add the tomato paste and cook for 1 minute, stirring constantly. 6. Add 2 cups of the chicken stock to the skillet and bring to a simmer, stirring with a wooden spoon to scrape up the flavorful browned bits off the bottom of the pan. Pour over the top of the chicken in the crock pot. 7. Cook on low for 4 hours, or until the chicken is extremely tender.

8. In a heavy medium saucepan over medium-high heat, combine the remaining 2 cups stock, the rice, red pepper flakes, lemon zest, and juice of one-half of the lemon, and season with salt. Bring to a boil, reduce the heat to low, and simmer, covered, until the rice is tender and has absorbed all the liquid, about 25 minutes. 9. To serve, spoon the rice onto plates and ladle the Catalonian chicken and vegetables over the top. Garnish with the olives and squeeze the juice from the remaining one-half lemon over the dish.

Garlic Chicken with Couscous

Prep time: 10 minutes | Cook time: 3½ hours | Serves 4

1 whole chicken, 3½ to 4 pounds(1.6 to 1.8 kg), cut into 6 to 8 pieces and patted dry
Coarse sea salt
Black pepper
1 tablespoon extra-virgin olive oil
1 medium yellow onion, halved and thinly sliced
6 cloves garlic, halved
2 teaspoons dried thyme
1 cup dry white wine
⅓ cup all-purpose flour
1 cup uncooked couscous
¼ chopped fresh parsley

1. Season the chicken with salt and pepper. 2. In a large skillet, heat the oil over medium-high heat. Add the chicken skin-side down and cook in batches until the skin is golden brown, about 4 minutes. Turn and cook an additional 2 minutes. 3. Add the onion, garlic, and thyme to the crock pot. 4. Top the contents of crock pot with chicken, skin-side up, in a tight layer. 5. In a small bowl, whisk together the wine and the flour until smooth, and add to the crock pot. 6. Cover and cook until the chicken is tender, about 3½ hours on high or 7 hours on low. 7. Cook the couscous according to package instructions. 8. Serve the chicken and sauce hot over the couscous, sprinkled with parsley.

Maple-Soy Glazed Chicken Drumsticks

Prep time: 10 minutes | Cook time: 8 hours | Serves 6

12 chicken drumsticks
½ cup pure maple syrup
¼ cup low-sodium soy sauce
1 teaspoon grated fresh ginger
1 teaspoon cornstarch
½ teaspoon garlic powder
¼ teaspoon freshly ground black pepper
4 scallions, sliced
1 teaspoon sesame seeds

1. Put the drumsticks in your crock pot. 2. In a small bowl, whisk together the maple syrup, soy sauce, ginger, cornstarch, garlic powder, and pepper. 3. Pour the sauce over the drumsticks and stir to coat. 4. Cover and cook on low for 8 hours. 5. Garnish with the scallions and sesame seeds before serving.

Turkey Tetrazzini

Prep time: 20 minutes | Cook time: 6 hours | Serves 4

Cooking spray or 1 tablespoon extra-virgin olive oil
3 cups diced cooked turkey
1 small onion, finely chopped
2 cups low-sodium chicken stock
1 cup heavy (whipping) cream
2 tablespoons dry sherry
1½ cups grated Parmesan cheese, plus more for garnish
4 ounces (113 g) cream cheese
1 teaspoon kosher salt, plus more for seasoning
½ teaspoon freshly ground black pepper, plus more for seasoning
⅛ teaspoon ground nutmeg
1 cup frozen peas

1. Use the cooking spray or olive oil to coat the inside (bottom and sides) of the crock pot. Add the turkey, onion, chicken stock, heavy cream, sherry, Parmesan, cream cheese, salt, pepper, and nutmeg. Stir to combine. Cover and cook on low for 6 hours. 2. About 25 minutes before serving, add the peas. Season with additional salt and pepper, as needed. When the peas have finished cooking, serve and garnish with extra grated Parmesan.

Cornish Hens and Veggies

Prep time: 15 minutes | Cook time: 8 hours | Serves 2

2 Cornish hens
½ teaspoon salt
½ teaspoon poultry seasoning
⅛ teaspoon freshly ground black pepper
1 small lemon, cut into eighths
1 cup sliced cremini mushrooms
2 carrots, sliced
1 onion, chopped
2 garlic cloves, minced
2 Yukon Gold potatoes, cubed
½ cup chicken stock

1. On a platter, sprinkle the hens with the salt, poultry seasoning, and pepper. Stuff the lemon slices into the hens' cavities and set aside. 2. In the crock pot, combine the mushrooms, carrots, onion, garlic, and potatoes. Top with the hens and pour the stock over everything. 3. Cover and cook on low for 8 hours, or until the hens register 165ºF (74ºC) on a meat thermometer. 4. Serve the hens with the vegetables.

Creamy Chicken Curry

Prep time: 20 minutes | Cook time: 2 to 4 hours | Serves 4 to 6

2 (10¾-ounce / 305-g) cans cream of mushroom soup
1 soup can water
2 teaspoons curry powder
⅓ to ½ cup chopped almonds, toasted
4 skinless chicken breast halves, cooked and cubed

1. Combine ingredients in slow cooker. 2. Cover and cook on low 2 to 4 hours. Stir occasionally. 3. Serve.

Cape Breton Chicken

Prep time: 15 minutes | Cook time: 7 hours | Serves 5

4 boneless, skinless chicken breast halves, uncooked, cubed
1 medium onion, chopped
1 medium green bell pepper, chopped
1 cup chopped celery
1 quart low-sodium stewed or crushed tomatoes
1 cup water
½ cup tomato paste
2 tablespoons Worcestershire sauce
2 tablespoons brown sugar
1 teaspoon black pepper

1. Combine all ingredients in slow cooker. 2. Cover. Cook on low 7 hours. 3. Serve.

Cashew Chicken and Snap Peas

Prep time: 15 minutes | Cook time: 6 hours | Serves 2

16 ounces (454 g) boneless, skinless chicken breasts, cut into 2-inch pieces
2 cups sugar snap peas, strings removed
1 teaspoon grated fresh ginger
1 teaspoon minced garlic
2 tablespoons low-sodium soy sauce
1 tablespoon ketchup
1 tablespoon rice vinegar
1 teaspoon honey
Pinch red pepper flakes
¼ cup toasted cashews
1 scallion, white and green parts, sliced thin

1. Put the chicken and sugar snap peas into the crock pot. 2. In a measuring cup or small bowl, whisk together the ginger, garlic, soy sauce, ketchup, vinegar, honey, and red pepper flakes. Pour the mixture over the chicken and snap peas. 3. Cover and cook on low for 6 hours. The chicken should be cooked through, and the snap peas should be tender, but not mushy. 4. Just before serving, stir in the cashews and scallions.

Whole Tandoori-Style Braised Chicken

Prep time: 10 minutes | Cook time: 4 to 8 hours | Serves 6

1 tablespoon freshly grated ginger
5 garlic cloves, minced
2 fresh green chiles, finely chopped
⅔ cup Greek yogurt
2 tablespoons mustard oil
1 tablespoon Kashmiri chili powder
1 tablespoon dried fenugreek leaves
1 tablespoon gram flour
2 teaspoons garam masala
1 teaspoon sea salt
1 teaspoon ground cumin
Juice of 1 large lemon
1 whole chicken, about 3⅓ pounds (1½ kg)
Handful fresh coriander leaves, chopped

1. Put the ginger, garlic, and green chiles in a spice grinder and grind to a paste. Empty into a large bowl and stir in all the other ingredients, except for the chicken and the coriander leaves. 2. Skin the chicken. Then, using a sharp knife, slash the chicken breasts and legs to allow the marinade to penetrate. 3. Marinate in the refrigerator for as long as you can leave it. (Overnight is fine.) 4. Preheat the crock pot on high. My cooker has a stand I can sit meat on, but if you don't have one, scrunch up some foil and put it in the bottom of the cooker. Pour a few tablespoons of water in the bottom of the cooker and place the chicken on the foil. 5. Cook on high for 4 hours, or on low for 6 to 8 hours. 6. Remove the chicken from the cooker and cut it into pieces. Sprinkle the chopped coriander leaves over the chicken and serve.

Chettinad Chicken

Prep time: 15 minutes | Cook time: 4 to 6 hours | Serves 6

1 tablespoon white poppy seeds
1 tablespoon coriander seeds
2 teaspoons cumin seeds
1 teaspoon fennel seeds
4 to 5 dried red chiles
2-inch piece cinnamon stick
6 green cardamom pods
4 cloves
1½ cups grated coconut
4 garlic cloves
1 tablespoon freshly grated ginger
2 tablespoons coconut oil
20 curry leaves
3 onions, finely sliced
2 star anise
4 tomatoes
1 teaspoon turmeric
Sea salt
1 teaspoon chili powder
12 chicken thighs on the bone, skinned and trimmed
Juice of 2 or 3 limes
Handful fresh coriander leaves, chopped

1. In a frying pan, toast the poppy seeds, coriander seeds, cumin seeds, fennel seeds, dried red chiles, cinnamon, green cardamom pods, and cloves until fragrant, about 1 minute. Remove from the pan and set aside to cool. Once cooled, grind to a fine powder in a spice grinder. 2. In the same pan, toast the grated coconut for 3 to 4 minutes until it just starts to turn golden. Remove from the pan and spread on a plate to cool. Once cooled, grind and mix with the ground spices. 3. Crush the garlic and ginger in a mortar and pestle and set aside. 4. Either heat the crock pot to sauté or use a pan on the stove. Heat the coconut oil and add the curry leaves, when they stop spluttering, add the sliced onions and fry them until they are light brown. Stir in the crushed garlic and ginger, and stir for a minute or two. 5. Add to the crock pot along with the ground spices and anise. Chop and add the tomatoes, the turmeric, and the salt, and stir in the chili powder. 6. Place the chicken pieces in the cooker, cover and cook on low for 6 hours, or on high for 4 hours, until tender and cooked through. 7. Check the seasoning and adjust if needed, squeeze in the lime juice, and serve topped with fresh coriander leaves.

Chicken with Lemon and Artichokes

Prep time: 10 minutes | Cook time: 6 to 8 hours | Serves 4

2 pounds (907 g) bone-in, skin-on chicken thighs
1 large onion, sliced
1 (15-ounce / 425-g) can artichoke hearts, drained, rinsed, and chopped
¼ cup freshly squeezed lemon juice
1 tablespoon extra-virgin olive oil
3 garlic cloves, minced
2 teaspoons dried thyme
1 teaspoon sea salt
½ teaspoon freshly ground black pepper
1 lemon, thinly sliced

1. In a crock pot, combine the chicken and onion. Top with the artichoke hearts. 2. In a small bowl, whisk together the lemon juice, olive oil, garlic, thyme, salt, and pepper. Pour the sauce into the crock pot. Top the chicken with lemon slices. 3. Cover the cooker and cook for 6 to 8 hours on Low heat.

Lime and Jalapeño Chicken Thighs

Prep time: 15 minutes | Cook time: 8 hours | Serves 4

4 bone-in, skinless chicken thighs
¼ cup honey
Juice of 2 limes
Zest of 1 lime
1 jalapeño pepper, seeded and minced
½ teaspoon garlic powder

½ teaspoon sea salt

¼ cup chopped fresh cilantro

1. Put the chicken thighs in your crock pot. 2. In a small bowl, whisk together the honey, lime juice, lime zest, jalapeño, garlic powder, and salt. 3. Pour the mixture over the chicken. 4. Cover and cook on low for 8 hours. 5. Garnish with the cilantro before serving.

Chicken in Mushroom Sauce

Prep time: 15 minutes | Cook time: 4 to 5 hours | Serves 4

4 boneless, skinless chicken breast halves
1 (10¾-ounce / 305-g) can cream of mushroom soup
1 cup sour cream
1 (7-ounce / 198-g) can mushroom stems and pieces, drained (optional)
4 bacon strips, cooked and crumbled, or ¼ cup precooked bacon crumbles

1. Place chicken in slow cooker. 2. In a mixing bowl, combine soup and sour cream, and mushroom pieces if you wish. Pour over chicken. 3. Cover and cook on low 4 to 5 hours, or until chicken is tender, but not dry. 4. Sprinkle with bacon before serving. 5. Serve.

Loretta's Hot Chicken

Prep time: 15 minutes | Cook time: 2 hours | Serves 12

8 cups cubed cooked chicken or turkey
1 medium onion, chopped
1 cup cubed American cheese
1 cup chopped celery
2 cups mayonnaise

1. Combine all ingredients except buns in slow cooker. 2. Cover. Cook on high 2 hours. 3. Serve.

Moroccan Chicken with Apricots, Almonds, and Olives

Prep time: 10 minutes | Cook time: 2 hours | Serves 4

3 pounds (1.4 kg) skinless chicken thighs
1 yellow onion, cut into ½-inch wedges
1 teaspoon ground cumin
½ teaspoon ground ginger
½ teaspoon ground coriander
¼ teaspoon ground cinnamon
¼ teaspoon cayenne pepper
Sea salt
Black pepper
1 bay leaf
⅓ cup chicken stock
1 (15-ounce / 425-g) can chickpeas, drained and rinsed
½ cup green olives
½ cup dried turkish apricots
⅓ cup sliced almonds, toasted

1. In a large bowl, mix the chicken thighs and the onion. Add the cumin, coriander, ginger, cinnamon, and cayenne and toss to coat. Season the spiced chicken and onion with salt and pepper. 2. Transfer the chicken and onion to the crock pot. Add the bay leaf and chicken stock to the crock pot. 3. Cover and cook on high for 2 hours. 4. Stir in the chickpeas, olives, and apricots. Cover and cook until the chicken is tender and cooked through and the apricots are plump, about 1 hour more. 5. Remove the bay leaf and season the juices with salt and pepper. 6. Meanwhile, preheat the oven to 350°F(180°C). Spread the almonds in a pie plate and toast for about 7 minutes, until fragrant and lightly golden. Watch them so they don't burn. 7. Spoon the hot chicken, vegetables, and juices into shallow bowls, sprinkle with the toasted almonds, and serve.

Mandarin Orange Chicken

Prep time: 20 minutes | Cook time: 4½ to 5½ hours | Serves 4

4 boneless, skinless chicken breast halves
1 medium onion, thinly sliced
¼ cup orange juice concentrate
1 teaspoon poultry seasoning
½ teaspoon salt
1 (11-ounce / 312-g) can mandarin oranges, drained, with 3 tablespoons juice reserved
2 tablespoons flour

1. Place chicken in slow cooker. 2. Combine onion, orange juice concentrate, poultry seasoning, and salt. Pour over chicken. 3. Cover. Cook on low 4 to 5 hours. 4. Remove chicken and keep warm. Reserve cooking juices. 5. In a saucepan, combine 3 tablespoons reserved mandarin orange juice and flour. Stir until smooth. 6. Stir in chicken cooking juices. Bring to a boil. Stir and cook for 2 minutes to thicken. 7. Stir in mandarin oranges. Pour over chicken. 8. Serve.

Curried Chicken Dinner

Prep time: 20 minutes | Cook time: 5 to 10 hours | Serves 6

1½ pounds (680 g) boneless, skinless chicken thighs, quartered
3 potatoes, peeled and cut into chunks
1 apple, chopped
2 tablespoons curry powder
1 (14½-ounce / 411-g) can chicken broth
1 medium onion, chopped (optional)

1. Place all ingredients in slow cooker. Mix together gently. 2. Cover and cook on low 8 to 10 hours, or on high 5 hours, or until chicken is tender but not dry. 3. Serve.

Mix-It-and-Run Chicken

Prep time: 10 minutes | Cook time: 8 to 10 hours | Serves 4

2 (15-ounce / 425-g) cans cut green beans, undrained
2 (10¾-ounce / 305-g) cans cream of mushroom soup
4 to 6 boneless, skinless chicken breast halves
½ teaspoon salt

1. Drain beans, reserving juice in a medium-sized mixing bowl. 2. Stir soups into bean juice, blending thoroughly. Set aside. 3. Place beans in slow cooker. Sprinkle with salt. 4. Place chicken in cooker. Sprinkle with salt. 5. Top with soup. 6. Cover and cook on low 8 to 10 hours, or until chicken is tender, but not dry or mushy.

One-Pot Easy Chicken

Prep time: 30 minutes | Cook time: 6 hours | Serves 6

- 6 to 8 potatoes, quartered
- 1 to 2 large onions, sliced
- 3 to 5 carrots, cubed
- 1 (5-pound / 2.3-kg) chicken, skin removed
- 1 small onion, chopped
- 1 teaspoon black pepper
- 1 tablespoon whole cloves
- 1 tablespoon garlic salt
- 1 tablespoon chopped fresh oregano
- 1 teaspoon dried rosemary
- ½ cup lemon juice or chicken broth

1. Layer potatoes, sliced onions, and carrots in bottom of slow cooker. 2. Rinse and pat chicken dry. In bowl mix together chopped onions, pepper, cloves, and garlic salt. Dredge chicken in seasonings. Place in cooker over vegetables. Spoon any remaining seasonings over chicken. 3. Sprinkle with oregano and rosemary. Pour lemon juice over chicken. 4. Cover. Cook on low 6 hours.

Chicken and Sun-Dried Tomatoes

Prep time: 20 minutes | Cook time: 4 to 6 hours | Serves 8

- 1 tablespoon olive oil
- 3 pounds (1.4 kg) boneless, skinless chicken breasts, cut in 8 serving pieces
- 2 garlic cloves, minced
- ½ cup white wine
- 1½ cups fat-free, low-sodium chicken stock
- 1 teaspoon dried basil
- ½ cup chopped, sun-dried tomatoes, cut into slivers

1. Heat oil in skillet. Add several pieces of chicken at a time, but make sure not to crowd the skillet so the chicken can brown evenly. 2. Transfer chicken to slow cooker as it finishes browning. 3. Add garlic, wine, chicken stock, and basil to skillet. Bring to a boil. Scrape up any bits from the bottom of the pan. 4. Pour over chicken. Scatter tomatoes over the top. 5. Cover. Cook on low 4 to 6 hours.

Italian Chicken Stew

Prep time: 20 minutes | Cook time: 3 to 6 hours | Serves 4

- 2 boneless, skinless chicken breast halves, uncooked, cut in 1½-inch pieces
- 1 (19-ounce / 539-g) can cannellini beans, drained and rinsed
- 1 (15½-ounce / 439-g) can kidney beans, drained and rinsed
- 1 (14½-ounce / 411-g) can low-sodium diced tomatoes, undrained
- 1½ teaspoons dried Italian seasoning
- 1 cup chopped celery
- 1 cup sliced carrots
- 2 small garlic cloves, coarsely chopped
- 1 cup water
- ½ cup dry red wine or low-fat chicken broth
- 3 tablespoons tomato paste
- 1 tablespoon sugar

1. Combine chicken, cannellini beans, kidney beans, tomatoes, celery, carrots, and garlic in slow cooker. Mix well. 2. In medium bowl, combine all remaining ingredients. Mix well. Pour over chicken and vegetables. Mix well. 3. Cover. Cook on low 5 to 6 hours, or on high 3 hours.

Chicken with Broccoli Rice

Prep time: 20 minutes | Cook time: 6 to 8 hours | Serves 6

- 1¼ cups long-grain rice, uncooked
- Pepper to taste
- 2 pounds (907 g) boneless, skinless chicken breasts, cut into strips
- 1 package Knorr's cream of broccoli dry soup mix
- 2½ cups chicken broth
- Nonstick cooking spray

1. Spray slow cooker with nonstick cooking spray. Place rice in cooker. Sprinkle with pepper. 2. Top with chicken pieces. 3. In a mixing bowl, combine soup mix and broth. Pour over chicken and rice. 4. Cover and cook on low 6 to 8 hours, or until rice and chicken are tender but not dry.

Chicken, Broccoli, and Rice Casserole

Prep time: 10 minutes | Cook time: 3 to 7 hours | Serves 8

- 1 cup long-grain rice, uncooked
- 3 cups water
- 2 teaspoons low-sodium chicken bouillon granules
- 1 (10¾-ounce / 305-g) can fat-free, low-sodium cream of chicken soup
- 2 cups chopped, cooked chicken breast
- ¼ teaspoon garlic powder
- 1 teaspoon onion salt
- 1 cup shredded, fat-free Cheddar cheese
- 1 (16-ounce / 454-g) bag frozen broccoli, thawed

1. Combine all ingredients except broccoli in slow cooker. 2. One hour before end of cooking time, stir in broccoli. 3. Cook on high for a total of 3 to 4 hours, or on low for a total of 6 to 7 hours.

Noodleless Lasagna

Prep time: 20 minutes | Cook time: 4 to 4½ hours | Serves 4

- 1½ pounds (680 g) fat-free ground turkey
- 1½ cups meat-free, low-sodium spaghetti sauce
- 8 ounces (227 g) sliced mushrooms
- 1½ cups fat-free ricotta cheese
- 1 egg, beaten
- 1 cup shredded Mozzarella cheese (part skim), divided
- 1½ teaspoons Italian seasoning
- 10 slices turkey pepperoni
- Nonfat cooking spray

1. Brown ground turkey in a nonstick skillet. 2. Add spaghetti sauce and mushrooms and mix with meat. 3. Pour half of turkey mixture into slow cooker sprayed with nonfat cooking spray. 4. In a small bowl, mix together the ricotta cheese, egg, ¼ cup of Mozzarella, and the Italian seasoning. Beat well with a fork. 5. Lay half of pepperoni slices on top of turkey mixture. 6. Spread half of cheese mixture over pepperoni. 7. Repeat layers, finishing by sprinkling the remaining Mozzarella on top. 8. Cover. Cook on low 4 to 4½ hours.

Chicken with Applesauce

Prep time: 20 minutes | Cook time: 2 to 3 hours | Serves 4

4 boneless, skinless chicken breast halves
Salt to taste
Pepper to taste
4 to 5 tablespoons oil
2 cups applesauce
¼ cup barbecue sauce
½ teaspoon poultry seasoning
2 teaspoons honey
½ teaspoon lemon juice

1. Season chicken with salt and pepper. Brown in oil for 5 minutes per side. 2. Cut up chicken into 1-inch chunks and transfer to slow cooker. 3. Combine remaining ingredients. Pour over chicken and mix together well. 4. Cover. Cook on high 2 to 3 hours, or until chicken is tender. 5. Serve.

Herby Barbecued Chicken

Prep time: 10 minutes | Cook time: 6 to 8 hours | Serves 4 to 6

1 whole chicken, cut up, or 8 of your favorite pieces
1 onion, thinly sliced
1 bottle Sweet Baby Ray's Barbecue Sauce
1 teaspoon dried oregano
1 teaspoon dried basil

1. Place chicken in slow cooker. 2. Mix onion slices, sauce, oregano, and basil together in a bowl. Pour over chicken, covering as well as possible. 3. Cover and cook on low 6 to 8 hours, or until chicken is tender but not dry.

Chicken and Bean Torta

Prep time: 20 minutes | Cook time: 4 to 5 hours | Serves 6

1 pound (454 g) uncooked boneless, skinless chicken breasts
1 medium onion
½ teaspoon garlic salt
¼ teaspoon black pepper
1 (15-ounce / 425-g) can ranch-style black beans
1 (15-ounce / 425-g) can low-sodium diced tomatoes with green chilies
4 tortillas
1½ cups shredded low-fat Cheddar cheese
Salsa
Fat-free sour cream
Lettuce
Tomatoes
Nonfat cooking spray

1. Cut chicken in small pieces. Brown with onion in nonstick skillet. Drain well. 2. Season with garlic salt and pepper. Stir in beans and tomatoes. 3. Place strips of foil on bottom and up sides of slow cooker, forming an X. Spray foil and cooker lightly with nonfat cooking spray. 4. Place 1 tortilla on bottom of cooker. Spoon on one-third of chicken mixture and one-quarter of the cheese. 5. Repeat layers, ending with a tortilla sprinkled with cheese on top. 6. Cover. Cook on low 4 to 5 hours. 7. Remove to platter using foil strips as handles. Gently pull out foil and discard. 8. Serve with salsa, sour cream, lettuce, and tomatoes.

Turkey in the Slow Cooker

Prep time: 5 minutes | Cook time: 1 to 5 hours | Serves 6 to 8

1 (3- to 5-pound / 1.4- to 2.3-kg) bone-in turkey breast
Salt and pepper to taste
2 carrots, cut in chunks
1 onion, cut in eighths
2 ribs celery, cut in chunks

1. Rinse turkey breast and pat dry. Season well inside with salt. 2. Place vegetables in bottom of slow cooker. Sprinkle with pepper. Place turkey breast on top of vegetables. 3. Cover and cook on high 1 to 3 hours, on low 4 to 5 hours, or until tender but not dry or mushy.

Chicken and Rice

Prep time: 10 minutes | Cook time: 5 to 6 hours | Serves 6

1 (10¾-ounce / 305-g) can cream of chicken soup
1 package dry onion soup mix
2½ cups water
1 cup long-grain rice, uncooked
6 ounces (170 g) boneless, skinless chicken breast tenders
¼ teaspoon black pepper

1. Combine all ingredients in slow cooker. 2. Cook on low 5 to 6 hours. 3. Stir occasionally.

Cranberry Barbecued Chicken

Prep time: 10 minutes | Cook time: 4 to 8 hours | Serves 6 to 8

1 (3- to 4-pound / 1.4- to 1.8-kg) chicken pieces
½ teaspoon salt
¼ teaspoon pepper
½ cup diced celery
½ cup diced onions
1 (16-ounce / 454-g) can whole berry cranberry sauce
1 cup barbecue sauce

1. Combine all ingredients in slow cooker. 2. Cover. Cook on high for 4 hours, or on low 6 to 8 hours.

Chicken, Corn, and Stuffing

Prep time: 5 minutes | Cook time: 2 to 2½ hours | Serves 4

4 boneless, skinless chicken breast halves
1 (6-ounce / 170-g) box stuffing mix for chicken
1 (16-ounce / 454-g) package frozen whole-kernel corn
Half a stick butter, melted
2 cups water

1. Place chicken in bottom of slow cooker. 2. Mix remaining ingredients together in a mixing bowl. Spoon over chicken. 3. Cover and cook on high 2 to 2½ hours, or until chicken is tender and the stuffing is dry.

Another Chicken in a Pot

Prep time: 10 minutes | Cook time: 3½ to 10 hours | Serves 4 to 6

1 (1-pound / 454-g) bag baby carrots
1 small onion, diced
1 (14½-ounce / 411-g) can green beans
1 (3-pound / 1.4-kg) whole chicken, cut into serving-size pieces
2 teaspoons salt
½ teaspoon black pepper
½ cup chicken broth
¼ cup white wine
½ to 1 teaspoon dried basil

1. Put carrots, onion, and beans on bottom of slow cooker. Add chicken. Top with salt, pepper, broth, and wine. Sprinkle with basil. 2. Cover. Cook on low 8 to 10 hours, or on high 3½ to 5 hours.

Turkey Meat Loaf

Prep time: 15 minutes | Cook time: 6 to 8 hours | Serves 8

1½ pounds (680 g) lean ground turkey
2 egg whites
⅓ cup ketchup
1 tablespoon Worcestershire sauce
1 teaspoon dried basil
½ teaspoon salt
½ teaspoon black pepper
2 small onions, chopped
2 potatoes, finely shredded
2 small red bell peppers, finely chopped

1. Combine all ingredients in a large bowl. 2. Shape into a loaf to fit in your slow cooker. Place in slow cooker. 3. Cover. Cook on low 6 to 8 hours.

1. Combine tomatoes, vinegar, onions, garlic, Italian seasonings, and basil in slow cooker. Turn to low. 2. Combine remaining ingredients, except flour and oil. Form into 1-inch balls. Dredge each ball in flour. Brown in oil in skillet over medium heat. Transfer to slow cooker. Stir into sauce. 3. Cover. Cook on low 6 to 8 hours. 4. Serve.

Sweet Potatoes and Chicken Curry

Prep time: 10 minutes | Cook time: 5¼ to 6¼ hours | Serves 4

4 boneless, skinless chicken breast halves
1 small onion, chopped
2 sweet potatoes (about 1½ pounds / 680 g), cubed
⅔ cup orange juice
1 garlic clove, minced
1 teaspoon chicken bouillon granules
1 teaspoon salt
¼ teaspoon pepper
4 teaspoons curry powder
2 tablespoons cornstarch
2 tablespoons cold water
Sliced green onions
Shredded coconut
Peanuts
Raisins

1. Place chicken in slow cooker. Cover with onions and sweet potatoes. 2. Combine orange juice, garlic, chicken bouillon granules, salt, pepper, and curry powder. Pour over vegetables. 3. Cover. Cook on low 5 to 6 hours. 4. Remove chicken and vegetables and keep warm. 5. Turn slow cooker to high. Dissolve cornstarch in cold water. Stir into sauce in slow cooker. Cover. Cook on high 15 to 20 minutes. 6. Serve topped with your choice of remaining ingredients.

Savory Stuffed Green Peppers

Prep time: 20 minutes | Cook time: 3 to 9 hours | Serves 8

8 small green peppers, tops removed and seeded
1 (10-ounce / 283-g) package frozen corn
¾ pound (340 g) 99% fat-free ground turkey
¾ pound (340 g) extra-lean ground beef
1 (8-ounce / 227-g) can low-sodium tomato sauce
½ teaspoon garlic powder
¼ teaspoon black pepper
1 cup shredded low-fat American cheese
½ teaspoon Worcestershire sauce
¼ cup chopped onions
3 tablespoons water
2 tablespoons ketchup

1. Wash peppers and drain well. Combine all ingredients except water and ketchup in mixing bowl. Stir well. 2. Stuff peppers ⅔ full. 3. Pour water in slow cooker. Arrange peppers on top. 4. Pour ketchup over peppers. 5. Cover. Cook on high 3 to 4 hours, or on low 7 to 9 hours.

Low-Fat Chicken Cacciatore

Prep time: 15 minutes | Cook time: 8 hours | Serves 10

2 pounds (907 g) uncooked boneless, skinless chicken breasts, cubed
½ pound (227 g) fresh mushrooms
1 bell pepper, chopped
1 medium-sized onion, chopped
1 (12-ounce / 340-g) can low-sodium chopped tomatoes
1 (6-ounce / 170-g) can low-sodium tomato paste
1 (12-ounce / 340-g) can low-sodium tomato sauce
½ teaspoon dried oregano
½ teaspoon dried basil
½ teaspoon garlic powder
½ teaspoon salt
½ teaspoon black pepper

1. Combine all ingredients in slow cooker. 2. Cover. Cook on low 8 hours. 3. Serve.

Savory Turkey Meatballs in Italian Sauce

Prep time: 30 minutes | Cook time: 6 to 8 hours | Serves 8

1 (28-ounce / 794-g) can crushed tomatoes
1 tablespoon red wine vinegar
1 medium onion, finely chopped
2 garlic cloves, minced
¼ teaspoon Italian herb seasoning
1 teaspoon dried basil
1 pound (454 g) ground turkey
⅛ teaspoon garlic powder
⅛ teaspoon black pepper
⅓ cup dried parsley
2 egg whites
¼ teaspoon dried minced onion
⅓ cup quick oats
¼ cup grated Parmesan cheese
¼ cup flour
Oil

Chicken and Potatoes Barbecue

Prep time: 10 minutes | Cook time: 4 to 9 hours | Serves 8

8 boneless, skinless chicken breast halves, divided
8 small or medium potatoes, quartered, divided
1 cup honey barbecue sauce
1 (16-ounce / 454-g) can jellied cranberry sauce
Nonfat cooking spray

1. Spray slow cooker with nonstick cooking spray. Place 4 chicken breasts in slow cooker. 2. Top with 4 cut-up potatoes. 3. Mix barbecue sauce and cranberry sauce together in a bowl. Spoon half the sauce over the chicken and potatoes in the cooker. 4. Place remaining breasts in cooker, followed by the remaining potato chunks. Pour rest of sauce over all. 5. Cover and cook on low 8 to 9 hours, or on high 4 hours, or until chicken and potatoes are tender but not dry.

Sausage Pasta

Prep time: 20 minutes | Cook time: 8 to 10 hours | Serves 6

1 pound (454 g) turkey sausage, cut in 1-inch chunks
1 cup chopped green and/or red bell peppers
1 cup chopped celery
1 cup chopped red onions
1 cup chopped green zucchini
1 (8-ounce / 227-g) can tomato paste
2 cups water
1 (14-ounce / 397-g) tomatoes, chopped
¼ cup cooking wine
1 tablespoon Italian seasoning
1 pound (454 g) pasta, cooked

1. Combine all ingredients except pasta in slow cooker. 2. Cover. Cook on low 8 to 10 hours. 3. Add pasta 10 minutes before serving.

One-Dish Chicken Supper

Prep time: 5 minutes | Cook time: 6 to 8 hours | Serves 4

4 boneless, skinless chicken breast halves
1 (10¾-ounce / 305-g) can cream of chicken or celery or mushroom soup
⅓ cup milk
1 package Stove Top stuffing mix and seasoning packet
1⅔ cups water

1. Place chicken in slow cooker. 2. Combine soup and milk. Pour over chicken. 3. Combine stuffing mix, seasoning packet, and water. Spoon over chicken. 4. Cover. Cook on low 6 to 8 hours.

Saucy Turkey Meatballs

Prep time: 20 minutes | Cook time: 6 to 8 hours | Serves 6

½ pound (227 g) lean ground turkey
1 cup oat bran
1 clove garlic, crushed
2 tablespoons water
1 tablespoon low-sodium soy sauce
3 egg whites
½ cup onions, diced
½ cup low-sodium chili sauce
½ cup grape jelly
¼ cup Dijon mustard

1. Combine turkey, oat bran, garlic, water, soy sauce, egg whites, and onions. Shape into 24 balls (1 tablespoon per ball). 2. Place meatballs on baking sheet and bake at 350° for 15 to 20 minutes until browned. (They can be made ahead and frozen.) 3. Mix together chili sauce, grape jelly, and Dijon mustard. 4. Combine meatballs and sauce in slow cooker. 5. Cover. Cook on low 6 to 8 hours.

Tender Turkey Breast

Prep time: 5 minutes | Cook time: 2 to 9 hours | Serves 10

1 (6-pound / 2.7-kg) boneless or bone-in turkey breast
2 to 3 tablespoons water

1. Place the turkey breast in the slow cooker. Add water. 2. Cover and cook on high 2 to 4 hours, or on low 4 to 9 hours, or until tender but not dry and mushy. 3. Turn over once during cooking time. 4. If you'd like to brown the turkey, place it in your oven and bake it uncovered at 325°F (165°C) for 15 to 20 minutes after it's finished cooking in the slow cooker.

Barbecued Turkey Legs

Prep time: 10 minutes | Cook time: 5 to 7 hours | Serves 4 to 6

4 turkey drumsticks
1 to 2 teaspoons salt
¼ to ½ teaspoon pepper
⅓ cup molasses
¼ cup vinegar
½ cup ketchup
3 tablespoons Worcestershire sauce
¾ teaspoon hickory smoke
2 tablespoons instant minced onion

1. Sprinkle turkey with salt and pepper. Place in slow cooker. 2. Combine remaining ingredients. Pour over turkey. 3. Cover. Cook on low 5 to 7 hours.

Slow-Cooked Turkey Dinner

Prep time: 15 minutes | Cook time: 7½ hours | Serves 4 to 6

1 onion, diced
6 small red potatoes, quartered
2 cups sliced carrots
1½ to 2 pounds (680 to 907 g) boneless, skinless turkey thighs
¼ cup flour
2 tablespoons dry onion soup mix
1 (10¾-ounce / 305-g) can cream of mushroom soup
⅔ cup chicken broth or water

1. Place vegetables in bottom of slow cooker. 2. Place turkey thighs over vegetables. 3. Combine remaining ingredients. Pour over turkey. 4. Cover. Cook on high 30 minutes. Reduce heat to low and cook 7 hours.

Herby Chicken and Stuffing

Prep time: 20 minutes | Cook time: 4½ to 5 hours | Serves 14 to 16

2½ cups chicken broth
1 cup butter, melted
½ cup chopped onions
½ cup chopped celery
1 (4-ounce / 113-g) can mushrooms, stems and pieces, drained
¼ cup dried parsley flakes
1½ teaspoons rubbed sage
1 teaspoon poultry seasoning
1 teaspoon salt
½ teaspoon pepper
12 cups day-old bread cubes (½-inch pieces)
2 eggs
1 (10¾-ounce / 305-g) can cream of chicken soup
5 to 6 cups cubed cooked chicken

1. Combine all ingredients except bread, eggs, soup, and chicken in saucepan. Simmer for 10 minutes. 2. Place bread cubes in large bowl. 3. Combine eggs and soup. Stir into broth mixture until smooth. Pour over bread and toss well. 4. Layer half of stuffing and then half of chicken into very large slow cooker (or two medium-sized cookers). Repeat layers. 5. Cover. Cook on low 4½ to 5 hours.

Chicken and Shrimp Casserole

Prep time: 20 minutes | Cook time: 3 to 8 hours | Serves 6

1¼ cups rice, uncooked
2 tablespoons butter, melted
3 cups fat-free, low-sodium chicken broth
1 cup water
3 cups cut-up, cooked skinless chicken breast
2 (4-ounce / 113-g) cans sliced mushrooms, drained
⅓ cup light soy sauce
1 (12-ounce / 340-g) package shelled frozen shrimp
8 green onions, chopped, 2 tablespoons reserved
⅔ cup slivered almonds

1. Combine rice and butter in slow cooker. Stir to coat rice well. 2. Add remaining ingredients except almonds and 2 tablespoons green onions. 3. Cover. Cook on low 6 to 8 hours, or on high 3 to 4 hours, until rice is tender. 4. Sprinkle almonds and green onions over top before serving.

Coq au Vin

Prep time: 25 minutes | Cook time: 5 to 6 hours | Serves 6

4 slices turkey bacon
1½ cups frozen pearl onions
1 cup fresh, sliced, button mushrooms
1 clove garlic, minced
1 teaspoon dried thyme leaves
¼ teaspoon coarse ground black pepper
6 boneless, skinless chicken breast halves
½ cup dry red wine
¾ cup fat-free, low-sodium chicken broth
¼ cup tomato paste
3 tablespoons flour

1. Cook bacon in medium skillet over medium heat. Drain and crumble. 2. Layer ingredients in slow cooker in the following order: onions, crumbled bacon, mushrooms, garlic, thyme, pepper, chicken, wine, and broth. 3. Cover. Cook on low 5 to 6 hours. 4. Remove chicken and vegetables. Cover. Keep warm. 5. Ladle ½ cup cooking liquid into small bowl. Allow to cool slightly. 6. Turn slow cooker to high. Cover. 7. Mix removed liquid, tomato paste, and flour until smooth. 8. Return tomato mixture to slow cooker. 9. Cover. Cook 15 minutes or until thickened. 10. Serve.

Southern Barbecue Spaghetti Sauce

Prep time: 20 minutes | Cook time: 4 to 5 hours | Serves 12

1 pound (454 g) lean ground turkey
2 medium onions, chopped
1½ cups sliced fresh mushrooms
1 medium green bell pepper, chopped
2 garlic cloves, minced
1 (14½-ounce / 411-g) can diced tomatoes, undrained
1 (12-ounce / 340-g) can tomato paste
1 (8-ounce / 227-g) can tomato sauce
1 cup ketchup
½ cup fat-free beef broth
2 tablespoons Worcestershire sauce
2 tablespoons brown sugar
1 tablespoon ground cumin
2 teaspoons chili powder
12 cups spaghetti, cooked

1. In a large nonstick skillet, cook the turkey, onions, mushrooms, green pepper, and garlic over medium heat until meat is no longer pink. Drain. 2. Transfer to slow cooker. Stir in tomatoes, tomato paste, tomato sauce, ketchup, broth, Worcestershire sauce, brown sugar, cumin, and chili powder. Mix well. 3. Cook on low 4 to 5 hours. Serve over spaghetti.

Chicken Vegetable Gala

Prep time: 15 minutes | Cook time: 6 to 8 hours | Serves 4

4 bone-in chicken breast halves
1 small head of cabbage, quartered
1 (1-pound / 454-g) package baby carrots
2 (14½-ounce / 411-g) cans Mexican-flavored stewed tomatoes

1. Place all ingredients in slow cooker in order listed. 2. Cover and cook on low 6 to 8 hours, or until chicken and vegetables are tender.

Lemon-Honey Chicken

Prep time: 5 minutes | Cook time: 8 hours | Serves 4 to 6

1 lemon
1 whole roasting chicken, rinsed
½ cup orange juice
½ cup honey

1. Pierce lemon with fork. Place in chicken cavity. Place chicken in slow cooker. 2. Combine orange juice and honey. Pour over chicken. 3. Cover. Cook on low 8 hours. Remove lemon and squeeze over chicken. 4. Carve chicken and serve.

One-Pot Chicken Dinner

Prep time: 15 minutes | Cook time: 3 to 6 hours | Serves 6

12 chicken drumsticks or thighs, skin removed
3 medium sweet potatoes, cut into 2-inch pieces
1 (12-ounce / 340-g) jar chicken gravy, or 1 (10¾-ounce / 305-g) can cream of chicken soup
2 tablespoons unbleached flour, if using chicken gravy
1 teaspoon dried parsley flakes (optional)
½ teaspoon dried rosemary (optional)
Salt and pepper to taste (optional)
1 (10-ounce / 283-g) package frozen cut green beans

1. Place chicken in slow cooker. Top with sweet potatoes chunks. 2. In small bowl, combine remaining ingredients, except beans, and mix until smooth. Pour over chicken. 3. Cover and cook on high 1½ hours, or on low 3½ hours. 4. One and one-half hours before serving, stir green beans into chicken mixture. Cover and cook on low 1 to 2 hours, or until chicken, sweet potatoes, and green beans are tender, but not dry or mushy.

Reuben Chicken Casserole

Prep time: 30 minutes | Cook time: 4 hours | Serves 6

2 (16-ounce / 454-g) cans sauerkraut, rinsed and drained, divided
1 cup Light Russian salad dressing, divided
6 boneless, skinless chicken breast halves, divided
1 tablespoon prepared mustard, divided
6 slices Swiss cheese
Fresh parsley for garnish (optional)

1. Place half the sauerkraut in the slow cooker. Drizzle with ⅓ cup dressing. 2. Top with 3 chicken breast halves. Spread half the mustard on top of the chicken. 3. Top with remaining sauerkraut and chicken breasts. Drizzle with another ⅓ cup dressing. (Save the remaining dressing until serving time.) 4. Cover and cook on low for 4 hours, or until the chicken is tender, but not dry or mushy. 5. To serve, place a breast half on each of 6 plates. Divide the sauerkraut over the chicken. Top each with a slice of cheese and a drizzle of the remaining dressing. Garnish with parsley if you wish, just before serving.

Chicken Breasts with Rosemary

Prep time: 10 minutes | Cook time: 3 to 6 hours | Serves 4

4 boneless, skinless chicken breast halves (4 ounces /113 g each)
1½ teaspoons balsamic vinegar
1 teaspoon minced garlic
1 tablespoon grated lemon rind
¼ teaspoon salt
⅛ teaspoon black pepper
½ cup dry white wine or reduced-sodium chicken broth
1 teaspoon finely chopped fresh rosemary, or ½ teaspoon dried
½ cup fresh diced tomato

1. Place chicken breasts in slow cooker. 2. Mix vinegar, garlic, lemon rind, salt, pepper, and wine. Pour over chicken. 3. Cover. Cook on low 6 hours, or on high 3 hours. 4. One-half hour before the end of the cooking time, stir in rosemary and fresh tomato.

Dad's Spicy Chicken Curry

Prep time: 25 minutes | Cook time: 6 to 8 hours | Serves 8

4 pounds (1.8 kg) chicken pieces, with bones
Water
2 onions, diced
1 (10-ounce / 283-g) package frozen chopped spinach, thawed and squeezed dry
1 cup plain yogurt
2 to 3 diced red potatoes
3 teaspoons salt
1 teaspoon garlic powder
1 teaspoon ground ginger
1 teaspoon ground cumin
1 teaspoon ground coriander
1 teaspoon pepper
1 teaspoon ground cloves
1 teaspoon ground cardamom
1 teaspoon ground cinnamon
½ teaspoon chili powder
1 teaspoon red pepper flakes
3 teaspoons turmeric

1. Place chicken in large slow cooker. Cover with water. 2. Cover. Cook on high 2 hours, or until tender. 3. Drain chicken. Remove from slow cooker. Cool briefly and cut/shred into small pieces. Return to slow cooker. 4. Add remaining ingredients. 5. Cover. Cook on low 4 to 6 hours, or until potatoes are tender. 6. Serve.

Chicken in a Hurry

Prep time: 10 minutes | Cook time: 4 to 8 hours | Serves 4 to 5

2½ to 3 pounds (1.1 to 1.4 kg) skinless chicken drumsticks
½ cup ketchup
1 package dry onion soup mix
¼ cup water
¼ cup brown sugar

1. Arrange chicken in slow cooker. 2. Combine remaining ingredients. Pour over chicken. 3. Cover. Cook on high 4 to 5 hours, or on low 7 to 8 hours.

Garlic-Lime Chicken

Prep time: 10 minutes | Cook time: 4 to 8 hours | Serves 5

5 chicken breast halves
½ cup soy sauce
¼ to ⅓ cup lime juice, according to your taste preference
1 tablespoon Worcestershire sauce
2 garlic cloves, minced, or 1 teaspoon garlic powder
½ teaspoon dry mustard
½ teaspoon ground pepper

1. Place chicken in slow cooker. 2. Combine remaining ingredients and pour over chicken. 3. Cover. Cook on high 4 to 6 hours, or on low 6 to 8 hours.

Come-Back-for-More Barbecued Chicken

Prep time: 10 minutes | Cook time: 6 to 8 hours | Serves 6 to 8

6 to 8 chicken breast halves
1 cup ketchup
⅓ cup Worcestershire sauce
½ cup brown sugar
1 teaspoon chili powder
½ cup water

1. Place chicken in slow cooker. 2. Whisk remaining ingredients in a large bowl. Pour sauce mixture over chicken. 3. Cover and cook on low 6 to 8 hours, or until chicken is tender but not overcooked.

Chicken-Vegetable Dish

Prep time: 10 minutes | Cook time: 2 to 5 hours | Serves 4

4 skinless bone-in chicken breast halves
1 (15-ounce / 425-g) can crushed tomatoes
1 (10-ounce / 283-g) package frozen green beans
2 cups water or chicken broth
1 cup brown rice, uncooked
1 cup sliced mushrooms
2 carrots, chopped
1 onion, chopped
½ teaspoon minced garlic
½ teaspoon herb-blend seasoning
¼ teaspoon dried tarragon

1. Combine all ingredients in slow cooker. 2. Cover. Cook on high 2 hours, and then on low 3 to 5 hours.

Chicken and Sausage Cacciatore

Prep time: 35 minutes | Cook time: 8 hours | Serves 4 to 6

1 large green pepper, sliced in 1-inch strips
1 cup sliced mushrooms
1 medium onion, sliced in rings
1 pound (454 g) skinless, boneless chicken breasts, browned
1 pound (454 g) Italian sausage, browned
½ teaspoon dried oregano
½ teaspoon dried basil
1½ cups Italian-style tomato sauce

1. Layer vegetables in slow cooker. 2. Top with meat. 3. Sprinkle with oregano and basil. 4. Top with tomato sauce. 5. Cover. Cook on low 8 hours. 6. Remove cover during last 30 minutes of cooking time to allow sauce to cook off and thicken. 7. Serve.

Healthy Chicken

Prep time: 10 minutes | Cook time: 3½ to 4 hours | Serves 8

3½ pounds (1.6 kg) chicken pieces or whole chicken, cut up
2 cups skim milk
5 cups rice or corn cereal, finely crushed
1 teaspoon salt
½ teaspoon black pepper

1. Remove skin from chicken. Dip in milk. 2. Put crumbs in a plastic bag. Drop chicken pieces into bag to coat with cereal. Shake well. 3. Place chicken pieces in slow cooker. Sprinkle with salt and pepper. 4. Cover. Cook on high 3½ to 4 hours.

Chicken Gumbo

Prep time: 25 minutes | Cook time: 3 to 10 hours | Serves 6 to 8

1 large onion, chopped
3 to 4 garlic cloves, minced
1 green pepper, diced
2 cups okra, sliced
2 cups tomatoes, chopped
4 cups chicken broth
1 pound (454 g) chicken breast, cut into 1-inch pieces
2 teaspoons Old Bay Seasoning

1. Combine all ingredients in slow cooker. 2. Cover. Cook on low 8 to 10 hours, or on high 3 to 4 hours. 3. Serve.

Can-You-Believe-It's-So-Simple Salsa Chicken

Prep time: 5 minutes | Cook time: 5 to 8 hours | Serves 4 to 6

4 to 6 boneless, skinless chicken breast halves
1 (16-ounce / 454-g) jar chunky-style salsa, your choice
of heat
2 cups shredded cheese, your choice of flavor

1. Place chicken in slow cooker. Pour salsa over chicken. 2. Cover and cook on low 5 to 8 hours, or until chicken is tender but not dry. 3. Top individual servings with shredded cheese and serve.

Pumpkin Black Bean Turkey Chili

Prep time: 20 minutes | Cook time: 7 to 8 hours | Serves 10 to 12

1 cup chopped onions
1 cup chopped yellow bell pepper
3 garlic cloves, minced
2 tablespoons oil
1½ teaspoons dried oregano
1½ to 2 teaspoons ground cumin
2 teaspoons chili powder
2 (15-ounce / 425-g) cans black beans, rinsed and drained
2½ cups cooked turkey, chopped
1 (16-ounce / 454-g) can pumpkin
1 (14½-ounce / 411-g) can diced tomatoes
3 cups chicken broth

1. Sauté onions, yellow pepper, and garlic in oil for 8 minutes, or until soft. 2. Stir in oregano, cumin, and chili powder. 3. Cook 1 minute. Transfer to slow cooker. Add remaining ingredients. 4. Cover. Cook on low 7 to 8 hours.

Chicken and Ham Gumbo

Prep time: 20 minutes | Cook time: 6 to 8 hours | Serves 4

1½ pounds (680 g) boneless, skinless chicken thighs, cubed
1 tablespoon oil
1 (10-ounce / 283-g) package frozen okra
½ pound (227 g) smoked ham, cut into small chunks
1½ cups coarsely chopped onions
1½ cups coarsely chopped green peppers
2 or 3 (10-ounce / 283-g) cans cannellini beans, drained
6 cups chicken broth
2 (10-ounce / 283-g) cans diced tomatoes with green chilies
2 tablespoons chopped fresh cilantro

1. Cook chicken pieces in oil in skillet until no longer pink. 2. Run hot water over okra until pieces separate easily. 3. Combine all ingredients but cilantro in slow cooker. 4. Cover. Cook on low 6 to 8 hours. Stir in cilantro before serving.

Chicken at a Whim

Prep time: 10 minutes | Cook time: 4½ hours | Serves 6 to 8

6 medium, boneless, skinless chicken breast halves
1 small onion, sliced
1 cup dry white wine, chicken broth, or water
1 (15-ounce / 425-g) can chicken broth
2 cups water
1 (6-ounce / 170-g) can sliced black olives, with juice
1 small can artichoke hearts, with juice
5 garlic cloves, minced
1 cup dry elbow macaroni or small shells
1 envelope dry savory garlic soup

1. Place chicken in slow cooker. Spread onion over chicken. 2. Combine remaining ingredients, except dry soup mix, and pour over chicken. Sprinkle with dry soup. 3. Cover. Cook on low 4½ hours.

Lemon Chicken

Prep time: 20 minutes | Cook time: 3½ to 4½ hours | Serves 6

6 boneless, skinless chicken breast halves
1 teaspoon dried oregano
½ teaspoon seasoned salt
¼ teaspoon black pepper
¼ cup water
3 tablespoons lemon juice
2 garlic cloves, minced
2 teaspoons chicken bouillon granules
2 teaspoons fresh parsley, minced

1. Pat chicken dry with paper towels. 2. Combine oregano, seasoned salt, and pepper. Rub over chicken. 3. Brown chicken in a nonstick skillet over medium heat. 4. Place chicken in slow cooker. 5. Combine water, lemon juice, garlic, and bouillon in skillet. Bring to a boil, stirring to loosen browned bits. Pour over chicken. 6. Cover. Cook on low 3 to 4 hours. 7. Baste chicken. Add parsley. 8. Remove lid and cook 15 to 30 minutes longer, allowing juices to thicken slightly. 9. Serve.

Cranberry Chicken

Prep time: 10 minutes | Cook time: 6 to 8 hours | Serves 6

6 chicken breast halves, divided
1 (8-ounce / 227-g) bottle Catalina or Creamy French salad dressing
1 envelope dry onion soup mix
1 (16-ounce / 454-g) can whole cranberry sauce

1. Place 3 chicken breasts in slow cooker. 2. Mix other ingredients together in a mixing bowl. Pour half the sauce over chicken in the cooker. 3. Repeat Steps 1 and 2. 4. Cover and cook on low 6 to 8 hours, or until chicken is tender but not dry.

Chapter 9　Fish and Seafood

Citrus Swordfish

Prep time: 10 minutes | Cook time: 1½ hours | Serves 2

Nonstick cooking oil spray
1½ pounds (680 g) swordfish fillets
Sea salt
Black pepper
1 yellow onion, chopped
5 tablespoons chopped fresh flat-leaf parsley
1 tablespoon olive oil
2 teaspoons lemon zest
2 teaspoons orange zest
Orange and lemon slices, for garnish
Fresh parsley sprigs, for garnish

1. Coat the interior of the crock pot crock with nonstick cooking oil spray. 2. Season the fish fillets with salt and pepper. Place the fish in the crock pot. 3. Distribute the onion, parsley, olive oil, lemon zest, and orange zest over fish. 4. Cover and cook on low for 1½ hours. 5. Serve hot, garnished with orange and lemon slices and sprigs of fresh parsley.

Simple Poached Turbot

Prep time: 10 minutes | Cook time: 50 minutes | Serves 4

1 cup vegetable or chicken stock
½ cup dry white wine
1 yellow onion, sliced
1 lemon, sliced
4 sprigs fresh dill
½ teaspoon sea salt
4 (6-ounce / 170-g) turbot fillets

1. Combine the stock and wine in the crock pot. Cover and heat on high for 20 to 30 minutes. 2. Add the onion, lemon, dill, salt, and turbot to the crock pot. Cover and cook on high for about 20 minutes, until the turbot is opaque and cooked through according to taste. Serve hot.

Honeyed Salmon

Prep time: 10 minutes | Cook time: 1 hour | Serves 6

6 (6-ounce / 170-g) salmon fillets
½ cup honey
2 tablespoons lime juice
3 tablespoons worcestershire sauce
1 tablespoon water
2 cloves garlic, minced
1 teaspoon ground ginger
½ teaspoon black pepper

1. Place the salmon fillets in the crock pot. 2. In medium bowl, whisk the honey, lime juice, Worcestershire sauce, water, garlic, ginger, and pepper. Pour sauce over salmon. 3. Cover and cook on high for 1 hour.

Creole Crayfish

Prep time: 10 minutes | Cook time: 3 to 4 hours | Serves 2

1½ cups diced celery
1 large yellow onion, chopped
2 small bell peppers, any colors, chopped
1 (8-ounce / 227-g) can tomato sauce
1 (28-ounce / 794-g) can whole tomatoes, broken up, with the juice
1 clove garlic, minced
½ teaspoon sea salt
¼ teaspoon black pepper
6 drops hot pepper sauce (like tabasco)
1 pound (454 g) precooked crayfish meat

1. Place the celery, onion, and bell peppers in the crock pot. Add the tomato sauce, tomatoes, and garlic. Sprinkle with the salt and pepper and add the hot sauce. 2. Cover and cook on high for 3 to 4 hours or on low for 6 to 8 hours. 3. About 30 minutes before the cooking time is completed, add the crayfish. 4. Serve hot.

Shrimp with Marinara Sauce

Prep time: 15 minutes | Cook time: 6 to 7 hours | Serves 4

1 (15-ounce / 425-g) can diced tomatoes, with the juice
1 (6-ounce / 170-g) can tomato paste
1 clove garlic, minced
2 tablespoons minced fresh flat-leaf parsley
½ teaspoon dried basil
1 teaspoon dried oregano
1 teaspoon garlic powder
1½ teaspoons sea salt
¼ teaspoon black pepper
1 pound (454 g) cooked shrimp, peeled and deveined
2 cups hot cooked spaghetti or linguine, for serving
½ cup grated parmesan cheese, for serving

1. Combine the tomatoes, tomato paste, and minced garlic in the crock pot. Sprinkle with the parsley, basil, oregano, garlic powder, salt, and pepper. 2. Cover and cook on low for 6 to 7 hours. 3. Turn up the heat to high, stir in the cooked shrimp, and cover and cook on high for about 15 minutes longer. 4. Serve hot over the cooked pasta. Top with Parmesan cheese.

Fish Chili

Prep time: 10 minutes | Cook time: 5 to 7 hours | Serves 6

1 (28-ounce / 794-g) can no-salt-added diced tomatoes
1 (15-ounce / 425-g) can reduced sodium white beans, drained and rinsed
1 (10-ounce / 283-g) can no-salt-added diced tomatoes with green chiles
1 (8-ounce / 227-g) can no-salt-added tomato sauce
3 garlic cloves, minced
1 small onion, diced
1 bell pepper, any color, seeded and diced
2 tablespoons chili powder
2 teaspoons ground cumin
1½ teaspoons paprika
1 teaspoon sea salt
1 teaspoon dried oregano
2 pounds (907 g) fresh or frozen fish fillets of your choice, cut into 2-inch pieces

1. In a crock pot, combine the tomatoes, beans, tomatoes with green chiles, tomato sauce, garlic, onion, bell pepper, chili powder, cumin, paprika, salt, and oregano. Stir to mix well. 2. Cover the cooker and cook for 5 to 7 hours on Low heat. 3. Stir in the fish, replace the cover on the cooker, and cook for 30 minutes on Low heat.

Scallop and Crab Cioppino

Prep time: 15 minutes | Cook time: 6½ hours | Serves 4

Cooking oil spray
1 medium yellow onion, finely chopped
4 cloves garlic, minced
1 (15-ounce / 425-g) can diced tomatoes, with the juice
1 (10-ounce / 283-g0 can diced tomatoes with green chiles
2 cups seafood stock
1 cup red wine
3 tablespoons chopped fresh basil
2 bay leaves
1 pound (454 g) cooked crabmeat, shredded
1½ pounds (680 g) scallops
Sea salt
Black pepper
¼ cup fresh flat-leaf parsley, for garnish

1. Coat a large sauté pan with cooking oil spray and heat over medium-high heat. Add the onion and sauté for about 5 minutes, until softened. 2. Add the garlic and sauté until golden and fragrant, about 2 minutes. 3. Transfer the onion and garlic to the crock pot, and add the tomatoes, tomatoes with green chiles, stock, wine, basil, and bay leaves. Cover and cook on low for 6 hours. 4. About 30 minutes before the cooking time is completed, add the crabmeat and scallops. Cover and cook on high for 30 minutes. The seafood will turn opaque. Season to taste with salt and pepper. Serve hot, garnished with parsley.

Seasoned Sole

Prep time: 5 minutes | Cook time: 2 to 4 hours | Serves 4

Nonstick cooking spray
2 pounds (907 g) fresh sole fillets
3 tablespoons freshly squeezed lime juice
2 tablespoons extra-virgin olive oil
2 garlic cloves, minced
1 tablespoon ground cumin
1½ teaspoons paprika
1 teaspoon sea salt
¼ cup fresh cilantro

1. Coat a slow-cooker insert with cooking spray, or line the bottom and sides with parchment paper or aluminum foil. 2. Place the sole in the prepared crock pot in a single layer, cutting it into pieces to fit if needed. 3. In a small bowl, whisk together the lime juice, olive oil, garlic, cumin, paprika, and salt until blended. Pour the sauce over the fish. 4. Cover the cooker and cook for 2 to 4 hours on Low heat. 5. Garnish with fresh cilantro for serving.

Spicy Tomato Basil Mussels

Prep time: 20 minutes | Cook time: 5½ hours | Serves 4

3 tablespoons olive oil
4 cloves garlic, minced
3 shallot cloves, minced
8 ounces (227 g) mushrooms, diced
1 (28-ounce / 794-g) can diced tomatoes, with the juice
¾ cup white wine
2 tablespoons dried oregano
½ tablespoon dried basil
½ teaspoon black pepper
1 teaspoon paprika
¼ teaspoon red pepper flakes
3 pounds (1.4 kg) mussels

1. In a large sauté pan, heat the olive oil over medium-high heat. Cook the garlic, shallots, and mushrooms for 2 to 3 minutes, until the garlic is just a bit brown and fragrant. Scrape the entire contents of the pan into the crock pot. 2. Add the tomatoes and white wine to the crock pot. Sprinkle with the oregano, basil, black pepper, paprika, and red pepper flakes. 3. Cover and cook on low for 4 to 5 hours, or on high for 2 to 3 hours. The mixture is done cooking when mushrooms are fork tender. 4. Clean and debeard the mussels. Discard any open mussels. 5. Increase the heat on the crock pot to high once the mushroom mixture is done. Add the cleaned mussels to the crock pot and secure the lid tightly. Cook for 30 more minutes. 6. To serve, ladle the mussels into bowls with plenty of broth. Discard any mussels that didn't open up during cooking. Serve hot, with crusty bread for sopping up the sauce.

Moroccan Fish

Prep time: 10 minutes | Cook time: 2 to 4 hours | Serves 4

Ras Al-Hanout:
¼ teaspoon ground cumin
¼ teaspoon ground ginger
¼ teaspoon ground turmeric
¼ teaspoon paprika
¼ teaspoon garlic powder
¼ teaspoon red pepper flakes
⅛ teaspoon ground cinnamon
⅛ teaspoon ground coriander
⅛ teaspoon ground nutmeg
⅛ teaspoon ground cloves
⅛ teaspoon sea salt
⅛ teaspoon freshly ground black pepper
Fish:
Nonstick cooking spray
2 pounds (907 g) fresh white-fleshed fish fillets of your choice
2 garlic cloves, minced

Make the Ras Al-Hanout: In a small bowl, stir together the cumin, ginger, turmeric, paprika, garlic powder, red pepper flakes, cinnamon, coriander, nutmeg, cloves, salt, and pepper. Make the Fish: 1. Coat a slow-cooker insert with cooking spray, or line the bottom and sides with parchment paper or aluminum foil. 2. Season the fish all over with the ras al-hanout and garlic. Place the fish in the prepared crock pot in a single layer, cutting it into pieces to fit if needed. 3. Cover the cooker and cook for 2 to 4 hours on Low heat.

Tomato-Basil Salmon

Prep time: 10 minutes | Cook time: 4 to 6 hours | Serves 4

1 (15-ounce / 425-g) can no-salt-added crushed tomatoes
½ cup chopped onion
4 teaspoons dried basil
3 garlic cloves, minced
2 pounds (907 g) fresh salmon fillets, skin on or off as preferred
1 teaspoon sea salt
¼ teaspoon freshly ground black pepper
¼ cup chopped fresh basil

1. In a crock pot, combine the tomatoes, onion, basil, and garlic. Stir to mix well. 2. Season the salmon all over with salt and pepper. Add the salmon to the crock pot, cutting it into pieces to fit if needed, and spoon some of the tomato mixture on top. 3. Cover the cooker and cook for 4 to 6 hours on Low heat. 4. Garnish with fresh basil for serving.

Sesame-Ginger Cod

Prep time: 10 minutes | Cook time: 4 to 6 hours | Serves 4

¼ cup low-sodium soy sauce
2 tablespoons balsamic vinegar
1 tablespoon freshly squeezed lemon juice
2 teaspoons extra-virgin olive oil
1 tablespoon ground ginger
½ teaspoon sea salt
¼ teaspoon freshly ground black pepper
Nonstick cooking spray
2 pounds (907 g) fresh cod fillets
½ teaspoon sesame seeds
4 scallions, green parts only, cut into 3-inch lengths

1. In a small bowl, whisk together the soy sauce, vinegar, lemon juice, olive oil, ginger, salt, and pepper until combined. Set aside. 2. Coat a slow-cooker insert with cooking spray and place the cod in the prepared crock pot. Pour the soy sauce mixture over the cod. 3. Cover the cooker and cook for 4 to 6 hours on Low heat. 4. Garnish with sesame seeds and scallions for serving.

Shrimp Risotto

Prep time: 10 minutes | Cook time: 4 to 6 hours | Serves 4

1½ cups raw arborio rice
4½ cups low-sodium chicken broth
½ cup diced onion
2 garlic cloves, minced
½ teaspoon sea salt
½ teaspoon dried parsley
¼ teaspoon freshly ground black pepper
1 pound (454 g) whole raw medium shrimp, peeled and deveined
¼ cup grated Parmesan cheese

1. In a crock pot, combine the rice, chicken broth, onion, garlic, salt, parsley, and pepper. Stir to mix well. 2. Cover the cooker and cook for 4 to 6 hours on Low heat. 3. Stir in the shrimp and Parmesan cheese. Replace the cover on the cooker and cook for 15 to 30 minutes on Low heat, or until the shrimp have turned pink and the cheese is melted.

Shrimp Foil Packets

Prep time: 15 minutes | Cook time: 4 to 6 hours | Serves 4

1½ pounds (680 g) whole raw medium shrimp, peeled, deveined, and divided into 4 (6-ounce / 170-g) portions
Sea salt
Freshly ground black pepper
2 teaspoons extra-virgin olive oil, divided
4 teaspoons balsamic vinegar, divided
4 garlic cloves, minced
1 red onion, cut into chunks
1 large zucchini, sliced
4 Roma tomatoes, chopped
4 teaspoons dried oregano, divided
Juice of 1 lemon

1. Place a large sheet of aluminum foil on a work surface. Lay one-quarter of the shrimp in the center of the foil and season it with salt and pepper. Drizzle with ½ teaspoon of olive oil and 1 teaspoon of vinegar. 2. Top the shrimp with one-quarter each of the garlic, onion, and zucchini, plus 1 tomato and 1 teaspoon of oregano. Place a second sheet of foil on top of the ingredients. Fold the corners over to seal the packet. 3. Repeat to make 3 more foil packets. Place the packets in a crock pot in a single layer, or stack them if needed. 4. Cover the cooker and cook for 4 to 6 hours on Low heat. 5. Be careful when serving: Very hot steam will release when you open the foil packets. Drizzle each opened packet with lemon juice for serving.

Herbed Tuna Steaks

Prep time: 10 minutes | Cook time: 4 to 6 hours | Serves 4

Nonstick cooking spray
4 (1-inch-thick) fresh tuna steaks (about 2 pounds / 907 g total)
1 teaspoon sea salt
¼ teaspoon freshly ground black pepper
2 teaspoons extra-virgin olive oil
2 teaspoons dried thyme
2 teaspoons dried rosemary

1. Coat a slow-cooker insert with cooking spray, or line the bottom and sides with parchment paper or aluminum foil. 2. Season the tuna steaks all over with salt and pepper and place them in the prepared crock pot in a single layer. Drizzle with the olive oil and sprinkle with the thyme and rosemary. 3. Cover the cooker and cook for 4 to 6 hours on Low heat.

Shrimp and Fish Chowder

Prep time: 20 minutes | Cook time: 4 to 6 hours | Serves 4

3 cups low-sodium vegetable broth
1 (28-ounce / 794-g) can no-salt-added crushed tomatoes
1 large bell pepper, any color, seeded and diced
1 large onion, diced
2 zucchini, chopped
3 garlic cloves, minced
1 teaspoon dried thyme
1 teaspoon dried basil
½ teaspoon sea salt
¼ teaspoon freshly ground black pepper
¼ teaspoon red pepper flakes
8 ounces (227 g) whole raw medium shrimp, peeled and deveined
8 ounces (227 g) fresh cod fillets, cut into 1-inch pieces

1. In a crock pot, combine the vegetable broth, tomatoes, bell pepper, onion, zucchini, garlic, thyme, basil, salt, black pepper, and red pepper flakes. Stir to mix well. 2. Cover the cooker and cook for 4 to 6 hours on Low heat. 3. Stir in the shrimp and cod. Replace the cover on the cooker and cook for 15 to 30 minutes on Low heat, or until the shrimp have turned pink and the cod is firm and flaky.

Red Snapper with Peppers and Potatoes

Prep time: 15 minutes | Cook time: 4 to 6 hours | Serves 4

1 pound (454 g) red potatoes, chopped
1 green bell pepper, seeded and sliced

1 red bell pepper, seeded and sliced
½ onion, sliced
1 (15-ounce / 425-g) can no-salt-added diced tomatoes
⅓ cup whole Kalamata olives, pitted
5 garlic cloves, minced
1 teaspoon dried thyme
1 teaspoon dried rosemary
Juice of 1 lemon
Sea salt
Freshly ground black pepper
1½ to 2 pounds (680 to 907 g) fresh red snapper fillets
2 lemons, thinly sliced
¼ cup chopped fresh parsley

1. In a crock pot, combine the potatoes, green and red bell peppers, onion, tomatoes, olives, garlic, thyme, rosemary, and lemon juice. Season with salt and black pepper. Stir to mix well. 2. Nestle the snapper into the vegetable mixture in a single layer, cutting it into pieces to fit if needed. Top it with lemon slices. 3. Cover the cooker and cook for 4 to 6 hours on Low heat, or until the potatoes are tender. 4. Garnish with fresh parsley for serving.

Italian Baccalà

Prep time: 2 to 3 hours | Cook time: 4 to 6 hours | Serves 4

1½ pounds (680 g) salt cod
1 (15-ounce / 425-g) can no-salt-added diced tomatoes
½ onion, chopped
2 garlic cloves, minced
½ teaspoon red pepper flakes
¼ cup chopped fresh parsley, plus more for garnish
Juice of ½ lemon

1. Wash the salt cod to remove any visible salt. Completely submerge the cod in a large bowl of water and let it soak for at least 2 to 3 hours. If you are soaking it for longer than 24 hours, change the water after 12 hours. 2. In a crock pot, combine the tomatoes, onion, garlic, red pepper flakes, parsley, and lemon juice. Stir to mix well. Drain the cod and add it to the crock pot, breaking it apart as necessary to make it fit. 3. Cover the cooker and cook for 4 to 6 hours on Low heat. 4. Garnish with the remaining fresh parsley for serving.

Low Country Seafood Boil

Prep time: 15 minutes | Cook time: 6 hours | Serves 8

8 medium red potatoes
2 large, sweet onions, such as Vidalia, quartered
2 pounds (907 g) smoked sausage, cut into 3-inch pieces
1 (3-ounce / 85-g) package seafood boil seasoning
1 (12-ounce / 340-g) bottle pale ale beer
10 cups water
4 ears of corn, halved
2 pounds (907 g) medium raw shrimp, shelled and deveined
Cocktail sauce, for serving
Hot sauce, for serving
½ cup melted butter, for serving
1 large lemon, cut into wedges, for garnish

1. In the crock pot, put the potatoes, onions, smoked sausage, seafood boil seasoning, beer, and water. Stir to combine. Cover and cook for 6 hours, or until the potatoes are tender when pierced with a fork. 2. About 45 minutes before serving, add the corn. Cover and continue cooking for 25 minutes. Add the shrimp, cover, and continue cooking until the shrimp are pink and no longer translucent. 3. Drain the crock pot, discard the cooking liquid, and serve the seafood with cocktail sauce, hot sauce, melted butter, and lemon wedges.

Smoked Salmon and Potato Casserole

Prep time: 10 minutes | Cook time: 8 hours | Serves 2

1 teaspoon butter, at room temperature, or extra-virgin olive oil
2 eggs
1 cup 2% milk
1 teaspoon dried dill
⅛ teaspoon sea salt
Freshly ground black pepper
2 medium russet potatoes, peeled and sliced thin
4 ounces (113 g) smoked salmon

1. Grease the inside of the crock pot with the butter. 2. In a small bowl, whisk together the eggs, milk, dill, salt, and a few grinds of the black pepper. 3. Spread one-third of the potatoes in a single layer on the bottom of the crock pot and top them with one-third of the salmon. Pour one-third of the egg mixture over the salmon. Repeat this layering with the remaining potatoes, salmon, and egg mixture. 4. Cover and cook on low for 8 hours or overnight.

Chapter 10   Desserts

Chai Spice Baked Apples

Prep time: 15 minutes | Cook time: 2 to 3 hours | Makes 5 apples

5 apples
½ cup water
½ cup crushed pecans (optional)
¼ cup melted coconut oil
1 teaspoon ground cinnamon
½ teaspoon ground ginger
¼ teaspoon ground cardamom
¼ teaspoon ground cloves

1. Core each apple, and peel off a thin strip from the top of each. 2. Add the water to the crock pot. Gently place each apple upright along the bottom. 3. In a small bowl, stir together the pecans (if using), coconut oil, cinnamon, ginger, cardamom, and cloves. Drizzle the mixture over the tops of the apples. 4. Cover the cooker and set to high. Cook for 2 to 3 hours, until the apples soften, and serve.

Cinnamon Pecans

Prep time: 15 minutes | Cook time: 3 to 4 hours | Makes about 3½ cups

1 tablespoon coconut oil
1 large egg white
2 tablespoons ground cinnamon
2 teaspoons vanilla extract
¼ cup maple syrup
2 tablespoons coconut sugar
¼ teaspoon sea salt
3 cups pecan halves

1. Coat the crock pot with the coconut oil. 2. In a medium bowl, whisk the egg white. 3. Add the cinnamon, vanilla, maple syrup, coconut sugar, and salt. Whisk well to combine. 4. Add the pecans and stir to coat. Pour the pecans into the crock pot. 5. Cover the cooker and set to low. Cook for 3 to 4 hours. 6. Remove the pecans from the crock pot and spread them on a baking sheet or other cooling surface. Let cool for 5 to 10 minutes before serving. Store in an airtight container at room temperature for up to 2 weeks.

Coconut-Vanilla Yogurt

Prep time: 15 minutes | Cook time: 1 to 2 hours | Makes about 3½ cups

3 (13½-ounce / 383-g) cans full-fat coconut milk
5 probiotic capsules (not pills)
1 teaspoon raw honey
½ teaspoon vanilla extract

1. Pour the coconut milk into the crock pot. 2. Cover the cooker and set to high. Cook for 1 to 2 hours, until the temperature of the milk reaches 180ºF measured with a candy thermometer. 3. Turn off the crock pot and allow the temperature of the milk to come down close to 100ºF. 4. Open the probiotic capsules and pour in the contents, along with the honey and vanilla. Stir well to combine. 5. Re-cover the crock pot, turn it off and unplug it, and wrap it in an insulating towel to keep warm overnight as it ferments. 6. Pour the yogurt into sterilized jars and refrigerate. The yogurt should thicken slightly in the refrigerator, where it will keep for up to 1 week.

Warm Cinnamon-Turmeric Almond Milk

Prep time: 15 minutes | Cook time: 3 to 4 hours | Makes 4 to 6 cups

4 cups unsweetened almond milk
4 cinnamon sticks
2 tablespoons coconut oil
1 (4-inch) piece turmeric root, roughly chopped
1 (2-inch) piece fresh ginger, roughly chopped
1 teaspoon raw honey, plus more to taste

1. In your crock pot, combine the almond milk, cinnamon sticks, coconut oil, turmeric, and ginger. 2. Cover the cooker and set to low. Cook for 3 to 4 hours. 3. Pour the contents of the cooker through a fine-mesh sieve into a clean container; discard the solids. 4. Starting with just 1 teaspoon, add raw honey to taste.

Creamy Dreamy Brown Rice Pudding

Prep time: 5 minutes | Cook time: 2 to 3 hours | Serves 6 to 8

Nonstick cooking spray (optional)
1 cup brown rice
4 cups unsweetened vanilla plant-based milk
¼ cup maple syrup or date syrup (optional)
2 teaspoons ground cinnamon
2 teaspoons vanilla extract
½ cup raisins, for topping (optional)

1. Coat the inside of the crock pot with cooking spray (if using) or line it with a crock pot liner. 2. Add the rice, milk, syrup (if using), cinnamon, and vanilla, and stir to combine. 3. Cover and cook on High for 2 to 3 hours or on Low for 3 to 4 hours, stirring when there is an hour left to check for doneness and your preference for the rice. Cook it longer for creamier pudding or shorter for a more toothsome texture. Just before serving, top with the raisins (if using) for extra sweetness and texture.

Pumpkin Pie Oatmeal Parfaits

Prep time: 20 minutes | Cook time: 7 hours | Makes 6 parfaits

Nonstick cooking spray (optional)
1 (15-ounce / 425-g) can coconut cream
2 cups steel-cut oats
4 cups water
1 (15-ounce / 425-g) can pumpkin purée
2 teaspoons ground cinnamon, divided
1 teaspoon ground nutmeg, divided
½ teaspoon ground cloves
½ teaspoon ground ginger
½ cup maple syrup, plus 3 to 4 tablespoons more for serving (optional)
1½ cups rolled oats
¾ cup chopped pecans (optional)

1. Coat the inside of the crock pot with cooking spray (if using) or line it with a crock pot liner. Place the unopened can of coconut cream into the refrigerator to chill. 2. Add the steel-cut oats, water, pumpkin purée, 1 teaspoon of cinnamon, ½ teaspoon of nutmeg, the cloves, ginger, and maple syrup (if using). Stir to combine. Cover and cook

on Low for 7 hours. After cooking, stir well. 3. While the steel-cut oats cook, preheat the oven to 350ºF (180ºC). On a parchment-lined baking sheet, spread out the rolled oats and pecans (if using) in a single layer and sprinkle with the remaining 1 teaspoon of cinnamon and ½ teaspoon of nutmeg. Bake for 10 minutes. Set the crumble aside to cool and store loosely covered at room temperature until the steel-cut oats are done cooking. 4. Just before serving, pour the cold coconut cream into a medium bowl. Using an electric beater, whip the cream for about 1 minute, until it becomes thick. 5. For each parfait, layer 3 tablespoons of the crumble, about ½ teaspoon of the maple syrup (if using), 2 to 3 tablespoons of the warm pumpkin oatmeal, and about 2 tablespoons of the whipped cream. Continue layering in this order until your glass is full, finishing with the whipped cream on top, a sprinkle of the crumble, and a tiny drizzle more of maple syrup.

Chocolate's Best Friends Brownies

Prep time: 15 minutes | Cook time: 3½ hours | Makes about 2 dozen brownies

1¼ cups oats
¾ cup white beans, drained, and rinsed
¾ cup plus 3 tablespoons maple syrup (optional)
¼ cup plus 2 tablespoons unsweetened applesauce
1½ teaspoons vanilla extract
1½ teaspoons baking powder
½ teaspoon salt (optional)
¾ cup unsweetened cocoa powder
½ teaspoon ground cinnamon
1 teaspoon instant coffee

1. Crumple two pieces of aluminum foil to form a ring around the interior base of the crock pot. Add a liner or piece of parchment and set the crock pot to Low to preheat. 2. Put the oats in a blender or food processor and process into oat flour. Pour it into a small bowl and set aside. 3. Add the beans, maple syrup (if using), applesauce, and vanilla to the blender and blend until well combined, about 1 minute. Add the oat flour, baking powder, salt (if using), cocoa powder, cinnamon, and instant coffee. Blend until smooth and thick, scraping down the sides as needed. 4. Spread the batter into the prepared crock pot. Cover and cook on Low for 3½ hours. Turn off the crock pot, remove the cover, and let the brownies cool completely before slicing, at least 1 hour. Store at room temperature for 2 to 3 days.

Peach Cobbler

Prep time: 15 minutes | Cook time: 1 to 2 hours | Serves 6 to 8

Filling:
2 (15-ounce / 425-g) cans peaches in juice
½ teaspoon ground cinnamon
½ teaspoon ground ginger
3 tablespoons maple syrup or date syrup (optional)
2 tablespoons cornstarch
Topping:
1 cup rolled oats
¼ teaspoon ground cinnamon
2 tablespoons coconut cream
1 tablespoon liquid from the canned peaches
4 tablespoons date syrup (optional)

1. Make the filling: Remove the peaches from the cans, reserving the juice. Slice the peaches into bite-size chunks and put them in the crock pot. Stir in the cinnamon, ginger, syrup (if using), and cornstarch. 2. Make the topping and cook: In a medium bowl, combine the oats, cinnamon, coconut cream, canned peach liquid, and date syrup (if using). Stir together until the oats are wet and crumbly. Sprinkle over the peaches in the crock pot. 3. To keep the condensation that forms on the inside of the lid away from the topping, stretch a clean dish towel or several layers of paper towels over the top of the crock pot, but not touching the food, and place the lid on top of the towel(s). If you skip this step, you will have a soggy result. Cook on High for 1 to 2 hours or on Low for 2 to 3 hours.

Gooey Bittersweet Chocolate Pudding Cake

Prep time: 15 minutes | Cook time: 3 to 4 hours | Serves 6 to 8

Cake:
1 cup whole-wheat flour
¼ cup cocoa powder
2 teaspoons baking powder
½ teaspoon ground cinnamon
¼ teaspoon salt (optional)
⅓ cup unsweetened applesauce
2 teaspoons vanilla extract
⅔ cup unsweetened vanilla or plain plant-based milk
2 tablespoons date syrup or maple syrup (optional)
Nonstick cooking spray (optional)
Pudding:
¼ cup cocoa powder
1 teaspoon instant coffee
½ cup date syrup or maple syrup (optional)
1 teaspoon vanilla extract
1 cup hot water

1. Make the cake: In a medium bowl, whisk together the flour, cocoa powder, baking powder, cinnamon, and salt (if using). 2. In a separate medium bowl, whisk together the applesauce, vanilla, milk, and date syrup (if using). Pour the applesauce mixture into the flour mixture and stir until just fully combined. Do not overmix. 3. Coat the inside of the crock pot with cooking spray (if using) or line it with a crock pot liner. Add the cake batter and spread it over the bottom of the crock pot. 4. Make the pudding: In a medium bowl, whisk together the cocoa powder, coffee, date syrup (if using), vanilla, and hot water. Pour over the cake ingredients in the crock pot. The mixture will be watery. 5. Cover and cook on Low for 3 to 4 hours. When it is ready to serve, the cake will look dry on top and will have achieved a pudding-like texture below the surface. Enjoy it immediately for best results.

Peach Brown Betty

Prep time: 20 minutes | Cook time: 6 hours | Serves 10

8 ripe peaches, peeled and cut into chunks
1 cup dried cranberries
2 tablespoons freshly squeezed lemon juice
3 tablespoons honey
3 cups cubed whole-wheat bread
1½ cups whole-wheat bread crumbs
⅓ cup coconut sugar
¼ teaspoon ground cardamom
⅓ cup melted coconut oil

1. In a 6-quart crock pot, mix the peaches, dried cranberries, lemon juice, and honey. 2. In a large bowl, mix the bread cubes, bread crumbs, coconut sugar, and cardamom. Drizzle the melted coconut oil over all and toss to coat. 3. Sprinkle the bread mixture on the fruit in the crock pot. 4. Cover and cook on low for 5 to 6 hours, or until the fruit is bubbling and the topping is browned.

Poppy's Carrot Cake

Prep time: 20 minutes | Cook time: 3 hours | Serves 6 to 8

Carrot Cake:
Nonstick cooking spray (optional)
1 tablespoon ground flaxseed
2½ tablespoons water
2¼ cups rolled oats, divided
1¾ teaspoons ground cinnamon
¾ teaspoon ground nutmeg
¾ teaspoon ground ginger
2 teaspoons baking powder
1 teaspoon baking soda
1 cup unsweetened plant-based milk
¾ cup raisins, divided
¼ cup unsweetened applesauce
⅓ cup date syrup or maple syrup (optional)
1 medium banana, peeled and broken into pieces
1 teaspoon vanilla extract
2 cups grated carrots
½ cup walnut pieces (optional)
Frosting:
¾ cup raw cashews
6 pitted Medjool dates, chopped
½ teaspoon ground ginger
⅓ to ½ cup water
2 tablespoons coconut cream

1. Prepare the crock pot by folding two long sheets of aluminum foil and placing them perpendicular to each other (crisscross) in the bottom of the crock pot to create "handles" that will come out over the top of the crock pot. Coat the inside of the crock pot and foil with cooking spray (if using) or line it with a crock pot liner. 2. Make the carrot cake: Make a flax egg in a small bowl by mixing together the flaxseed and the water. Set aside. 3. In a blender or food processor, combine 1¾ cups of oats, the cinnamon, nutmeg, ginger, baking powder, and baking soda. Blend until the oats are turned into a flour. Pour into a large bowl and set aside. Add the remaining ½ cup of whole oats to the dry ingredients. 4. Without rinsing the blender or food processor, add the milk, ¼ cup of raisins, applesauce, syrup (if using), banana, vanilla, and the flax egg. Process until smooth and the raisins are broken down. Pour over the dry ingredients. Add the carrots, the remaining ½ cup of raisins, and the walnuts (if using), and stir well to combine. 5. Pour the mixture into the prepared crock pot. Stretch a clean dish towel or a few layers of paper towels over the top of the crock pot and cover. Cook on Low for 3 hours. The carrot cake is ready when a toothpick inserted in the center comes out clean. Remove the insert from the crock pot and cool on a wire rack for at least 30 minutes before removing the cake from the insert. Allow to cool completely before frosting. 6. Make the frosting: Put the cashews, dates, and ginger in a blender or food processor. Cover with just enough water to submerge the cashews and dates. Let the mixture soak for up to 1 hour to soften. Add the coconut cream and blend well until creamy. The frosting will thicken slightly as it sits.

"Here Comes Autumn" Apple Crisp

Prep time: 15 minutes | Cook time: 2 to 3 hours | Serves 4 to 6

Apple Base:
6 apples (about 2 pounds / 907 g), any variety, cored and thinly sliced
1 tablespoon lemon juice
2 tablespoons maple syrup (optional)
½ cup rolled oats
3 tablespoons maple syrup (optional)
1 teaspoon ground cinnamon
½ teaspoon grated nutmeg
Topping:
¾ cup chopped pecans
½ cup almond meal or almond flour
½ teaspoon ground cinnamon
¼ teaspoon grated nutmeg

1. Make the apple base: Put the apples in the crock pot and sprinkle with the lemon juice, tossing well to coat the apples completely. Stir in the maple syrup (if using), cinnamon, and nutmeg until the syrup and spices cover every apple slice. Spread the apples out in an even layer. 2. Make the topping and cook: In a medium bowl, combine the pecans, almond meal or flour, oats, maple syrup (if using), cinnamon, and nutmeg. Mix well until crumbles form. Spoon the mixture evenly over the apples. 3. To keep the condensation that forms on the inside of the lid away from the topping, stretch a clean dish towel or several layers of paper towels across the top of the crock pot, but not touching the food, and place the lid on top of the towel(s). If you skip this step, you will have a soggy result rather than a crunchy crumble. 4. Cook on High for 2 to 3 hours or on Low for 4 to 5 hours, until the apples are soft and cooked through.

Apple-Granola Bake

Prep time: 10 minutes | Cook time: 6 to 8 hours | Serves 6

Nonstick cooking spray
2 cups steel-cut oats
2 apples, finely diced, divided
⅓ cup semisweet chocolate chips, divided
1 teaspoon baking powder
1 teaspoon ground cinnamon
½ teaspoon salt
2 cups almond milk
¼ cup honey or maple syrup
1 ripe banana, mashed
1 large egg
1 tablespoon pure vanilla extract
1 banana, cut into ½-inch slices

1. Spray the crock pot generously with nonstick cooking spray. 2. In a large bowl, mix together the oats, 1 of the diced apples, about half of the chocolate chips, and the baking powder, cinnamon, and salt. 3. In a separate large bowl, whisk together the almond milk, honey, mashed banana, egg, and vanilla. The honey might clump up at first; just keep whisking. 4. Pour the oat mixture into the crock pot. Add the remaining apple and chocolate chips, and spread the banana slices on top. 5. Pour the honey mixture on top of everything. Gently shake the crock pot to make sure all of the dry mixture is completely wet. 6. Cook on low for 6 to 8 hours, or until the oatmeal is set, and serve. (You'll know it's done when you insert a knife and it comes out clean.)

Apple-Peach Crumble

Prep time: 20 minutes | Cook time: 5 hours | Serves 8

6 large Granny Smith apples, peeled and cut into chunks
4 large peaches, peeled and sliced
3 tablespoons honey
2 tablespoons lemon juice
1 cup almond flour
1 teaspoon ground cinnamon
3 cups quick-cooking oatmeal
⅓ cup coconut sugar
½ cup slivered almonds
½ cup melted coconut oil

1. In a 6-quart crock pot, mix the apples, peaches, honey, and lemon juice. 2. In a large bowl, mix the almond flour, cinnamon, oatmeal, coconut sugar, and almonds until well combined. 3. Add the coconut

oil and mix until crumbly. 4. Sprinkle the almond mixture over the fruit in the crock pot. 5. Cover and cook on low for 4 to 5 hours, or until the fruit is tender and the crumble is bubbling around the edges.

Berry Crisp

Prep time: 20 minutes | Cook time: 6 hours | Serves 12

3 cups frozen organic blueberries
3 cups frozen organic raspberries
3 cups frozen organic strawberries
2 tablespoons lemon juice
2½ cups rolled oats
1 cup whole-wheat flour
⅓ cup maple sugar
1 teaspoon ground cinnamon
⅓ cup coconut melted oil

1. Do not thaw the berries. In a 6-quart crock pot, mix the frozen berries. Drizzle with the lemon juice. 2. In a large bowl, mix the oats, flour, maple sugar, and cinnamon until well combined. Stir in the melted coconut oil until crumbly. 3. Sprinkle the oat mixture over the fruit in the crock pot. 4. Cover and cook on low for 5 to 6 hours, or until the fruit is bubbling and the topping is browned.

Nutty Baked Apples

Prep time: 20 minutes | Cook time: 6 hours | Serves 8

8 large apples
2 tablespoons freshly squeezed lemon juice
1½ cups buckwheat flakes
1 cup chopped walnuts
⅓ cup coconut sugar
1 teaspoon ground cinnamon
¼ teaspoon salt
6 tablespoons unsalted butter, cut into pieces
½ cup apple juice

1. Peel a strip of skin around the top of each apple to prevent splitting. Carefully remove the apple core, making sure not to cut all the way through to the bottom. Brush the apples with lemon juice and set aside. 2. In a medium bowl, mix the buckwheat flakes, walnuts, coconut sugar, cinnamon, and salt. 3. Drizzle the melted butter over the buckwheat mixture and mix until crumbly. Use this mixture to stuff the apples, rounding the stuffing on top of each apple. 4. In a 6-quart crock pot, place the stuffed apples. Pour the apple juice around the apples. 5. Cover and cook on low for 4 to 6 hours, or until the apples are very tender.

Spiced Carrot Pudding

Prep time: 20 minutes | Cook time: 7 hours | Serves 12

3 cups finely grated carrots
1½ cups chopped pecans
1 cup golden raisins
1 cup almond flour
1 cup coconut flour
½ cup coconut sugar
1 teaspoon baking powder
1½ teaspoons ground cinnamon
2 eggs, beaten
2 cups canned coconut milk

1. In a 6-quart crock pot, mix all of the ingredients. Cover and cook on low for 5 to 7 hours, or until the pudding is set. 2. Serve warm, either plain or with softly whipped heavy cream.

Apple-Oatmeal Bread Pudding

Prep time: 20 minutes | Cook time: 8 hours | Serves 8

8 slices oatmeal bread, cubed
2 cups quick-cooking oatmeal
3 apples, peeled and chopped
1 cup dried cranberries
⅓ cup coconut sugar
1 teaspoon ground cinnamon
2 teaspoons vanilla extract
3 eggs, beaten
2 cups canned coconut milk
3 tablespoons melted coconut oil

1. In a 6-quart crock pot, mix the bread cubes, oatmeal, apples, and cranberries. 2. In a large bowl, mix the coconut sugar, cinnamon, vanilla, eggs, coconut milk, and melted coconut oil, and mix until well combined. Pour into the crock pot. 3. Cover and cook on low for 6 to 8 hours, or until a food thermometer registers 165°F (74°C).

Fruited Rice Pudding

Prep time: 20 minutes | Cook time: 6 hours | Serves 16

6 cups canned coconut milk
3 cups water
1⅔ cups brown Arborio rice
½ cup coconut sugar
2 tablespoons coconut oil
1 cup raisins
1 tablespoon vanilla extract
1 cup dark chocolate chips (optional)

1. In a 6-quart crock pot, mix the coconut milk and water. Add the rice and coconut sugar and mix. Add the coconut oil and the raisins. 2. Cover and cook on low for 5 to 6 hours, or until the rice is very tender. 3. Stir in the vanilla. If using, serve the pudding with the chocolate chips sprinkled on top.

Clean Eating Brownies

Prep time: 20 minutes | Cook time: 5 hours | Serves 12

1½ cups whole-wheat pastry flour
¾ cup unsweetened cocoa powder
1 teaspoon baking powder
5 tablespoons melted coconut oil
1 cup mashed ripe bananas (about 2 medium)
1 cup mashed peeled ripe pears
½ cup coconut sugar
½ cup honey
4 eggs
2 teaspoons vanilla extract

1. Tear off two long strips of heavy-duty foil and fold to make long thin strips. Place in a 6-quart crock pot to make an X. Then line the crock pot with parchment paper on top of the foil. 2. In a medium bowl, combine the whole-wheat pastry flour, cocoa powder, and baking powder and stir to mix. 3. In another medium bowl, combine the melted coconut oil, mashed bananas, mashed pears, coconut sugar, honey, eggs, and vanilla and mix well. 4. Stir the banana mixture into the flour mixture just until combined. 5. Spoon the batter into the crock pot onto the parchment paper. 6. Cover and cook on low for 4 to 5 hours or until a toothpick inserted near the center comes out with just a few moist crumbs attached to it. 7. Carefully remove the brownie, using the foil sling. Let cool, then remove the brownie from the parchment paper and cut into squares to serve.

Upside-Down Chocolate Pudding Cake

Prep time: 15 minutes | Cook time: 2 to 3 hours | Serves 8

1 cup dry all-purpose baking mix	divided
1 cup sugar, divided	½ cup milk
3 tablespoons unsweetened cocoa powder, plus ⅓ cup,	1 teaspoon vanilla
	1⅔ cups hot water
	Nonstick cooking spray

1. Spray inside of slow cooker with nonstick cooking spray. 2. In a bowl, mix together baking mix, ½ cup sugar, 3 tablespoons cocoa powder, milk, and vanilla. Spoon batter evenly into slow cooker. 3. In a clean bowl, mix remaining ½ cup sugar, ⅓ cup cocoa powder, and hot water together. Pour over batter in slow cooker. Do not stir. 4. Cover and cook on high 2 to 3 hours, or until toothpick inserted in center of cake comes out clean.

Hot Fudge Cake

Prep time: 10 minutes | Cook time: 1½ to 1¾ hours | Serves 8

1¾ cups brown sugar, divided	½ cup skim milk
1 cup flour	2 tablespoons butter, melted
3 tablespoons, plus ¼ cup, unsweetened cocoa, divided	½ teaspoon vanilla
	1¾ cups boiling water
1½ teaspoons baking powder	Nonfat cooking spray
½ teaspoon salt	

1. In a mixing bowl, mix together 1 cup brown sugar, flour, 3 tablespoons cocoa, baking powder, and salt. 2. Stir in milk, butter, and vanilla. 3. Pour into slow cooker sprayed with nonfat cooking spray. 4. In a separate bowl, mix together ¾ cup brown sugar and ¼ cup cocoa. Sprinkle over batter in the slow cooker. Do not stir. 5. Pour boiling water over mixture. Do not stir. 6. Cover. Cook on high 1½ to 1¾ hours, or until toothpick inserted into cake comes out clean.

Cranberry Pudding

Prep time: 20 minutes | Cook time: 3 to 4 hours | Serves 8 to 10

Pudding:	
1⅓ cups flour	½ cup water
½ teaspoon salt	Butter Sauce:
2 teaspoons baking soda	1 cup confectioners sugar
⅓ cup boiling water	½ cup heavy cream or evaporated milk
½ cup dark molasses	
2 cups whole cranberries	½ cup butter
½ cup chopped nuts	1 teaspoon vanilla

1. Mix together flour and salt. 2. Dissolve soda in boiling water. Add to flour and salt. 3. Stir in molasses. Blend well. 4. Fold in cranberries and nuts. 5. Pour into well greased and floured bread or cake pan that will sit in your cooker. Cover with greased foil. 6. Pour ½ cup water into cooker. Place foil-covered pan in cooker. Cover with cooker lid and steam on high 3 to 4 hours, or until pudding tests done with a wooden pick. 7. Remove pan and uncover. Let stand 5 minutes, then unmold. 8. To make butter sauce, mix together all ingredients in saucepan. Cook, stirring over medium heat until sugar dissolves.

Peanut Butter Cake

Prep time: 10 minutes | Cook time: 2 to 3 hours | Serves 6

2 cups yellow cake mix	½ cup water
⅓ cup crunchy peanut butter	

1. Combine all ingredients in electric mixer bowl. Beat with electric mixer about 2 minutes. 2. Pour batter into greased and floured baking pan insert, designed to fit inside your slow cooker. 3. Place baking pan insert into slow cooker. Cover with 8 paper towels. 4. Cover cooker. Cook on high 2 to 3 hours, or until toothpick inserted into center of cake comes out clean. About 30 minutes before the end of the cooking time, remove the cooker's lid, but keep the paper towels in place. 5. When cake is fully cooked, remove insert from slow cooker. Turn insert upside-down on a serving plate and remove cake.

Chocolate Peanut Butter Cake

Prep time: 10 minutes | Cook time: 2 to 2½ hours | Serves 8 to 10

2 cups dry milk chocolate cake mix	6 tablespoons peanut butter
	2 eggs
½ cup water	½ cup chopped nuts

1. Combine all ingredients in electric mixer bowl. Beat for 2 minutes. 2. Spray interior of a baking insert, designed to fit into your slow cooker. Flour interior of greased insert. Pour batter into insert. Place insert in slow cooker. 3. Cover insert with 8 paper towels. 4. Cover cooker. Cook on high 2 to 2½ hours, or until toothpick inserted into center of cake comes out clean. 5. Allow cake to cool. Then invert onto a serving plate, cut, and serve.

Brownies with Nuts

Prep time: 15 minutes | Cook time: 3 hours | Makes 24 brownies

Half a stick butter, melted	1 (23-ounce / 652-g) package brownie mix
1 cup chopped nuts, divided	

1. Pour melted butter into a baking insert designed to fit into your slow cooker. Swirl butter around to grease sides of insert. 2. Sprinkle butter with half the nuts. 3. In a bowl, mix brownies according to package directions. Spoon half the batter into the baking insert, trying to cover the nuts evenly. 4. Add remaining half of nuts. Spoon in remaining batter. 5. Place insert in slow cooker. Cover insert with 8 paper towels. 6. Cover cooker. Cook on high 3 hours. Do not check or remove cover until last hour of cooking. Then insert toothpick into center of brownies. If it comes out clean, the brownies are finished. If it doesn't, continue cooking another 15 minutes. Check

again. Repeat until pick comes out clean. 7. When finished cooking, uncover cooker and baking insert. Let brownies stand 5 minutes. 8. Invert insert onto serving plate. Cut brownies with a plastic knife (so the crumbs don't drag). Serve warm.

Scandinavian Fruit Soup

Prep time: 5 minutes | Cook time: 8 hours | Serves 12

- 1 cup dried apricots
- 1 cup dried sliced apples
- 1 cup dried pitted prunes
- 1 cup canned pitted red cherries
- ½ cup quick-cooking tapioca
- 1 cup grape juice or red wine
- 3 cups water, or more
- ½ cup orange juice
- ¼ cup lemon juice
- 1 tablespoon grated orange peel
- ½ cup brown sugar

1. Combine apricots, apples, prunes, cherries, tapioca, and grape juice in slow cooker. Cover with water. 2. Cook on low for at least 8 hours. 3. Before serving, stir in remaining ingredients. 4. Serve warm or cold.

Apple Crisp

Prep time: 10 minutes | Cook time: 2 to 3 hours | Serves 6 to 8

- 1 quart canned apple pie filling
- ¾ cup quick oatmeal
- ½ cup brown sugar
- ½ cup flour
- ¼ cup butter, at room temperature

1. Place pie filling in slow cooker. 2. Combine remaining ingredients until crumbly. Sprinkle over apple filling. 3. Cover. Cook on low 2 to 3 hours.

Easy Chocolate Clusters

Prep time: 5 minutes | Cook time: 2 hours | Makes 3½ dozen clusters

- 2 pounds (907 g) white coating chocolate, broken into small pieces
- 2 cups semisweet chocolate chips
- 1 (4-ounce / 113-g) package sweet German chocolate
- 1 (24-ounce / 680-g) jar roasted peanuts

1. Combine coating chocolate, chocolate chips, and German chocolate. Cover and cook on high 1 hour. Reduce heat to low and cook 1 hour longer, or until chocolate is melted, stirring every 15 minutes. 2. Stir in peanuts. Mix well. 3. Drop by teaspoonfuls onto waxed paper. Let stand until set. Store at room temperature.

Dried Fruit

Prep time: 5 minutes | Cook time: 4 to 8 hours | Serves 3 to 4

- 2 cups mixed dried fruit
- ¼ cup water

1. Place dried fruit in slow cooker. Add water. 2. Cover. Cook on low 4 to 8 hours. 3. Serve warm.

Apple Appeal

Prep time: 10 minutes | Cook time: 4 to 5 hours | Serves 6

- 6 baking apples, peeled, cored, and quartered
- ¼ teaspoon nutmeg
- 2 tablespoons sugar
- ¾ teaspoon Asian five-spice powder
- ¼ cup apple juice

1. Place prepared apples in slow cooker. 2. In a small mixing bowl, combine all remaining ingredients. 3. Pour into slow cooker, stirring gently to coat apples. 4. Cover and cook on low 4 to 5 hours, or until apples are as tender as you want them. 5. Serve the apples sliced or mashed and warm, cold, or at room-temperature.

Peanut Butter and Hot Fudge Pudding Cake

Prep time: 10 minutes | Cook time: 2 to 3 hours | Serves 6

- ½ cup flour
- ¼ cup sugar
- ¾ teaspoon baking powder
- ⅓ cup milk
- 1 tablespoon oil
- ½ teaspoon vanilla
- ¼ cup peanut butter
- ½ cup sugar
- 3 tablespoons unsweetened cocoa powder
- 1 cup boiling water
- Vanilla ice cream

1. Combine flour, ¼ cup sugar, and baking powder. Add milk, oil, and vanilla. Mix until smooth. Stir in peanut butter. Pour into slow cooker. 2. Mix together ½ cup sugar and cocoa powder. 3. Gradually stir in boiling water. Pour mixture over batter in slow cooker. Do not stir. Cover and cook on high 2 to 3 hours, or until toothpick inserted comes out clean. 4. Serve warm with ice cream.

Carmeled Pears 'n Wine

Prep time: 10 minutes | Cook time: 4 to 6 hours | Serves 6

- 6 medium fresh pears with stems
- 1 cup white wine
- ½ cup sugar
- ½ cup water
- 3 tablespoons lemon juice
- 2 apple cinnamon sticks, each about 2½ to 3 inch long
- 3 whole dried cloves
- ¼ teaspoon ground nutmeg
- 6 tablespoons fat-free caramel apple dip

1. Peel pears, leaving whole with stems intact. 2. Place upright in slow cooker. Shave bottom if needed to level fruit. 3. Combine wine, sugar, water, lemon juice, cinnamon, cloves, and nutmeg. Pour over pears. 4. Cook on low 4 to 6 hours, or until pears are tender. 5. Cool pears in liquid. 6. Transfer pears to individual serving dishes. Place 2 teaspoons cooking liquid in bottom of each dish. 7. Microwave caramel dip for 20 seconds and stir. Repeat until heated through. 8. Drizzle caramel over pears and serve.

Chocolate Rice Pudding

Prep time: 10 minutes | Cook time: 2½ to 3½ hours | Serves 4

4 cups white rice, cooked
¾ cup sugar
¼ cup baking cocoa powder
3 tablespoons butter, melted
1 teaspoon vanilla
2 (12-ounce / 340-g) cans evaporated milk
Whipped cream
Sliced toasted almonds
Maraschino cherries

1. Combine first 6 ingredients in greased slow cooker. 2. Cover. Cook on low 2½ to 3½ hours, or until liquid is absorbed. 3. Serve warm or chilled. Top individual servings with a dollop of whipped cream, sliced toasted almonds, and a maraschino cherry.

Vanilla Bean Rice Pudding

Prep time: 10 minutes | Cook time: 2½ to 4 hours | Serves 12

6 cups fat-free milk
1½ cups converted rice, uncooked
1 cup sugar
1 cup raisins
1 tablespoon butter or margarine, melted
½ teaspoon salt
1 vanilla bean, split
1 large egg
½ teaspoon ground cinnamon
1 (8-ounce / 227-g) carton fat-free sour cream

1. Combine milk, rice, sugar, raisins, butter, and salt in slow cooker. Stir well. 2. Scrape seeds from vanilla bean. Add seeds and bean to milk mixture. 3. Cover with lid and cook on high 2½ to 4 hours, or just until rice is tender and most of liquid is absorbed. 4. Place egg in small bowl. Stir well with a whisk and gradually add ½ cup hot rice mixture to egg. 5. Return egg mixture to slow cooker, stirring constantly with whisk. Cook 1 minute while stirring. Remove inner vessel from slow cooker. 6. Let stand 5 minutes. Mix in cinnamon and sour cream. Discard vanilla bean. 7. Serve warm, not hot, or refrigerate until fully chilled.

Fruit Dessert Topping

Prep time: 20 minutes | Cook time: 3½ to 4¾ hours | Makes 6 cups

3 tart apples, peeled and sliced
3 pears, peeled and sliced
1 tablespoon lemon juice
½ cup packed brown sugar
½ cup maple syrup
¼ cup butter, melted
½ cup chopped pecans
¼ cup raisins
2 cinnamon sticks
1 tablespoon cornstarch
2 tablespoons cold water

1. Toss apples and pears in lemon juice in slow cooker. 2. Combine brown sugar, maple syrup, and butter. Pour over fruit. 3. Stir in pecans, raisins, and cinnamon sticks. 4. Cover. Cook on low 3 to 4 hours. 5. Combine cornstarch and water until smooth. Gradually stir into slow cooker. 6. Cover. Cook on high 30 to 40 minutes, or until thickened. 7. Discard cinnamon sticks. Serve.

Caramel Apples

Prep time: 15 minutes | Cook time: 4 to 6 hours | Serves 4

4 very large tart apples, cored
½ cup apple juice
8 tablespoons brown sugar
12 hot cinnamon candies
4 tablespoons butter
8 caramel candies
¼ teaspoon ground cinnamon
Whipped cream

1. Remove ½-inch-wide strip of peel off the top of each apple and place apples in slow cooker. 2. Pour apple juice over apples. 3. Fill the center of each apple with 2 tablespoons brown sugar, 3 hot cinnamon candies, 1 tablespoon butter, and 2 caramel candies. Sprinkle with cinnamon. 4. Cover and cook on low 4 to 6 hours, or until tender. 5. Serve hot with whipped cream.

Tapioca

Prep time: 10 minutes | Cook time: 3½ hours | Serves 10 to 12

2 quarts whole milk
1¼ cups sugar
1 cup dry small pearl tapioca
4 eggs
1 teaspoon vanilla
Whipped topping (optional)

1. Combine milk and sugar in slow cooker, stirring until sugar is dissolved as well as possible. Stir in tapioca. 2. Cover and cook on high 3 hours. 3. In a small mixing bowl, beat eggs slightly. Beat in vanilla and about 1 cup hot milk from slow cooker. When well mixed, stir into slow cooker. 4. Cover and cook on high 20 more minutes. 5. Chill for several hours. Serve with whipped topping if you wish.

Chunky Cranberry Applesauce

Prep time: 15 minutes | Cook time: 3 to 4 hours | Serves 6

6 baking apple, peeled or unpeeled, cut into 1-inch cubes
½ cup apple juice
½ cup fresh or frozen cranberries
¼ cup sugar
¼ teaspoon ground cinnamon (optional)

Combine all ingredients in slow cooker. 2. Cover and cook on low 3 to 4 hours, or until apples are as soft as you like them. 3. Serve warm, or refrigerate and serve chilled.

Fruit and Nut "Baked" Apples

Prep time: 25 minutes | Cook time: 1½ to 3 hours | Serves 4

4 large firm baking apples
1 tablespoon lemon juice
⅓ cup chopped dried apricots
⅓ cup chopped walnuts or pecans
3 tablespoons packed brown sugar
½ teaspoon cinnamon
2 tablespoons butter, melted
½ cup water or apple juice

4 pecan halves (optional)

1. Scoop out center of apples creating a cavity 1½ inches wide and stopping ½ inch from the bottom of each. Peel top of each apple down about 1 inch. Brush edges with lemon juice. 2. Mix together apricots, nuts, brown sugar, and cinnamon. Stir in butter. Spoon mixture evenly into apples. 3. Put ½ cup water or juice in bottom of slow cooker. Put 2 apples in bottom, and 2 apples above, but not squarely on top of other apples. Cover and cook on low 1½ to 3 hours, or until tender. 4. Serve warm or at room temperature. Top each apple with a pecan half, if desired.

Appendix Measurement Conversion Chart

MEASUREMENT CONVERSION CHART

VOLUME EQUIVALENTS (DRY)

US STANDARD	METRIC (APPROXIMATE)
1/8 teaspoon	0.5 mL
1/4 teaspoon	1 mL
1/2 teaspoon	2 mL
3/4 teaspoon	4 mL
1 teaspoon	5 mL
1 tablespoon	15 mL
1/4 cup	59 mL
1/2 cup	118 mL
3/4 cup	177 mL
1 cup	235 mL
2 cups	475 mL
3 cups	700 mL
4 cups	1 L

VOLUME EQUIVALENTS (LIQUID)

US STANDARD	US STANDARD (OUNCES)	METRIC (APPROXIMATE)
2 tablespoons	1 fl.oz.	30 mL
1/4 cup	2 fl.oz.	60 mL
1/2 cup	4 fl.oz.	120 mL
1 cup	8 fl.oz.	240 mL
1 1/2 cup	12 fl.oz.	355 mL
2 cups or 1 pint	16 fl.oz.	475 mL
4 cups or 1 quart	32 fl.oz.	1 L
1 gallon	128 fl.oz.	4 L

TEMPERATURES EQUIVALENTS

FAHRENHEIT(F)	CELSIUS(C) (APPROXIMATE)
225 °F	107 °C
250 °F	120 °C
275 °F	135 °C
300 °F	150 °C
325 °F	160 °C
350 °F	180 °C
375 °F	190 °C
400 °F	205 °C
425 °F	220 °C
450 °F	235 °C
475 °F	245 °C
500 °F	260 °C

WEIGHT EQUIVALENTS

US STANDARD	METRIC (APPROXIMATE)
1 ounce	28 g
2 ounces	57 g
5 ounces	142 g
10 ounces	284 g
15 ounces	425 g
16 ounces (1 pound)	455 g
1.5 pounds	680 g
2 pounds	907 g

Printed in Great Britain
by Amazon